The Bishop's Curse

Raff Ellis

A battle of wills in the early American Catholic Church
Between a layman, his priest and his bishop

The Bishop's Curse

PROLIX PRESS, Orlando, Florida
ISBN 9 781620 509081
Hardcover $30.00

Library of Congress Cataloging-in-Publication Data
Ellis, Raff
The Bishop's Curse
A battle of wills in the early American Catholic Church
Between a layman, his priest and his bishop

/Raff Ellis

1. Ellis, Raff - 2. Irish/American History/Biography
3. Carthage (NY) Biography 4. Roman Catholic Church
History 5. New York State History 6. St. James Parish.

Cover design by Chris Ellis
Entropy Design

raff.ellis@yahoo.com
www.raffellis.com

Prolix Press
Orlando, Fl 32817

To those fearless immigrants of hardy Irish stock who, in order to escape starvation and persecution, risked their lives to make the perilous journey to reach the "promised land" of America. Many perished in the attempt; many found they were not welcome; many were greeted by discrimination; and many were taken advantage of at every opportunity. Yet they, along with many other immigrant ethnicities, persisted and persevered to build lives and careers that placed them in the pantheon of architects of American culture.

The brazen hypocrite who moans
O'er others' sins, yet dares dissemble
His own foul guilt, whereat the stones
Of Sodom's self might blush and tremble!
Thy power and pride shall cease below
The scoff of every tongue and nation,
And men thy name shall only know
As meaning guilt and desolation."

From *Song of the Irish-American Regiments*
by Richard D'Alton Williams
Irish poet/physician/revolutionary
b. Dublin, Ireland 1842
d. Thibodeaux, La. 1862

INTRODUCTION

The winds of rebellion in these United States gusted with alternating frequency all through the 1850s. Although they waxed and waned, and at times died down completely, by the start of the following decade they blew across the nation with a tempest-like ferocity, culminating with the onset of the great Civil War in the spring of 1861.

Of lesser moment perhaps was a church rebellion that erupted in the small village of Carthage, a hamlet tucked away in the northern reaches of New York State. The revolt would pit several Irish Catholic immigrants in a struggle against their priest and bishop, a conflict-by their Church's reckoning-that would put them at risk of losing their immortal souls.

The clash was the direct consequence of laws enacted by early American Protestant-led legislatures. The statutes were meant to establish rules for the administration of religious societies. The enactment of these decrees betrayed the lawmakers' servile adherence to an underlying principle of the centuries-old Protestant Reformation-namely, the separation of church and state.

These civil laws established a trustee system that put the governance of local churches in the hands of local laymen, a condition that was alien to the Roman Church. The Church's opposition betrayed the insecurity it still felt due to Martin Luther's schism begun some three centuries before. The notion that laypersons could have a say in ecclesiastical matters was a direct challenge to the Catholic Church's long-established authoritarian rule. The clergy were indoctrinated to believe they were intercessors between man and God, a principle that left no room for debate.

The struggle that developed between bishops and the lay trustees was by no means limited to Carthage. Several other parishes were also in rebellion over ownership of the deeds to church property and control of the decision making process.

The trustees, who had come from a land where church and state were inextricably and oppressively intertwined, were unwilling to give up their newfound power. The bishops, for their part, were unwilling to let the situation stand.

The rebellion at St. James Parish in Carthage, where this particular drama unfolded, festered over a period of years and manifested itself in verbal vituperations from the pulpit and letters to their bishop, along with a smattering of civil suits between parishioners and their priest.

The story of this struggle, no doubt duly embellished, long outlived its participants, and was whispered about and handed down to succeeding generations by the town's residents. Religious historians who wrote of the incident, *ex post facto,* harshly judged the Carthage congregation for its temerity and disobedience to the Church. Thus the rebels acquired a reputation for being unduly litigious, truculent, fractious, mulish, and even anticlerical. Stories, delivered in *sotto voce,* spoke of "black Masses" and other indignities that had threatened the Church's hierarchal order.

The dissenting members of St. James parish had come to America to escape the persecution, poverty, and political impotence endured under their former English masters. They were thus loath to relinquish any of their newfound freedoms. Arriving penniless for the most part, they dug in with their callused hands and sweaty brows to help carve out a settlement in the wilderness of the former Oneida Indian Territory. Whatever success they had was due to an independence of spirit and dedication to the drudgery required to survive in a hostile environment.

Take a journey now back to a time and place where a confluence of seemingly simple circumstances would cause an eruption that would affect the lives of many innocent bystanders.

Chapter 1

Carthage, New York, January 1861

"That bastard priest!"

Richard Gallagher bolted upright from his ample oak desk in the back of his spacious store. His large hands clenched the offending letter a messenger had delivered to his furniture emporium some ten minutes before. The elaborate penmanship with elongated curls and serifs, along with the red sealing wax securing the envelope's flap, announced its importance. Gallagher ran his fingers over the raised impress, embossed with the signet of the Most Reverend Dr. John McCloskey, Bishop of Albany. When he finally slid his silver dagger-shaped letter opener under the seal, freeing it from its mooring, he exposed the words that evoked his curse. He plopped back down into his stuffed chair and scanned the words anew.

> ... the Holy Roman Catholic Church's decision that you hereby be excommunicated from its membership rolls and henceforth denied the sacraments of salvation...

The sharp words jumped off the page to penetrate his soul. The lanky man abruptly stood up again, violently shaking his head, disheveling his thick, prematurely gray-streaked hair. With tightened jaw, he began pacing the rear of his store before sinking back into his chair for a third time. With great effort, he resisted the impulse to crumple the letter into a heap and throw it into his wastebasket.

"That bastard priest!" he muttered once again.

***

Kilhewire Parish, County Westmeath, Ireland, March 1825

A muffled knock at the door of his tiny thatch-roofed cottage aroused John Gallagher from fitful slumber. His wife Mary stirred, lifted her head, opened her eyes to slits and eyed the door through the dim light. Gallagher put his index finger to his lips and Mary remained silent, although apprehensively so. The tall man swung his legs over the side of his pallet and shoved his feet into his ragged slippers, which stood guard at his bedside. He took a few steps across the floor and looked up at the loft to see if the three boys sequestered there had been disturbed by this unexpected intrusion. Seeing no sign of such, he shuffled over the dirt floor to the rude door and whispered, "Who's there?"

"Open up, Jack," the voice on the other side whispered back. "It's me, Tommy."

Gallagher lifted and gently slid the latch to unbolt the planked entryway and let it open a crack. He peered into the darkness to ensure it was indeed his friend, another tenant farmer from down the lane. Warily, he eased the door further ajar and his stubby neighbor seized the opportunity to wriggle his way inside, closely followed by a whiff of chimney smoke that hung heavily in the chilly outside air. Although the peat fire was banked since the children went to bed, the two men sought the warmth of the dying clods, taking seats on the bench in front of the hearth.

"I've come with bad news," said Tommy.

"And what bad news would that be?"

"You're to be evicted."

A pause ensued, followed by a surprisingly calm, "And you know this how?"

"I have a source in the constabulary, a peeler from an Anglican family I've known for years. The order is to be executed next week."

"After all the work I've done, we're to be put off?" Gallagher said with rising anger, struggling to keep his voice down. If pressed to tell, he'd admit he wasn't surprised but angry nonetheless. "Those goddamned English aren't satisfied with ownin' nearly all of our soil. They want every inch. That bastard landlord has threatened more than once to raise the rent or put us off. Bad enough I have to give him two of every three potatoes I raise. Well, I been savin' for this day and now's time to risk the trip to the New World."

"Nay, I'll not be goin'." Tommy's words surged in resentment as they spilled from deep in his barreled chest. "This is my land, where I was born and where I'll die. The English be damned!"

"Shh, ye'll wake the wee 'uns," Gallagher cautioned, and added, "And if 'tis dyin' you'll be wantin', those bastards are more than willin' to oblige ya, if ya take my meanin'."

"Aye, perhaps they will," said Tommy, his voice descending into resignation. "Anyway, I thought you should know. I'd best be gettin' back to my place. The bastards think we're all plottin' agin' 'em and are really enforcin' the curfew, so I'll take to the hedgerows to duck the peelers, the same way I come."

"Mind yerself, and thanks for the warnin'." Gallagher sighed in resignation as he let his friend out, surveyed his surroundings, and seeing nothing amiss, softly closed and relatched the door. He shuffled back over to his bed still motioning to his wife to be still. "No need to alarm the kiddies," he whispered as he slid back under the covers.

In the loft directly above his parent's sleeping niche, seven-year-old Richard lay alongside his two younger brothers. They had each gone to bed wishing they could have had larger helpings of the meatless potato stew, but in spite of their rumbling bellies had finally fallen asleep. Only Richard was roused by the visitor's intrusion. He turned down the rough woolen blanket and inched closer to the edge of the garret, straining to hear the conversational echoes wafting up from below. After the neighbor left he lay awake staring up at the slanted rafters, mind racing and fretting over this news and what it meant. We're to be put off? he said to himself over and over. His father's grumbling about the ill-humored English landlord hadn't gone unnoticed, but he never dreamed it would go this far. He'd ask his da about it tomorrow, he resolved and tried to get back to sleep. An hour passed before the boy returned to the arms of Morpheus, only to have a disturbing nightmare about the loathsome landlord, pitchfork in hand, marching the Gallaghers off their farm.

When he awoke, the bleary-eyed Richard clambered down the ladder to see his worried father seated at their coarse dining table, in muted conversation with his ma. "We have to go now," his father said to a somber Mary, emphasizing the "now." Hearing his da's proclamation, the lad suddenly realized he had been forewarned. Each time his ma sent him to the root cellar, the dwindling potato bin grimly forecast a menu of smaller portions at mealtimes. The farm's two acres, at the limit of what the law allowed, just didn't permit John Gallagher to raise enough of those life sustaining tubers to feed his family, much less pay the rent. The blight that had come intermittently over the last few years only exacerbated the problem.

"Maybe the Church will do something," Mary said.

"Nay, there's too many of us," John replied. "They're overwhelmed and most of 'em are in hiding."

Richard thought back to the time he answered the door when two strange men came calling. "We're sorry, so sorry," he heard the visitors say over and over to his parents. They seemed kind enough, but their well-kept clothing carried an odor neither of sheep nor sod, which puzzled the boy.

"'Tis the smell of charity," his da said when asked. Richard took to sniffing his own well-worn garb to see if he also had the smell of charity, something he now deemed quite undesirable.

Neighbor Tommy's news had triggered John Gallagher's nascent escape plan. With furrowed brow the words came forth even more determinedly; "We have to go now or we'll never get out." With that final pronouncement he rose and traced the few steps over to the fireplace where he reached for the loose stone behind which his life's savings were secreted in a miniature tin strongbox. "I hope this will be enough," he said as he pulled the smooth rock away from its neighbors. He eased out and opened the small container and reflexively began fingering the small mound of silver coins that he'd hoarded over seven long years. "The fare's as cheap as it's gonna' get so we'd better plan on takin' advantage. We'll take passage to British North America."

"How much is it now?" Mary asked.

"'Tis 15 shillings* each for us, half for the wee ones. The English bastards always try to kill at least two birds with the same stone. They want to be rid of us and need people in their territories over there. And they don't want us goin' to America. But that's where we're gonna' end up. They hate the Yankees almost as much as they hate us 'cause they're still smartin' over the last war."

"Who are the Yankees?" the rapt Richard interrupted.

"That's what they call people who live in America."

The boy raced across the room and hustled up the ladder to wake his brothers. "We're gonna' be Yankees," he shouted.

"Who're the Yankees?" the boys asked in unison while rubbing the sleep from their eyes.

"Them's the people fightin' those 'savages' across the ocean." Richard had paid close attention to his teacher at the hedge school when his class was told about the primitive Indians that lived in America.

"It don't matter what the English want," the elder Gallagher continued from below. "Most of the Irish end up in the United States anyway. I've heard stories about livin' up in those northern wilds. It's almost as hard scrapin' out a livin' there 'tis here. If I could, we'd take passage to New York or Boston, but that'd cost 5£ each, almost ten times what it costs goin' to the English lands. It's barely manageable now, so that's where we'll be a'goin'. 'Tis better to risk the crossin' than be forced to choose which child gets his supper."

After young Richard and his five-year-old brother Patrick had prepared for school, his da brushed back the shock of black hair always tumbling down the older boy's forehead as he cautioned, "Youse boyos mustn't say nothin' to anybody, not even your schoolmaster. Get on to school now, and mind what I said. There are spies everywhere." He prized learning dearly, as did most of his countrymen, but had become sharply suspicious and trusted no one.

"I won't say nothin', Da," said Richard as he and Patrick trundled off to school.

Richard's teacher was an underground priest who was hiding from the British because the infamous Penal Laws outlawed both schooling and church for the Catholic Irish. These activities were always talked about in whispers for the boy's schoolmaster was indeed a fugitive. The cleric, in addition to teaching at the hedge school, also said clandestine Masses in a barn or behind a pile of rocks in a remote pasture. In exchange for teaching the children, the priest lived on whatever the peasantry could spare, often as little as a pound of butter or a piece of peat sod.

The secret schools got their name from pupils huddling out of sight behind one of the many hedgerows to take their lessons, weather permitting. They gathered in barns when it was not. The children, although they knew their schoolmaster's station, weren't permitted to call him "Father" for fear someone might slip and cause his discovery and subsequent imprisonment.

While meandering over the expansive green pastures to the distant schoolhouse-barn, Richard replayed in his mind the disturbing news that had descended on his family. "I'm gonna' miss school," he said absentmindedly to his brother as they passed the few sheep grazing nearby, "and tellin' the folks about learnin' Latin and Greek." He knew the reports of school activities, eagerly delivered at dinnertime, made his parents proud.

"You need a good education boyo," his da said in encouragement, for he himself had learned his readin', 'ritin', and 'rithmetic at a hedge school.

"The only thing I don't like about school," Richard said when the boys got home that afternoon, "is that the other lads are always talkin' about eatin'. It makes it hard to pay attention to our schoolmaster." The hungrier the youngsters became the more obsessed they were with food, and could not put such thoughts out of mind. Richard didn't like being reminded of the scant portions that made up his family's meals at home.

"Aye, 'tis understandable," said his da, "the whole country's starvin'."

"And little Terry Farrell didn't show up today. I asked about him and they said he'd passed away."

Richard didn't understand "passed away," but one of the older boys said, "It just means you're dead, stupid." This revelation so shocked him he vowed to never again ask about absent kids. He couldn't help scanning the faces of his classmates, wondering if any of the others might also "pass away."

"I'll be missin' school," Richard sighed as the family sat over their meager evening meal.

"There'll be plenty of schools in America," assured his da.

"Richie got into a fight," Patrick blurted.

The parents looked alarmed as his da asked, "Why, boyo, why?"

Richard shot a piercing glance at his sibling that had no visible effect on the tale-teller.

"A big kid called him stupid," Patrick added.

Richard's anger had flashed, embarrassed he didn't know what "passed away" meant, and resented being called stupid in front of the other boys. He charged the bigger boy and pushed him to the ground. His antagonist jumped up and retaliated with a punch to Richard's head. The clamor of cheering boys brought the schoolmaster who rushed to separate the writhing pair. "I'm surprised you've enough energy to fight," the priest said.

"Mustn't do that boyo," his ma said waggling a finger at her son. "We're not a family of low class scrappers, you hear?"

"Aye, Ma," the boy replied, his head bowed in insincere contrition. *And I'll do it again if he calls me stupid. I ain't stupid!*

The boy turned his thoughts to the many things he wouldn't miss upon leaving his homeland. He had watched his mother working in the evenings knitting sweaters to sell, while his da complained the price she was getting was barely enough to pay for the wool. "You're workin' for buttons," he said in exasperation. Many Irish women toiled in cottage industries making various products to sell that helped their families make ends meet. The elusive ends, however, no longer met-in fact they weren't coming close enough to exchange a greeting.

"Buttons," Richard thought, we can't eat buttons!

"I won't miss Ma comin' down with the fevers either," he said to his brothers. "And I won't miss havin' to tell you blokes to be quiet 'cause Ma's ailin'." Richard didn't have to mention he also wouldn't miss being hated by the English.

"We're ready to go," the elder Gallagher announced two days later.

"We'll not take any rags with us," their ma said as she supervised the packing. However, filling the handbags required judicious sorting because there was scant difference in the quality of their clothing. The parents had four large fabric satchels, one each for them and two additional for the three boys. "We'll bundle up the blankets and coats with this rope and let the poor wretches who take this place have whatever's left," said Mary Gallagher as she supervised the packing.

"I doubt anybody will be takin' this place," said her husband bitterly. "They're turnin' our farms into pastureland to raise more sheep."

The family rose early the next day and traveled on foot the short distance from Kilhewire to Mullingar, where they took a horse-drawn barge down the Royal Canal to Dublin. The journey would take thirteen long hours, but Richard and his brothers would treat the outing like a picnic. Spring had burst forth and the scent of wildflowers blooming above the waterline penetrated their nostrils. The sun peeked out to warm them, and the two older boys lay on their bellies to gaze over the side and stare at the tadpoles making jagged arcs just below the surface. Occasionally they saw a large carp go lazily by. "Oh, Da," Richard exclaimed, "can we catch a fish?"

"No, boyo," Gallagher laughed, "we've no poles to catch a fish."

The lad was disappointed but continued staring at the ripples in the barge's wake, even though it made him dizzy. His eyes glassed over as he became caught up in daydreaming about the adventure of going to America.

When finally they docked at Dublin, the wide-eyed Gallagher children gawked at the sheer size of the place. As they made their way off the barge, Richard and Patrick wrinkled up their noses at the lingering whiff of fresh caught fish permeating the air. It was foreign to them, and decidedly unpleasant. This prompted Richard to have his first misgivings about this adventure.

Gallagher soon learned the last of the three Dublin-Liverpool Steam Packet Co. boats that made daily trips across the sea had departed. He arranged to board the family overnight at the hotel owned by the Royal Canal Company. For a shilling the five Gallaghers squeezed into a room with one bed. The parents and youngest boy William slept on the bed while Richard and Patrick lay on a blanket on the floor. Richard whispered to his brother that he didn't like it much because the room was dusty and had a dank odor that reminded him of the smell of the root cellar after a heavy rain.

An uneasy sleep ended with the dawn. The troupe arose and speedily descended the rickety hotel stairs, happy to abandon the derelict accommodations. They soon boarded the first steam-powered paddlewheeler to take them across the sea to Liverpool, a journey of eight hours.

Unlike the barge trip, this experience was anything but picnic-like. The steam engine's thumping pistons rhythmically shook the deck with each stroke, frightening the children. "'Tis normal," John Gallagher assured his brood. But Richard could feel his pounding heart keeping time with the pulsating engine.

"Why can't we go down?" Richard pleaded to his Da.
There was no shelter from the inclement weather rolling in from the northern Irish Sea. The wind and rain whipped them mercilessly as the Gallagher family huddled together with the rest of the passengers on the open upper deck.

"The damn fools think more of their animals than they do of us Irish," his father replied, straining to be heard over the howling of the wind and the drumbeat of the engine. "They're the only ones allowed below."

As the steamer bucked the waves, there soon came a point at which young Richard re-voiced his doubts about the wisdom of this journey, especially when his ma began coughing. "Are you sure we should be goin' Da?" he said, spitting the salt taste from his mouth. The fun had on the barge had been transformed into the miserable reality of life on the open sea, and the boy didn't like it one bit. Sensing his father might also have regrets, Richard studied his face intently. But the elder Gallagher's stoic visage betrayed no remorse.

"There's no turnin' back," John Gallagher whispered to his wife.

CHAPTER 2

"Look at all those people!" Richard said as he pointed to the ragged human horde lining the Liverpool wharves.

"They're all waitin' for their chance to escape," said his da. Mary shuddered with sadness.

The steam packet had arrived at low tide and the exposed, barnacle encrusted piers frightened Richard the closer they came to it. The boy held his da's hand ever more tightly as the wind-weary travelers struggled up the gangplank. They scarcely noticed the hungry seagulls' serenading squawks from the gray-blue skies above. When they alighted on the dock proper, Richard asked about the line of beggars cadging handouts. "Aye, 'tis a shame," his da said somberly. "No matter how bad off we are there's always worse."

The elder Gallagher reminded his clan once again to "be on the watch for blacklegs"* mingling among the unwary émigrés. Such shady characters lurked about waiting for newcomers and the opportunity to cozen them out of their passage money. The grapevine, fed by the letters emigrants sent home, had forewarned Gallagher to buy the tickets at Mullingar before starting the journey. What little money was left would have to tide them over until their ship, the *Exmouth Castle* arrived.

The vagaries of wind and weather accommodated no accurate ship scheduling, so Gallagher's inquiry to the harbormaster about the *Exmouth* was met with the hackneyed phrase, "Expected any day now." He fingered the leather purse attached to his belt and decided they had enough money to do as they did in Dublin-find lodgings to wait out their ship's arrival.

"We can manage a few days," he said casting a wary eye down the narrow cobblestone street. He cringed at the score of wretches lining the gutter, unfortunates who had recently been added to the ever-increasing roll of those who could no longer afford food, much less lodging.

"Hey, mate, need a room?" One of the many boarding house shills trolling the docks for customers called out to Gallagher.

"Aye, how much?"

"I can get you a nice room for your whole tribe for one and six."

After a bit of negotiation, it was decided a room could actually be had for a shilling, same as in Dublin.

The agent, a lean specimen of about twenty, bowed politely in a manner ordinarily reserved for a person of higher station and led the Gallaghers down the smooth cobblestoned street past even more hapless beggars soliciting alms. "Can you spare a few pence?" they pleaded, but Gallagher had no coins to spare.

"Some of the bloody ships never come in a'tall," their escort whispered, "and these poor bastards are left to beg in the slums of this pitiful place. I'm one of the luckier ones." He then admitted he also was a stranded Irishman who had, through a friend of a friend, secured an agent's job. This gave him a place to stay and a few scraps to eat, all of which helped keep him a half step ahead of the starving street people they passed.

"Look," Richard whispered to his brothers as they walked by the emaciated multitude, "those people are Irish, just like us." Even a seven-year-old could recognize his kinsmen by their dress and demeanor.

Weeping silently as they walked, Mary was overcome by a feeling of despair. "Oh, these poor, poor people," she murmured while trying to hide the tears worming their way down her cheeks.

"God forbid this happens to us," Gallagher said softly.

The observant Richard, responding to his mother's sadness, fought to hold back a sympathetic welling in his eyes.

Poverty had worked relentlessly against the Irish people and gave their enemies one more bone to pick with them.

Their bedraggled appearance, along with occasional outbursts of compensatory boisterous behavior, only reaffirmed the stereotype the English had affixed to their Celtic cousins. "They're no more than drunks and criminals and we'd best be rid of them," a voice was heard to say as they passed a pub. Richard didn't need to be reminded, for even children his age could sense the wrath of entrenched hostility.

Unwittingly, the stranded Irish only served to intensify the English disdain. Their popular "rugged individualist" belief held that anyone who really desired to better himself could do so by dint of hard work. This dogma was unremittingly advocated by scholar, economist, and clergyman Thomas Malthus, and adopted by even the poorest of his countrymen who fared no better than the Irish. "They show no restraint in their procreation and the sooner their excesses are checked by famine and disease, the better," Malthus preached. He pointedly aimed at those who refused to convert to Anglicism. Ironically, the clergyman saw no conflict between his attitude and the precepts of his Christian religion. "We'd best be rid of these papists. They're all part of the Roman conspiracy against us," he railed in his sermons.

When the subject of conversion came up, Richard's da had always uttered in defiance, "Catholic we are and Catholic we'll remain."

The Gallaghers' guide paused in front of a ramshackle structure with a crude and defeated HOTEL sign hanging askew over the entrance. "It's seen better days, no doubt," John Gallagher said as he appraised the weathered clapboard structure. The squeaking of the boards as the family trooped in only served to confirm the antiquity of the place. Happy to reach their lodgings, if for no other reason than to relinquish the depressing street, the family was shown to a room on the third floor, one little different from the lodgings they had occupied in Dublin.

"I hope we don't have to stay here long," Richard whispered to his brothers. The Gallaghers soon settled in with grim resignation to await the arrival of their ship.

Early the next morning, Richard and his da returned to the harbor to check ship arrivals. Lady Luck smiled on them as the three-masted brig *Exmouth Castle* pulled into Waterloo Dock as they watched. Its hold was stuffed with timber from British North America.

"Look at how big it is," Richard exclaimed as he stared at the name engraved into a wooden plank curving aft from the ship's prow. The harbor master informed them the vessel required another day to unload, and install bunks before the gangplank could be put in place for boarding. The ship was built in 1818 and regularly made lumber runs from the New World to Great Britain and was returning for more of the same. Rather than deadhead back, the owners found it economically desirable to take on government-subsidized émigrés, even at the low fare of 15s. It was much better than no fare at all.

The next day the Gallaghers mingled among the anxious mob of passengers, waiting patiently for the signal to board. When a gong was struck, everyone made a mad dash up the gangplank. They had heard stories of ships abruptly pulling away from the dock, intent on taking advantage of the tide. Crowds of easily entertained spectators lined the wharf to watch the scramble. The jostling soon became frenzied and disordered, and the gangplank's continual shifting and swaying made many justifiably fearful.

"Hold tight!" Gallagher hollered, but he could barely be heard above the din as he cradled the youngest in his arms. Mary, her body quivering with fright, clasped the hands of the two other boys and joined in the mad rush to board the *Exmouth*. The family breathed a sigh of relief after they made it aboard without any untoward incident.

No sooner had the Gallaghers boarded when the *Exmouth* was abruptly towed away from the dock. Two stragglers fell into the water as the gangplank was yanked away from the ship. A loud splash announced a mishap and was accompanied by shrill shrieks from the gathered gawkers. "Ooh, lookee there," they shouted to the idling dinghies below. "Man overboard!" Enterprising boatmen at Liverpool dock stood ready to fish floundering travelers out of the water-for a price.

"This must'a been what it was like in Paris when crowds gathered at the guillotine to watch Robespierre's victims," said a gentleman standing next to Gallagher.

"Aye, so, I've heard," Gallagher said as he took stock of the man clad in black and clutching a familiar church missal. The look of religion ringed the man, or so he thought.

The crowd that cheered when two men fell into River Mersey also cheered when they were fished out. They roared their approval when the ship passed through the dock gate to the open sea, either in congratulations for a successful departure or in happiness to be rid of yet another clump of unwanted humanity. And the passengers waved and cheered in return, relieved and elated to finally quit the shores of England.

"I won't wave at those bastards," Gallagher muttered in disgust," and Richard hurriedly put his hand down.

Once below in the belly of the Exmouth, Gallagher laid claim to one of the hastily rigged bunks at the rear of the hold. It measured six by six feet and, according to rule, had to accommodate the entire family. Each adult was allotted a width of eighteen inches, with half that for a child. For the Gallaghers, that came to 54 inches, leaving room for one more child.

"Ye'll have to make do with that crib. It'll hold a family of six," said a sailor supervising the mad rush for accommodations. "Ye'll have to make room for everybody." A neighbor put one of their children in with the Gallaghers and no one gave this a second thought.

Gallagher hadn't bought one of the straw mattresses being hawked by vendors on the dock, so the family had to sleep on the planks. "Couldn't afford it," he lamented to Mary. They had to make do with the blankets they brought with them, spread over the boards. Everyone lay on their sides to make the cheek to jowl accommodations workable.

Once through the dock gate and out on the open sea, the *Exmouth* headed back towards Ireland from whence the Gallagher's had come. The captain decided his course based on the prevailing winds, and on this day, the air currents pushed them north around Mallin Head. This was where the voyage to British North America, soon to become more popularly known as Canada, would commence in earnest.

“What's that noise?” the frightened Richard asked his da after they had gotten underway.

No experienced traveler himself, the elder Gallagher's furrowed brow showed he was just as anxious about the loud groaning that assaulted their ears. But one of the crew told them to put aside their fears. “Not to worry, 'tis normal. The timbers are flexin' their muscles,” he chortled.

After a few days on the sea the passengers no longer noticed the sounds of the ship and they settled into a monotonous routine.

“This smells better than those rooms we had to stay in,” Richard observed. The woody odors of fresh cut lumber pleased his nostrils and he started thinking it might be a pleasant voyage after all. The boy looked in awe down the length of the hold at the mass of humanity occupying sleeping quarters on either side of the narrow gangway. "How many people are in 'ere?" he asked his Da.

"Too many," was the reply. "They count the wee ones as half a regular passenger, so there's half again as many here as should be." Although the *Exmouth* was officially registered to carry 165 passengers, the owners boosted the rolls by counting two children as one adult-a legality permitted by British maritime law.

Now on a steady course for the New World, the *Exmouth* pitched and rolled with the wind-whipped waves, a development for which most of the 241 passengers' constitutions proved intolerant. Many became seasick and vomited up their meager rations. The malady took no pity on the Gallagher family, with the exception of Richard, who pranced about the ship thumbing his nose at the ever-present *mal de mer*.

"Da and Ma don't look so good," Richard whispered to Patrick a week into the voyage. Indeed his parents had gotten quite green around the gills and looked as wretched as the other unfortunates. Mother Mary began coughing again.

"It really stinks in 'ere," Richard said to his ma two weeks into the journey. The pleasant scent of wood had been overcome by the odors of human excrement.

"Aye, my son, it does." She turned to her husband and asked, "Will they never clean up?"

"'Tis no fault of our people," he said. "When you're as sick as they are you kin'not help if you din'not make it to a slop pot." The elder Gallagher joined the cleaning parties by lowering buckets with long ropes into the ocean to capture seawater, which they then sloshed on the floor of their compartment.

"I'm not sure 'tis makin' it better," Mary said.

"We hafta try to do somethin'," her husband replied.

To avoid the unpleasant conditions below, Richard spent as much time on deck as the breezy April weather permitted. Surveying the crew as they went about their duties, he took special note of the sailors who ascended the ropes to the crow's nest. One day he impulsively decided to climb up to the perch himself. Only a few steps into the adventure, he felt a heavy hand tugging on his leg as he heard a voice say, "Nay, you can't go there!" The old salt who had grabbed his leg and pulled him down then said, "Not even cabin boys are allowed."

Richard's spirits were abruptly dampened for he wanted to view the ocean from aloft, optimistically thinking he might be able to see America from up there.

As the Exmouth labored ever onward over the choppy Atlantic, gaunt looks and wan pallor decorated the faces of nearly every passenger. "How are you feeling?" the man with the missal asked Gallagher.

"Why ya askin'?"

"I've heard the plague's aboard."

"Do ya think I look sick? I'm as healthy as anyone 'ere." Gallagher's voice rose in protest because he knew shunning those who might be sick had become a common, if imprecise, practice. And he did not want to be labeled a disease carrier. Nonetheless, although he resented being singled out, he felt compelled to issue a warning to his family to be careful, and not to go near people who looked sick.

Richard began eying everyone, especially the younger children, and continually cautioned his brothers to stay away from this or that child. "They all look sick," he finally said in exasperation to his Da. And it was indeed difficult to find healthy looking specimens among the multitude.

The conditions the Irish endured in their homeland had ill prepared them for the rigors of the journey, a journey made harsher by uncaring and unscrupulous ship owners. The bad food worsened as the voyage progressed and only added to their misery. The bread became hard and moldy and the scarce portions of mutton hadn't fared much better.

"They say there's typhus aboard," John Gallagher whispered to Mary. The contagion had stolen aboard as an invisible passenger. What he heard as a rumor soon proved true as an outbreak on the *Exmouth* saw the Grim Reaper begin to systematically pluck his prey from the rolls of the weak-the children and the elderly. "Everybody's gettin' scared," Gallagher said. "They're tellin' stories of burials at sea and even ships disappearing never to be heard from again."

Mary shuddered anew and hugged her children ever more tightly, as if to protect them from the unseen menace.

Early one morning, three weeks into the voyage, Richard was awakened by a sharp shriek. "What was that?" the startled boy asked as he lurched upright.

His Ma, along with several others, also abruptly sat up, peering into the dim light of the breaking dawn. Mary could see a distraught mother, a few bunks forward, gently cradling her child. The woman stroked and rocked her infant girl, as if trying to make the child show some sign of life.

Finally her husband put his arm around her and said, "'Tis no use. We'd best prepare for the burial." The mother's wailing and uncontrollable sobbing transfused the entire compartment and as if on cue many women began sobbing in unison.

"She's passed away, hasn't she, Ma?" Richard said while watching tears course down his mother's face.

A few women rose in an attempt to console the bereaved mother, but they could neither stem her tears nor alleviate her sorrow. Richard's gaze transfixed on the scene as one of the women wrapped the infant in a blanket that would serve as the baby's funereal cloth. The man with the missal, who had let it be known that he was a deacon at secret church services back in Ireland, soon appeared. A small makeshift funeral procession languorously emerged from the hold, led by the lay cleric mumbling Latin prayers from his black book.

After the convoy reached the upper deck, Richard followed even though he had been told to remain behind. He somberly watched as the tightly wrapped waif was gently consigned to the deep. The wails of the bereaved mother drowned out the sympathetic moaning of the wind while everyone dutifully made the sign of the cross and prayed. Richard wondered if any more such processions would be made before the *Exmouth's* journey concluded.

Lingering on deck after the funeral procession returned below, Richard heard a voice say, "If you think it's bad on this 'ere ship, believe me there's plenty worse." It was the same sailor who had befriended Richard after pulling him down from the rigging. Staring at the earring in the old salt's left lobe, the boy wondered how the man could talk while puffing on the clay pipe clenched between his teeth. "We don't lose as many as others I know," the sailor added. He proceeded to relate his experience on a variety of ships crossing the Atlantic, as Richard listened, both in fear and wonderment.

The boy took to roaming the ship most of his waking hours, causing his parents to continually worry about him. Having heard about such phenomenon, his da warned Richard about being swept overboard by a rogue wave. But the ghastly images of dead children being lowered into the sea trumped any concern he had for his own safety. *I'll not stay below,* he thought. *'Tis where everybody's gettin' sick.*

"The boy's stubborn," his father said to his wife.

"Aye, the lad's got a mind of his own," replied Mary.

After six long weeks on the briny, and none too soon as far as Richard was concerned, the ship docked at the port of Grande Isle, Quebec. The lad watched with excited interest as seamen and stevedores looped large hawsers over the piers and prepared to lay down the gangplank.

Like everyone else aboard, the Gallaghers were eager to quit the ship and put the voyage behind them. "Let's pray and give thanks for our safe journey," said John Gallagher. With wobbly sea legs, they threaded their way down the gang-plank onto the Massive dock and into the teeming throng of immigrants hustling to and fro.

Confusion reigned over the crowded expanse of pier as most did not know where they should go or what they should do. "Hang on tight!" was the oft-repeated instruction as the Gallagher family formed a chain of hands to keep them from being separated by the crowd.

British government officials herded the disembarked into groups for processing and begin their introduction to life in the sparsely settled country. The prosperous looking bureaucrats meant to funnel these people to the more unpopulated western and northern territories where they would be given land to farm. "All ye have to do," they said, "is work the land for five years and the acreage will be yours to keep." The government felt after that period of time, the newcomers would be so invested in their farms they would remain there permanently.

“They want to put us in their wilderness,” Gallagher said, betraying his wariness of the scheme.

Conspiring to foil the British plan were the land and labor agents from America who also prowled the docks at Grande Isle. "We've got lots of land too," announced an agent from the Holland Company in Buffalo, New York. "We've thousands of acres acquired in treaties with the Indians. We're looking for people to settle on them. You can get land on the cheap!"

American canal building was in full swing and operatives of construction companies were on hand to entice needed labor. The willing and desperate-for-work Irish were more than eager to hear these offers. The competition for able bodies became fierce as agents shouted out the needs of Massachusetts, New Hampshire, and various parts of New York State.

“We'll go to that place called the Mohawk Valley. The land’s fertile I'm told,” Gallagher said to his wife. "We’ll do well there.” His friend Seamus Cunningham had settled in a community called Utica in Central New York, and that was where his mind was set to follow.

An agent from the Holland Land Company accosted him and said, "I'll arrange passage on a barge that will transport your family down to Western New York. That's where my company has its lands. You can be very happy there." Gallagher sprang at the offer, and the last leg of his family's journey was soon underway.

The pilgrimage proved to be quite scenic and impressed Richard with sights he never saw or could even imagine back home. "Look there!" he exclaimed to his brothers as he pointed to the Adirondack Mountains off in the distance. His brothers also gawked in wonderment.

The long trip took them down the Richelieu River to the recently completed Champlain Canal. The barge stopped along the way to discharge and take on passengers at Plattsburg and Burlington. Soon they were on the Erie Canal, which stretched nearly to Buffalo. As the trip wore on, the sheer vastness of the land impressed the Gallaghers, especially young Richard.

When finally they reached Utica, Gallagher and his family rushed to disembark, even though the Holland Company lands lay further to the west.

"This is where Cunningham told me to get off," he said when other passengers told him they still had miles to go. "Nay, we'll go no further." Despite the protests, the family alighted, intending to unite with their friend from the Auld Sod.

"We're all Yankees now," Richard said proudly to his brothers.

CHAPTER 3

"We'll make room for ye 'til you're settled," Gallagher's friend Cunningham said. "I'll tell you all you need to know to get started. For now, rest your bones. I know the trip can take its toll." The family had arrived with the help of an Erie Canal dockworker at the Utica port who was alerted to be on the lookout for them.

Gallagher became a tenant farmer again, only this time it was for his friend Cunningham. The two older boys enrolled in school, and soon they all became acclimated to life in America. Although he didn't mind doing farm chores after school, Richard didn't look forward to them either. When given the choice, he opted for driving a team or helping repair a wagon instead of working in the fields. His da noticed the boy's hands were always looking for something else to do besides pulling weeds.

Twelve months after arrival, the Gallagher tribe grew by one as they celebrated the birth of John, Jr. The family's increase prompted the elder Gallagher to work even harder, and three years later, with his friend's help, acquired a quarter section of his own and had a community barnraising. His family had become firmly established in their new life in America.

"'Tis ours, not some bloody landlords," Gallagher said with pride as he looked over his property. Although their home wasn't much bigger than the one they left in Ireland, there was no equivalence as far as the family was concerned.

As the years passed, Richard appreciated the family's good fortune the most. "I love America," he often repeated with pride.

To the bullies at school, Richard looked an easy mark but it took only a fight or two to convince them to look elsewhere. The lean and angular lad didn't have rippling muscles, and lacking such might deceive an antagonist at first, but most soon learned to think twice before challenging the shy immigrant farm boy.

Meals at the Gallagher household seemed to be extravagant celebrations by comparison to those back in Ireland. But letters from home, passed from neighbor to neighbor tempered the family's joy. Richard's parents felt guilty about the poor wretches left behind to the mercy of the English. "We must give thanks," their da said to the family each time they sat at the table in their humble home. "America, 'tis indeed the land of plenty. Maybe someday," he said to his boys, "you'll help others and repay the debt we owe." Richard took this admonition to heart as he devoutly bowed his head in prayer.

Richard's parents, after the initial salubrious effects of relocation had passed, began suffering bouts of sickness that couldn't be explained by doctors. Their faces became drawn, bodies thin, and they coughed a lot. The physicians said it was the result of what they went through back home. "It's left a permanent mark, I'm afraid." The boys sadly realized there was nothing they could do.

The days and weeks laboriously and uneventfully passed and soon Richard was poised to enter the eighth and last grade of his education.

"I'm not much for farmin'," he said to his Da.

"Aye, I've known that for some time." Although all of the boys were accomplished at working the soil, only John, Jr. seemed willing and fitted to embrace the farm work as a vocation. Richard came to loathe the barn odors because they aroused olfactory memories of the *Exmouth* stench, which in turn brought back thoughts of sickness and death.

"I like makin' things, Da," Richard said, and he took every opportunity to work in the farm's small smithy. He repaired the wagons, tempered the iron for the carriage rims, and shod the horses with a fervor that proved to his father it was better to let him ply a trade than drive a plow horse or work in the fields. "I'd rather be buildin' or fixin' somethin' than workin' in dirt," Richard admitted.

When his eighth grade schooling was finished, Richard's speech had become indistinguishable from native born boys. He summoned his Irish brogue only when he wanted to tease his countrymen. "Da, I'd like to try cabinetmaking as my trade," he said one day, and the boy was soon placed as an apprentice in a woodworking shop in Utica.

Richard would learn that sickness and death was not confined to Ireland or the *Exmouth Castle*. By the time his twenty-first birthday approached in 1838, both his parents had passed away. Their fevers and periodic relapses that had vexed them during those malnourished days in Ireland increased in frequency and dealt them both a final blow, just thirteen years after arriving in America. Richard's da passed away, only one week after his ma. The rigors of farm life had exacerbated the couple's already compromised constitutions, and the doctor said it was consumption that did them in.

"'Tis a blessing. They're in a better place," the priest said, but Richard spontaneously disagreed.

"Nay, Father, 'tis not a blessing for us." The Gallagher boys had listened to the prolonged death rattles from both their parents, and none could see how their passing away could in any way be a blessing. "I respect what you say, padre," Richard added, but in his heart he reserved judgment as to whether this was God's doing. *More like the work of the Devil,* he thought.

Richard's cabinetmaking apprenticeship was nearing its end. He had attacked his profession with an enthusiasm his master craftsman said showed promise of a bright future. "We cabinetmakers can build anything that's made from wood," he said and Richard learned to make all types of furniture from hutches to caskets-with equal skill. He had become so adept at crafting chairs that he decided to specialize in them. Proud of his workmanship, he would run his hands over the smooth arms of a completed piece, and carefully carve his name on the bottom of the seat. He loved the scent of sawdust, which reminded him of his first few pleasant days on the *Exmouth Castle*. Many customers, after seeing his signature on a chair, specifically asked him to custom craft their seating needs. This, of course, made the lad exceedingly, and rightfully proud.

It wasn't long after his apprenticeship concluded that an ego-deflating anvil dropped. "I'm afraid you'll have to find some other place to ply your trade. There's too many young lads ready to take your place," the master craftsman announced. Richard had hoped against hope he could remain where he was. Although the news was not a complete shock, the young man frowned dejectedly as the master craftsman continued. "I hate to lose you, son, but there's too many shops and not enough work. I'll give you a good recommend if ye'd like."

Richard carried the news home on a visibly sagging back and told his brothers, "I've been sacked. I've got to find another job." With Patrick and William pitching in, they scoured ads from the local and New York sheets. Most of the cabinetmaker notices were for jobs far away from Utica.

Richard spent several days writing to prospective cabinet shops across three states and could do no more than await their replies.

"Here's one that looks interesting," he said to his brothers one evening. The opportunity that caught his eye was in a small town called Champion, some sixty miles to the northwest of Utica. "It's on the shores of the Black River, not that far away."

Coincidently, a companion article in the paper described the manufacturing plants being thrown up at a frantic pace in the area, on both sides of the River. Champion's bustling sister town of Carthage, formerly called Long Falls, had grown to over 1,500 by 1835.

"Just look at that," Richard exclaimed to his brothers, "they've got a blast furnace, potash manufactory, flax mill, two saw mills, a tannery, gristmill, forge, rolling mill, nail works, axe factory, and carding mill! Those workers will need good furniture." He was right; there was ample opportunity here for a young and ambitious man like himself.

Not only did the news article extol the economic opportunities awaiting the area's immigrants, but also told the story of the prominent land developer Count James Le Ray de Chaumont. The man had fled France during the Revolution and had acquired thousands of acres that encompassed the better part of three counties. The devout count had also endowed a thriving church in Carthage that when established in 1818, was only the fourth Catholic Church in all of New York State.

"And they've got a church named St. James," he reported to his brothers. Richard knew it was rare for such a small hamlet to have a Catholic Church as many larger towns had no Sunday services at all. Had he been old enough and less bewildered, he might have remembered Le Ray's agents roaming the docks of Grand Isle looking for workers and farmers when his family arrived back in 1825.

Richard wrote an inquiry to the cabinetmaker, Mr. Roswell Woolson, and made sure to include a copy of the letter of reference he'd received from his former employer. It was the middle of 1839 and Woolson, who had an established cabinet shop in a place called Champion, New York, said he needed a junior partner.

Richard fidgeted as he awaited a reply, thinking his recommendation was favorable enough to receive a quick response. He was disappointed when four weeks went by without an answer. Finally, a letter arrived that his long fingers anxiously ripped open. "If Mr. Gallagher desires to make a trip up to Champion, Mr. Woolson will be happy to interview him for the open position."

Richard was torn. The cost of the trip would tax his finances, and a hard day's travel over those roads would take him further from Utica than he'd been since arriving in

America. After agonizing over the decision for a day, he said, "I'll go." Early the next day he packed a bag, climbed aboard the buckboard, and brother William drove him to the stage depot. After he doled out the fare for passage, he waved goodbye to William and boarded a coach to Boonville. From there he changed to another stage for High Falls where they stopped at the line's inn for a bite to eat and a pair of fresh horses. The coach then proceeded to Lowville and finally dropped him off at Champion.

He discovered upon inquiry that Woolson's shop was just up the street from the stage depot. He banged on the door only to be answered by a loud barking dog that was standing guard inside. The weather-beaten cabinet shop was closed for the day so he went to the adjoining house, knocked on the door and asked, "Do ya know where I might find the cabinetmaker Woolson?"

"Are you Gallagher?" asked the short, stocky man who guarded the entranceway. Upon receiving the lad's vigorous nodding assent he said, "I'm Woolson. Well, you've gotten here late," he said a bit gruffly. "We'll have to put you up for the evening and go to the shop tomorrow."

Richard, disappointed at the tepid welcome, affected a wary attitude towards both the Englishman and his missus, as they bade him to come into the kitchen. Mrs. Woolson sporadically conversed with the lad as he attacked a plate of cold mutton, while the master of the house remained silent. Richard could not constrain his exuberance as he prattled on about his bumpy ride and his woodworking experience while the owl-like Woolson sat on his perch puffing a clay pipe. Mrs. Woolson soon warmed to the lad and he noticed her face had taken on a kindly, sort of matronly, look. She had, he learned, borne no sons, been brought up in a proper New England home, and was obviously a product of good breeding. She made sure the weary traveler had enough to eat before escorting him to his small room on the second floor.

Richard, however, still didn't know what to make of Mr. Woolson.

The exhausted traveler collapsed onto the trundle bed and was soon fast asleep. When he was called early the next morning, he rose to rub his eyes, feeling as though he he'd been asleep for only a few minutes. *I'll be needing more rest than that,* he thought.

After breakfast, Woolson, with Richard trailing behind, waddled over the short distance to open the shop. "Quiet, Cromwell," the owner hollered to his growling dog.

Following a safe distance behind, Richard surveyed the wood shop. It's quite a bit smaller than the one in Utica, he calculated, and the equipment is a bit older. But he didn't think it was a problem he couldn't handle.

"Let's see what you can do," Woolson said cautiously, whereupon Richard grabbed the leather apron that hung on a wall hook, draped it over his body and went over to the lathe to prepare to turn a piece of oak stock into a chair leg. He was at the machine for but fifteen minutes when Woolson became animated, moved closer and exclaimed, "Stop! You're hired!" He stuck out his stubby mitt as an invitation for Richard to seal the bargain. The pair of calloused hands met in midair and clasped in a firm handshake, signaling the beginning their partnership.

If there was one thing Woolson respected, it was craftsmanship. Woodworking was the commonest denominator for most of his friendships. As improbable as this seemed to Richard just twelve hours before, Woolson had done a complete turnabout, color came to his face as his frown melted away. The New Hampshire Yankee had never met a competent wood turner he didn't at least try to like. And his now friendly face, framed by a neatly trimmed but graying beard, beamed a wide, tobacco-stained, toothy smile. Upon second appraisal, Richard thought the gnomish Woolson could be a man he might actually enjoy working with.

"Ye'll stay at my home, of course," his new partner said. Richard was familiar with the practice of master craftsmen boarding their workers, especially because of the general shortage of lodgings in these fast growing towns. Census takers found it rare to encounter households without nonfamily members residing there.

"The place is small," Richard wrote to his brothers a week after arriving. "'Tis a lot smaller than Utica but the town they call Carthage over on the east side of the Black River looks to be quite a bit bigger." Champion was but a collection of farms, a few homes, a forge, and three factories on the riverbank. Gallagher didn't mind the diminutive setting, nor its rutted streets, which turned to mud after a rain. He was just happy to be placed in a permanent situation with an opportunity to start making some real money. "It don't bother me none," he wrote, when describing the small inconveniences he had to put up with. "Woolson's a nice chap, and he likes to joke around and makes me laugh a lot." Richard had few occasions to joke at the cabinet shop in Utica, but he thought that was due to his master craftsman being much more serious than Woolson. "Rozzie, I call him, is making me feel right at home," he wrote, unable to mask his obvious satisfaction.

A week after his arrival, Woolson sent Richard on a trek over the rickety bridge to Carthage to purchase supplies unavailable in Champion. As the buggy rattled across the bridge and made its way up State Street, the young man gawked at the business district. *The stores got boardwalks out front just like Utica,* he observed. He wished they had them in Champion so he wouldn't get his boots muddied up. He picked up the grit paper and wood glue as instructed and instead of immediately heading back across the bridge, drove the buggy up the street past St. James Church.

As he did a U-turn in front of the church he thought he must come back for a visit soon.

Chapter 4

It was a nice day for a walk, Richard conceded as he sauntered over the bridge to Carthage. He had on his Sunday best, which weren't so much fancy as they were clean. His outfit was plucked off the clothesline in back of Woolson's house just two hours before. He tried to remember the last time he'd worn his tight-fitting coat that even without a vest was much too snug. With the gait of a conquering hero, he tugged at his slightly askew shoestring tie that was knotted as best he knew how. Given he hadn't much opportunity to practice such costumery, he thought himself quite acceptable. His only pair of boots, scraped of Champion mud, lacked a coat of polish, but this gave little concern.

"Nice day," he said to everyone he passed. And indeed it was. The sun shone brightly and the few puffy snow-white clouds dancing above the gentle breeze gave no hint of raining on his parade. He tipped his cap to the women and tossed smiles at the hoop-skirted young misses. A warm blush in his cheeks swiftly followed this gesture, as the soft fragrances exuded by these ladies tantalized his nostrils. *Looking good, yesiree, looking good,* he said to himself, as he eyed the ladies ever more closely. The animal passion welling up within him surprised as much as it pleased. He had been so busy with learning his trade and securing financial permanence he hadn't found time to indulge that side of his nature.

He was on his way to visit St. James Church, which he had scouted two days before. After a brisk jaunt up State Street hill, he reached the large clapboarded building where a dozen or so people congregated outside, enjoying the late summer sunshine.

"Mornin'," he said again and again to the polite nods of the people conversing in front of the house of worship. They wore Sunday clothes a peg or two better than Richard's. "What time is Mass?" he inquired.

"Oh, there's no Mass today," a short, chubby lady piped up. "We've no priest, don' cha know? And who might you be?"

Richard was unused to being accosted by women whom he thought should leave such interrogation to men. "I'm new here. Name's Richard Gallagher from County Westmeath. I've just taken a job in Champion with Mr. Woolson." *Why did I say that,* he wondered? *Why did I feel I had to mention my Irish ancestry? After all I've been in the country for fourteen years.*

"Welcome Mr. Gallagher," the lady said with a head toss that signaled her approval. "I'm Nancy Walsh. You can call me Aunt Nancy. Everybody else does. We're from County Monahan" she said mockingly, returning the favor of Irish ancestry. "Let me introduce you to my brothers," she said taking him by the arm.

A rush of blush invaded Richard's cheeks as he regretted the mention of his Irish provenance. He hastily added, "I've actually just come from Utica, where my family's lived since coming to America, to take this job over in Champion." He thereupon shook hands with Patrick, James, and Anthony Walsh, the unmistakable brothers of Aunt Nancy.

In the subsequent conversation he learned the Walsh clan, as did a majority of the Irish, lived at a Settlement some five miles south of town, just over the Lewis County line. All were farmers except Anthony, who plied the shoemaker's trade.

Gallagher felt a heavy hand on his shoulder from a fellow who awaited no introduction. "I'm George O'Leary," said the stocky, ruddy-faced man whose features jutted out from under a green Tam O'Shanter. Richard turned and took the proffered mitt but wasn't prepared for the knuckle-crunching grip that followed. It choked his hand, making him wince appreciably-to the laughter of the men who knew what was coming.

"That's quite a grip you've got there," Richard said, alternately massaging and flapping his wounded paw while nervously trying to laugh it off. *Son of a bitch,* he thought, *I wasn't ready for that. Was he trying to embarrass me?*

"I like to welcome newcomers properly," said O'Leary with a twinkle in his eye.

"The Squire's got a bit of a mean streak," said James Walsh with a wave of his hand. "But he don't mean nothin' by it. It's those shoemaker hands, doncha know. Now yee've been properly initiated into the Irish community."

In the animated conversation that ensued, Richard was disappointed to again hear there was no local pastor, and that a missionary from Watertown-some sixteen miles to the west-served the parish, and then only when it fit his schedule. "'Tis a shame," boomed Nancy Walsh. "We've a place large enough to house 400 people, and we often have that many on those days when we have a priest."

"We might get a visit every two or three months," said her brother James, the words tumbling sadly out of his tanned and weathered face.

"This has to change," Richard said firmly. "Have you written to the bishop?"

"Aye, of course we've written," said Patrick Walsh as the bystanders nodded their affirmation. "But what does a bishop down in New York know of us folk up here on the edge of the wilderness? He thinks we're still living among the savages."

"Humbug! They don't know what it's like up here," said Aunt Nancy, not waiting her turn to speak. "The Diocese of New York covers the entire State! And, they claim there's a shortage of priests, especially in these northern parts."

"This is not good," said Richard, his voice straining to reach a lower register.

"We could use some new blood around here," said O'Leary. Although a shoemaker by trade, he was one highly respected as having learnin'. "Are you fixin' to become a member of the parish?"

"Of course," said Richard.

The introductions continued as he met a pair of grunting old farmers, Farrel Neary and Ed Galvin, identified as trustees of St. James Church. Neary and Galvin were the earliest Irish immigrants to land in Carthage. Gallagher soon felt comfortable among these people, but not with quite the same warmth he had established with Woolson.

"We're holding Sunday school for the kiddies inside," said Aunt Nancy.

"I'm still puzzled as to why a parish this size don't have a priest of its own," Richard said again, even though he knew the answer. "We'll have to work on this," he repeated. "Now I must go in to say my prayers."

"He's a pious one, ain't he?" whispered Aunt Nancy as Richard headed towards the church entrance.

"Maybe he's just puttin' on airs," scoffed brother Patrick. "Thinks he can influence the bishop, does he?"

"There ya go," scolded Aunt Nancy. "You don't think any-body's as holy as you. Maybe he will influence the bishop. Lord knows you've tried. And look what it's gotten us."

Richard traversed the boards leading up to the church and walked through the tall double doors. Once inside, he looked around, and was pleased by what he saw. Rows of oak pews graced either side of the center aisle, leaving walkways next to the outside walls of the building. He walked up the middle aisle to the altar rail and knelt to say his prayers.

As had become his habit, he beseeched the almighty on behalf of his departed parents and to give thanksgiving for his safe arrival to the New World. When he finished his supplications and returned outside, the Walsh brothers approached and invited the new member to their next Saturday night get-together, which had become a ritual at the Settlement. "Come on down next Saturday. Ye'll get to meet everyone, and we have good food and dancin'," he said with a wink.

"I'll have to think on it," said Richard. His previous cabinetmaking cohorts in Utica never invited him to go dancing so he hadn't had the opportunity to learn, although he harbored the dream of doing so. It would be useful for meeting the ladies that much he knew. He hadn't cultivated a drinking habit either. *Don't want to be seen as just another drunken Irish bum,* he'd often thought, wary of fulfilling the English stereotype.

"Oh, come on, you'll enjoy it," brother James piped up. "You'll meet some pretty lasses as well," he added with a hearty laugh. "You're not married, are you?"

"Nay, nay," Richard said. "Haven't had time to think on that." The comment about pretty lasses did jog his loins, so he said he'd try to make it. *Might be good for me after a week of hard work,* he mused.

After bidding his newly introduced fellow congregants goodbye, Richard walked back over the bridge to Woolson's house. His boss had just gotten back from attending services at the Methodist Episcopal Church, only a block up the street from St. James. "I could have given you a lift if you'd spoken up. How did you find it?" he asked.

"It was alright," said Richard. "No priest."

"Aye, I hear they been having problems getting a regular minister."

"I hope we can do something about that. I met lots of nice people though. And they've invited me to their Settlement on Saturday."

Richard gave Woolson a rundown of whom he'd met, and in return got his opinion of these people-including whom he might want to stay away from. "The Walshes are good people," he said. "And O'Leary's all right. But that Aunt Nancy's a regular busybody ain't she?"

Richard let out a chortle, "So she's got a reputation, eh?"

"She'll be fixin' you up with one of her colleens, that one. Funny, she ain't never had a beau of her own but delights in matchmakin'. Maybe that's her only way of gettin' to go to weddings. It'd be good for you to go down to the party on

Saturday, but you gotta be careful. They can get a bit wild. Take Bessie, I'll have no use for the horse on Saturday night."

The following Saturday afternoon, Richard found himself sitting on the seat in Woolson's trap, reins in hand, clicking his tongue at Bessie as they headed down Mechanic Street towards the Irish Settlement. There was hesitancy in his movement as he flicked the lash lightly on the horse's hind-quarters. *What am I getting myself into?* he wondered.

Upon arriving at the Settlement, Richard parked his buggy alongside the line of carriages and looped Bessie's straps around the hitching rail. He walked towards the commotion that met his ears and ended up at the Settlement's town square where he found the festivities already underway. The aroma of mutton turning on a spit filled the air along with the faint odor of what he thought was spilt beer.

"Well, hellooo there Westmeath boyo," a voice boomed as Aunt Nancy spied the bachelor. "I see you decided to join us," she said, a bit too enthusiastically for Richard's taste.

"Thanks for the invite," came the shy response as others also came to offer their welcomes. The rosy-cheeked Nancy took the bashful boy by the arm and led him into the gathering for a round of introductions. The blizzard of names tattooing his eardrums could not possibly be remembered. Nancy also made sure they passed by the row of young ladies seated around the square's grassy perimeter. Mildly aroused, Richard bowed and shook hands with each and every lass. The girls giggled and fluttered their eyes at the handsome newcomer, and Richard's cheeks took on an even-deeper blush. Aunt Nancy gave a knowing wink to the ladies, and they responded with even broader smiles.

The arrival of another rooster in the barnyard was greeted with muted squawks of hostility from the young bucks standing by. Richard was so focused on the ladies he didn't notice the scowls being launched in his direction.

"Come and get a plate of vittles," Nancy said as she led Richard to the eating area. There he found a row of tables covered with all sorts of familiar Irish food, including stew and scones, which he really loved. The visitor was prodded to fill a plate and was handed a mug of beer as he went to sit among the men, most of whom had already finished eating.

"So, what do you think of our little gathering?" James Walsh inquired.

"It's very nice," came the somewhat self-conscious reply. "We never had these kinds of get-togethers back where I lived."

"You didn't? What was wrong with your people?"

"Our farms were quite spread out," said Richard. "We didn't have a gathering place like this nearby. I guess we never mustered up the same traditions you folks have here."

"You'll find sticking together will benefit us all. We're in this together, you know," said Patrick Walsh. "There's enough hating here to go 'round for all us newcomers."

"America seems different," Richard volunteered as several pairs of eyebrows at the table rose in unison. "Different kinds seem to get along better here than back home."

"'Tis true," said James, "up to a point." His voice of experience was persuasive as he jabbed a forefinger in Richard's direction. "It's not like the Auld Sod, that's for sure. But the hatin' exists. You're a bit short in the tooth but yee'll see it soon enough." Richard sensed a hint of condescension but let it pass.

"My boss Woolson seems a very nice chap. He's accepted me without any reservations. At least that I can see." Since arriving in America, Richard had met many people whom he might have instinctively considered enemies back in Ireland. But he soon came to believe they were of a different ilk than those who came banging on the Gallagher's door in the middle of the night back in Kilhewire. Or even those who cheered his departure from the wharves of Liverpool. "I never thought that I'd be working with an Englishman. Roswell Woolson don't seem to have any of the notions about Irish I saw back home."

"Oh, he's a good man," O'Leary volunteered. "I've found him to be as honest as the day is long. He's a New Hampshire Yankee, don't ya know. I think he's been here longer even than Farrel Neary."

"Come on, have another beer." Jimmie Walsh waved his mug, beckoning him towards the keg.

"No, thanks, one's plenty for me," said Richard to the raised eyebrows of several of the revelers-along with chuckles from the younger boys.

"Well, the dancin's starting up. Pick a nice colleen and take a trip around the square," said Aunt Nancy who had just come back to check-up on her visitor.

"I'm no good at it."

"Posh," replied Nancy. "Any of these girls will be happy to teach you."

"Maybe you can do the honors, Nan," said O'Leary, a man who obviously placed great store in his wit. Nancy was eight years Richard's senior and not at all attractive to him, although his manners wouldn't allow him to be so crass as to mention that. He didn't much take to her loud and assertive demeanor, and wished the members of the fair sex behaved more like his ma.

"No thanks, Ma'am." His polite refusal went for naught, however, as Nancy grabbed his arm and pulled him out onto the green. As the stumbling Richard clumsily clung to Nancy, they gracelessly weaved around the other dancers, eliciting gales of laughter, especially from the girls. The tall, fidgety Richard with his short-armed, flailing and foot-stomping partner, tickled the bystanders. The more the spectators laughed, the more bewildered the discomfited lad became.

"Kinda stiff, ain't he?" said Jimmie Walsh.

"I hope he's better at writin' letters to the bishop than he is at dancin'. Maybe he'd loosen up with some Irish whiskey," said Patrick as he tapped the personal pint he kept concealed in his coat pocket.

What ensued for Gallagher, who looked like an awkward giant stomping on an anthill, was total embarrassment, and he reddened appreciably. He tried looking down at his partner's feet to get an idea of what he was supposed to do, while punishing the ground with his size thirteen boots, all out of time with the music. The more he concentrated on his feet the more he bumped into other whirling and footslogging dancers. It was obvious Terpsichore had not spoken to him, and altogether probable it might not have mattered even if she had. Although Richard tried to be a good sport about it, he was completely flustered and when the music paused, eased his way off the dancing green and receded into the crowd. When sure no one was paying attention, he stole off, retrieved the carriage and was soon on his way back to Champion.

"I won't be doing that again real soon," he remorsefully confided to Bessie.

CHAPTER 5

Richard had waited an entire week to cross the river to visit St. James again, hoping his initiation into the Irish community had been forgotten before he had to meet any of them again. Yet, he knew he couldn't avoid them forever, not if he wanted to worship at their church, which he fervently did.

"Well, look who's 'ere," Aunt Nancy's voice boomed, "our dancing Westmeath boy!"

Gallagher smiled wanly as he greeted everyone but his eyes narrowed at Aunt Nancy's words. Nonetheless, he couldn't avoid her as she took his arm and led him to a young lady who was standing off to the side of the church entrance. "Here's a girl who's been dyin' to meet ya," she boomed. "Meet Miss Charlotte Cunningham."

The young girl, who looked about eighteen by Richard's reckoning, bowed slightly and flashed a broad smile revealing a sparkling, if a bit crooked, set of white teeth. Her Sunday best brought back memories of the dresses his ma used to make. It was a simple creation with no hoops or stays. "How do you do," said Charlotte as she offered her dainty hand in greeting. "I saw you at the Settlement last week, but we never got a chance to dance," she said, suppressing a muffled laugh.

"Well, you're lucky in that," Richard replied with a downward glance. "Are you related to the Cunninghams down Utica way?"

The girl threw off the question with a laugh. "There's way too many Cunninghams. Maybe next time we'll get to dance," she said with a twinkle, placing a hand on her hip and leaning to one side as if to invite Richard to come closer.

Now where'd she learn that? Gallagher wondered as his interest became aroused. But before he could entertain the idea of accepting the overture, a young man rushed over to insinuate himself between the couple. "Excuse me," he said gruffly. "Charlotte, isn't it time we went inside for prayers?"

The girl blushed before an ashen veil fell across her face. "I wasn't ready to go in just yet," she said sharply as she dropped her arm and stiffened upright. Richard, whose muscles had involuntarily tensed, could see the girl wasn't as attached to this boy as he wanted to convey.

"Nice to have met ya," Richard said as he reluctantly turned away to rejoin the gathering of men. He wondered why Aunt Nancy had introduced him if the girl was spoken for. Was he supposed to compete for a farm girl? He chuckled at the self-styled boyfriend whom he vaguely remembered from the crowd of roosters he saw down at the Settlement. He felt no need to create a bad impression by getting into a broil in front of the church. *Must avoid Aunt Nancy at future gatherings,* he thought, but reckoned this might be hard to do.

After his praying was done, Richard went window shopping up and down both sides of State Street. He was getting acclimated to the town and liked to bask in the air of civility it projected. Several of the buildings gracing both sides of the thoroughfare reached three stories high. And he could tell from the names on a few that men from Ireland owned them. Yes, he thought, I've made the right choice. This will be a good place for me to settle down and raise a family.

***

As the months wore on, Richard worked tirelessly to improve his financial prospects. His reputation for making fine furniture was the most important thing in his life, more important even than courting farm girls, he said to Woolson. His hard work was paying off and he became firmly established as the best man to make your chair, on either side of the River. Woolson's business was on the increase, due in great part to his junior partner's labors. It became increasingly clear to Roswell he would soon have to consider making Gallagher a full partner.

For the first time in his young life, Gallagher was making a decent living. His savings grew as he continued to observe and learn what he could from Woolson. He had long ago put aside the man's adherence to the Episcopal faith and knew his first impression had been way off the mark. Their fast friendship had exceeded the boundaries of their business relationship, a development he had not anticipated.

"He's got a way with the tools of the trade," Woolson was heard to say about Richard more than once, "and can really make the lathe hum." A year into the partnership, Richard had begun to outpace the owner in crafting a variety of furniture pieces, both in quantity and quality.

Rozzie began needling Richard about being single. "You don't even have a girlfriend yet. Don't you like girls?" Outside of a few dates with the Settlement's Charlotte, he hadn't been seen with any other lady. "All work and no play makes Jack a dull boy, so they say," added Woolson.

Richard did his best to feign anger. "What do ya mean by that?" he blushed.

Woolson laughed at this pretense as his ample, apron-bound belly bounced in rhythm with each chuckle. "How old are ye now? Going on twenty-three? And still not starting a family? What's a fine specimen of a man like you doing single? Didn't the Irish lassie over at the Settlement suit you?" Woolson enjoyed teasing his partner.

Richard, found too many of these good-natured jibes hitting home. "I don't know, Rozzie," he responded. "I'm not ready for marriage. It's a big step. If you take a girl out hereabouts, everybody starts asking 'when's the wedding'"?

"Oh, you'll find the right lass soon, especially with your financial prospects. You won't get away. That Walsh woman has it in her mind to mate you with one of those Settlement girls."

"They don't interest me," Richard sighed. But it was a half-truth, for he did find a few to be attractive, although none were what he had in mind for a long term relationship. Sure he'd dated the buxom Charlotte Cunningham but found her a bit eager, too forward. The romance hadn't gotten past a kiss or two despite signals from the girl she was eager for more. "There's not a lot of refinement there, if you take my meaning."

"Getting snobby, are you?" Woolson teased. "I hope you're not going to behave like some of the English I know."

Richard reddened anew because Rozzie was again hitting close to home. "I know it sounds odd coming from me, but I've been reading some of your books and I like those stories about English gentry. It gives me something to look forward to."

"Well if a refined English girl is what you think you'd like, I've got just the lady for you." Woolson then brought up a young woman named Maria Sherwood. "Her father was a medical doctor who passed away some ten years ago. She lives with her brother, a sawyer I've done a lot of business with." His eyes twinkled as he began warming to the idea of being a matchmaker.

Gallagher feigned perfunctory interest and as offhandedly as he could, and then asked about the woman's religion. "Is she a church-going woman?"

"She goes to my church."

"Nay, I don't think she'd be right for me, Rozzie," he said, obviously unprepared to consider marriage to a Protestant woman.

But Woolson wasn't easily put off and two weeks later, unbeknownst to Richard, invited the woman and her brother to Sunday dinner. "Richard Gallagher, this is William Sherwood," Woolson said, "and his sister, Miss Maria Sherwood."

"How do you do?" Richard stammered, taken aback by the woman's beauty. He shook William Sherwood's hand while unable to stop staring at the man's sister. He wondered why this pretty lady, who exuded the scent of spring wildflowers, hadn't yet married. He surveyed her attire and saw her tightly cinched blue satin dress was quite a bit fancier than those worn by the Settlement girls.

He recalled Woolson mentioning Miss Sherwood had many suitors over the last few years but she had deemed none suitable. "They be all farmers, as rough hewn as the logs her brother makes into lumber," Woolson assumed. "She doesn't see herself tied to farm life and enjoys conversation like the ones she was privy to between her father and mother when they were alive." Even though her age was drifting upward past the traditional marriage years, Maria Sherwood had decided to wait until a better prospect came along.

"How do you do?" cooed Maria as she extended a dainty, lace-gloved hand to Richard. He was torn about what to do next. *Should I kiss it,* he wondered, *or should I give it a gentle shake like the girls down at the Settlement seem to expect?* The English gentlemen in Woolson's books took every opportunity to kiss a lady's hand. He decided to softly shake the proffered limb, and they all sat down to converse and get to know one another better.

Richard found himself at pains to stop his eyes from fixating on Miss Sherwood as he continued to inhale the pleasant fragrance wafting from the vision seated across from him. *She can't be twenty-one,* he thought as he searched his mind for the information Woolson had given when discussing the lady. He thought she looked eighteen at most. The transfixed young man silently gave thanks to the gods she hadn't yet found a husband. He resolved to pay attention because this could develop into something serious. Even though it was the first time he'd laid his hungry eyes on her, he wondered why the attraction was so sudden. It was a question for which his flustered mind had no answer.

After the roast beef dinner and apple pie dessert-during which many pleasantries were passed that everyone seemed to enjoy, except William Sherwood-the party retreated to the parlor to continue the small talk. Mrs. Woolson soon began serving the steaming chicory-coffee she had prepared in her small kitchen. Their conversation turned to the Black River Canal and its potential impact on the area, but Richard wasn't really paying attention. Maria's pixyish ways so distracted and intrigued him that his thoughts could focus only on her. Maria laughed easily and often, and after interjecting a comment, hid all but those dancing blue eyes behind her fan, making it impossible for Richard to divine her thoughts. The smitten young man listened intently whenever Maria took her turn to discuss topics that, due to their variety and depth, quite often surprised and pleased him.

"Wasn't that tornado in Mississippi just awful?" Maria exclaimed. "Why just three months ago over 300 souls perished. I hope we never have that kind of weather here."

Richard hadn't kept up with the news so he thought it best to remain silent while everyone listened attentively to the grisly recitation of death and destruction in Natchez, Mississippi. It became obvious to him the lady was not only well informed but also commanded a refined usage of the English language. As the conversation trekked across a variety of topics, Richard learned Maria was also acquainted with Shakespeare and Keats, personages he knew by name only. His thoughts alternated between the subject at hand and her appearance. Her dress showed a petite figure to great advantage. Soft brown curls framed a delicate oval face housing those blue eyes that not only sparkled but set off fireworks whenever she looked at him. He felt they could penetrate his innermost secrets. When she occasionally pursed the lips of her small mouth to emphasize a point, Richard's cheeks warmed and he began fantasizing about kissing those self-same lips. He was taken prisoner by Maria's manner and found himself at a loss for words. The more the lady spun her spell, the deeper his attraction became. He wondered if this could be what they called love.

As the evening drew to a close and the Sherwoods rose to leave, Richard resisted an impulse to ask Maria's guardian if he could come courting. It was a bit too soon for that, even for life on the frontier he decided, although it was definitely on his mind.

After the Sherwoods left, the ever-keen Woolson asked Richard what he thought about Maria Sherwood, even though he knew the answer. "I think you like her a little," he teased.

"She... she... seemed alright," Richard finally admitted.

"Maria appeared to like you too. It'll take a little persuasion of the brother, but I think I can bring him around."

"Do you really think so?" Richard replied, in a rising voice, betraying anticipation.

"I'm going to have to get you married off, or you'll be no good to me in the shop. Your mind will be on the lady and you're liable to saw your hand off. Now that would not be a pretty sight."

"It wouldn't hurt for you to make a discreet inquiry, would it?"

"Let's see what I can do. I've set this in motion, so I've an obligation to bring it to the next step."

After falling asleep, Richard dreamed he saw Maria Sherwood beckon him as she floated atop a white cloud. "Come to me..." her voice repeated over and over. After a night of tossing and turning, Richard came down to breakfast with a bright smile on his face.

CHAPTER 6

"You know, Roswell, I'm not at all sure this is best for Maria." In the back of William Sherwood's mind was the thought left unspoken that his sister should not become involved with a Catholic, much less an Irish Catholic. Woolson saw his courtship idea foundering. He knew Sherwood was a cautious man, one who carefully chopped trees to make sure they fell in just the right direction. Woolson figured he'd have to convince him that if Maria's fell for Gallagher, it would be the right direction. Of course a good dose of Maria's pleading wouldn't hurt either.

Corresponding problems took root in Gallagher's mind as well. He appreciated that the English Protestant Woolson had accepted his Catholicism, seemingly without reservation, and wondered why he shouldn't adopt the same attitude towards the Sherwoods. He debated with himself, thinking friendship was one thing but marriage quite another. Yet the prospect of forming a union with this lady became the central focus of his thoughts. Was it enough he was attracted to her and wanted her to be the mother of his children? Or did marriage also require a compatibility of religious beliefs? Wrestling with this dilemma occupied much of his time.

Richard had encountered many men of differing national origins in his short life but had developed social relationships with only a few. The smaller towns of Champion and Carthage gave him opportunities to come in contact with a more diversified group of English, French, and Germans. Cities like Utica seemed to engender a clannishness that wasn't as obvious in this smaller place, the Irish Settlement aside. His attitude towards his former English oppressors, although greatly mellowed from his years in America, had not totally disappeared.

Two weeks later, in spite of his initial concerns about religion and ethnicity, William Sherwood reluctantly agreed to a courtship between Maria and Richard. The couple met regularly and properly at Sherwood's modest home. A few weeks into their courtship Richard felt it was time to take the next step, to do something more than sit on the front porch with their *de facto* chaperone lurking in the background. It was the edge of wilderness, after all, and few couples had time to follow fancy courtship formalities.

"Do you think you'd like to take an excursion with me up the Black River next Sunday morning?" he asked Maria.

"Why yes, Richard, I'd like that very much. But don't you have to go to church?"

"No, we haven't had a priest in over two months. Don't know when one will be coming by."

That Maria was willing to forgo services at her church, which had no ministerial shortage, for a date with him made the lad feel she was serious about him. And he attached great importance to this observation.

When Sunday rolled round, Richard urged Bessie over to the Sherwood residence, and with hat in hand knocked on the door. Maria's unsmiling brother answered and greeted with a tart, "Oh, it's you."

Maria soon came clattering down the stairs, and with a cheery "Good morning, Richard!" she breezed by her brother.

Richard's countenance took on a rosy glow whenever Maria came into view. Her brother's obvious disapproval of him did nothing to dampen this reaction. He offered his hand and, as always, her slightest touch sent shivers up his back, making his arm quiver involuntarily. They walked out to the carriage and Maria allowed Richard to boost her up to the box, a chore he loved.

"Bessie smells clean and fresh," Maria remarked. "Did you just groom her?"

Richard sheepishly admitted he had, but didn't add that all his preparations aimed squarely at having this outing come off perfectly. As they rode off, Maria was all a'jabber, excitedly making small talk while her attentive beau, as had become customary, listened intently.

"So, what have you been doing, Richard?" she inquired after a bit, thinking it might be good to encourage her bashful beau to get a few words in.

"I finished a real fine chair yesterday, in Queen Anne style. I'll make one for you if you like."

"Oh, that would be lovely." Maria beamed.

Soon the carriage rode onto the bridge that crossed the river to Carthage. "My, my," Maria exclaimed, "is this structure safe? My brother said there's some concern over the soundness of it."

"There's been talk of putting in a new one, it's just a matter of someone raising the money," Richard replied as the carriage rumbled to its destination.

At bridge's end, Richard pulled on the right rein to maneuver Bessie onto Water Street where the excursion boat was docked and waiting.

"Oh my, we'll have lots of company," Maria said excitedly, as she glanced at the large crowd gathered for the pleasure trip up river to Lowville. She could hardly contain her enthusiasm at the prospect of spending a whole day with her handsome suitor.

The wharf area was busy as usual, but today there was an added attraction. Rev. J. N. Webb, pastor of the Baptist Church, was conducting a christening in the shallows down river from the boat dock. As the couple looked on, the minister led a half-dozen aspirants into the stream to waist-high depth. He began the ritual dunking of each convert according to the rite's traditional baptismal ceremony. He pinched their noses shut and tipped them backwards into the dark waters of the river while his flock on shore accompanied the ritual by loudly singing Rimbault's "Oh happy day... when Jesus washed my sins away."

Richard didn't know the lyrics, but Maria instinctively began mouthing the words as if to sing along. "Oh, so you know that one," Richard remarked. Maria didn't catch the hint of sarcasm in his voice, or if she did, she wisely chose to ignore it.

"Oh, yes, it's a beautiful song," Maria glowed. Richard began wondering just how entrenched his lady was in these Protestant hymns and customs. "It was written by an English clergyman," Maria added.

All the better, Richard thought, but decided to keep that deliberation to himself.

The *Cornelia II* majestically awaited as Richard stood in line to purchase tickets. "I'm told the boat gets its name from the wife of one of the major stockholders, Vincent Le Ray," Richard said. "Vincent is the son of Count James Le Ray, the man who started St. James parish. The original *Cornelia* was built back in 1832 at a cost of $6,000."

"Oh, how nice," Maria replied, feigning an interest to convince her beau that knowledge of these matters was important.

"It's a fairly new vessel that was built to replace the original, which was the first steamboat to navigate the river south to High Falls," Richard continued. "I hope we don't have the bad luck she had." His dissertation forged ahead with details about how the original unwieldy vessel had drafted too deep and ran aground several times. "Its only saving grace was that it proved you could navigate the forty-two miles up to High Falls. They tell me back five years ago, before I came here, she broke loose from her moorings, went over the dam and smashed up on the rocks below. They salvaged the engine and it's being used in the iron mines up north. Le Ray took a big loss on the deal, but everyone thinks he could well afford it."

"Yes, I remember that," Maria replied, recalling the event was big news back then.

Whenever the opportunity arose, Richard enjoyed displaying his knowledge of the history of the place he now called home. It helped emphasize his commitment to the area where he had come to earn his fortune and raise a family.

Maria tightly held her beau's arm and smiled contentedly, unconcerned about a few of the onlookers' prudish stares. She was truly proud to be seen with her escort.

Gallagher fished out the 38½¢ fare for each from the leather pouch attached to his belt and plunked the coins down on the counter. Tickets in hand, the couple followed the other passengers down the gangplank to board the flat-bottomed paddle-wheeler for the eagerly anticipated outing.

The pair barely listened as Captain Sweet shouted the details of the excursion through his megaphone. "We'll make six miles an hour when we get steam up, so our trip upriver will take about two and a half hours. It'll be a fair bit less coming back on the current," he added.

As soon as the last passengers boarded, the *Cornelia's* whistle tooted its readiness and the gangplank was stowed. The captain rang the ship's bell three times, a signal to the engineer to stoke the boiler with more wood. At his urging of the throttle, a shower of sparks ushered up the stack and a long plume of smoke trailed the boat's stern as they inched away from the dock. Richard could taste the flavor of burning wood in his mouth and instinctively spat into the river. "Sorry, dear," he said, worried his impulsive act might be offensive, but she just smiled.

As the *Cornelia* gained speed a gentle May morning breeze bathed the couple's faces, which only added to their pleasure. The smiling Maria, with her long curls fluttering from under her straw hat, looked up at her escort just as a gust nearly blew her hat away. But the alert Richard caught it just in time. "You'd best tie that ribbon," he said as he gently placed the chapeau back on her head.

"Isn't the scenery beautiful!" Maria couldn't hide her excitement as she pointed towards the shore. "Look at those trees!" The front rank of the dense pine forests crowded the waterline, as if to dare anyone to enter their forbidding thickets. "It looks as wild and uncivilized as nature intended."

The couple was having a marvelous time chatting and observing nature, but the scene that interested them most, if pressed to admit it… was each other.

Captain Sweet used his megaphone to periodically punctuate the trip with short spiels about each point of interest. As the boat traveled further away from civilization, the scent of the river took on a cleaner fresher smell. Its odors carried no hint of the many bass, pike and pickerel lurking below.

All too quickly, as far as the couple was concerned, the *Cornelia* arrived at the Lowville dock. The gangplank was put in place and the passengers disembarked to be greeted by an array of picnic tables on which a buffet lunch had been placed, ready to stuff the hungry sojourners.

"Look at this, Richard! There's wurst, and baked ham, and fried chicken, and sauerkraut. And look at the bread!" Maria pointed to the many dark loaves stacked before them, which served to betray the German character of Lowville. Richard sniffed and salivated as a brass band began playing lively tunes, which only added to everyone's enjoyment.

The two lovebirds sampled each of the several varieties of food. They took turns feeding little bites to each other. After lunch was consumed Richard suggested they go for a stroll to get away from the crowd. "I've got to walk off this meal," he said. "Let's see if we can find a spot to be alone." From the moment they landed he'd been plotting to get Maria away from all those prying eyes. His quickened breath gave away his anxiety.

The couple took a path leading away from the picnic area and once they had gone a sufficient distance, Richard veered off the trail into a sparse thicket that obscured their view of the crowd. He took Maria's face into his hands, looked deeply into her eyes and said, "I've been waiting a long time for this." He bent down and kissed his love, flush on those lips he had admired for so long. There was no objection from Maria and no doubt in Richard's mind she was a willing participant in this show of love. *This must be what heaven is like,* thought

Richard as their lips pressed together and his arms tightly encircled Maria's waist.

"Oh, Richard," cooed Maria, "I think I'm falling in love."

Richard couldn't stop kissing his love and finally she had to gently push him away. "We mustn't overdo," she said, as softly as her rising ardor permitted.

The aroused young man let out a long sigh as he released his grip. "I know I'm in love," he whispered. The soft words came out with such deep conviction that Maria thought, if only her brother heard them his objections would melt away.

After what seemed too short a time, the *Cornelia's* steam whistle signaled the couple to return to the dock. The pair skipped down the path hand in hand to join the laughing and chattering crowd. The knowing glances of some of the passengers caused Maria to blush but Richard beamed with pride. Soon the steamer was plowing down the Black River on its way back to Carthage.

The trip came to its inevitable end when Richard deposited Maria back at her doorstep. "I had a wonderful time," she said rather giddily as Richard held her hand. Before he had a chance for another kiss, the door abruptly opened and Maria's unsmiling brother appeared.

"You've been gone a long time," he barked.

"Oh, was it long?" Maria said with feigned surprise. "It was wonderful. Good bye, Richard," she liltingly added as she floated into the house and up the steps to her room.

The young man couldn't help but look back before he mounted the buggy. He caught a glimpse of Maria looking down at him from her bedroom window, and his heart took another skip. He was hardly touching the seat of the trap as he guided Bessie back to Woolson's place.

"Have a good time?" Woolson asked.

"It was good," Richard replied, but couldn't hide the twinkle in his eyes.

"I bet it was," the older man said with a chuckle. "I bet it was."

CHAPTER 7

The courtship of Richard and Maria continued into the year 1841 as they basked in the benefits that deep love bestows on the young. They had overcome any lingering concerns about ethnicity and religion, as Maria and Richard became totally devoted to each other. "I love his expressive, steel-gray eyes and the passion he shows for everything he talks about," she mentioned to her brother, who grunted, remained skeptical, and wondered how he might derail this romance.

The couple's religious beliefs, in particular Maria's Episcopalian faith, were often the subject of conversation. Without any prodding, Maria spontaneously offered, "If you choose to have me as your wife, Richard, I'll gladly embrace your Catholic religion." She knew in her heart this was an essential condition for marriage to this devout Irishman, and she wanted him to know she was ready to accept and follow. Coincidentally, it was also one of the easier religious bridges to cross. Maria knew many Episcopalians had made that same journey to Catholicism, even some of their clergy.

Richard's eyebrows knitted together in surprise for he expected his intended to fight for her denomination. "You make me so happy. I know you'll make a good Catholic."

Maria's brother continued to be unhappy at the progression of the courtship, which came as no surprise to the lovebirds. He was an elder in the Methodist Episcopal Church, as was his father before him. His reservations not only concerned religious differences, but also the Irish reputation for copious alcoholic consumption and raucous behavior. On this issue he was an adherent of Malthus' principles, which thoroughly denigrated the Irish. He consciously avoided conversation with Richard unless the situation demanded it. "Your brother doesn't like me much," her suitor said.

"Oh, don't worry about him, dear. He'll come around," Maria responded with a confident glow.

But the woman had underestimated her brother's resolve. One day a farmer from Deer River by the name of Manning showed up at the Sherwood's door. Hat in hand he had come to see if Maria Sherwood might accept a courtship entreaty from him. He wouldn't mention that William Sherwood had put him up to the visit by inferring his sister was available. Sherwood welcomed him warmly into their home as he called up to Maria, "We've a visitor. Come down please."

Maria was puzzled but obeyed her brother's command. She was sharply taken aback when her brother explained who the man was and what his purpose was. "No, no," she said in a firm but quivering voice. "I'm not available for any such consideration!"

"You must not be rude," her brother scolded as the red-faced suitor fidgeted nervously. He was obviously unprepared for such a reaction.

"It is you, dear brother, who is being rude," Maria hissed through clenched teeth. "You gave me no warning and put Mr. Manning's hopes up for no good reason. I'm sorry but this cannot be." With that pronouncement she bid good day, turned and retreated up the steps to her room.

Embarrassed, Sherwood now faced an angry visitor. "What kind of fool do you make me?" he shouted at the mumbled apology, then turned heel and stormed out of the house.

William Sherwood had vastly underestimated his sway over his sister and her commitment to this Gallagher chap. He would now have to resign himself to the fact that Maria's mind was made up and there was naught he could do. Yet, he still felt an obligation to ensure this was a proper match. So, with no prospect of stopping the courtship, he leaned on Woolson for advice. "What do you make of Gallagher?" he inquired, and listened carefully to Woolson's opinion.

"Gallagher's a hard-worker and has excellent financial prospects. I fear he'll be striking out on his own one of these days. And I've never seen him take a drink stronger than an occasional beer. I think he's disposed towards temperance."

Sherwood's resistance reluctantly lessened, in no small measure due to the suitor's generous nature. Gallagher gave Maria presents at every occasion, such as a gold bracelet on her birthday, an extravagant gift by the sawyer's reckoning. Finally, he acceded to the union, largely because of Woolson's endorsement, but also because he stood little chance of stopping his strong-willed sister.

"Let's set a date for the wedding," Richard said.

"Of course," Maria gaily replied. "When would you like?"

"I understand the priest is due here next month, in June, so let's make it then."

Two months had passed since Father Gibson had been in Carthage so his scheduled visit was anxiously anticipated. Several parishioners would plan baptisms, weddings, and a few First Communions. The Gallagher-Sherwood nuptials were added to the sacramental services list.

"There'll be no need for you to be re-baptized," Richard informed his intended. According to the Catholic Church rubric, an Episcopal christening was recognized as valid in their communion, so Maria would be accepted as one who had already been saved.

Richard couldn't hide his happiness, even absentmindedly humming while at work, usually to the accompaniment of Woolson's chuckling. *The boy's anxious to get married,* Woolson thought. *I may have missed my calling as a matchmaker.*

Saturday was furniture delivery day because cabinet-makers knew it was the best time to catch customers at home, not only to accept the goods, but also to receive payment. Richard was away when an agitated Dennis Cunningham arrived unannounced at Woolson's shop. "Is Gallagher here?" he gruffly asked.

"Nay, he's out deliverin' furniture," answered Woolson, surprised to see the man who had never visited his shop before. "Should be back within the hour."

"I'll wait," said the nervous Cunningham.

"Suit yourself."

Woolson knew the Settlement widower to be the father of Charlotte Cunningham, the girl Richard had sported about a few times. His eyes trailed the man as he dragged his weary body out the shop doors to begin a vigil atop his buckboard. He was naturally curious as to what this visitation could be about. The news of Gallagher's impending nuptials had certainly made the rounds down to the Settlement, so he speculated it might have to do with Charlotte Cunningham's hopes being dashed. But that shouldn't be a reason for her father to come calling on Gallagher. A feeling of foreboding overtook Woolson as he studied the fidgeting grim-faced farmer sitting in the box of his wagon, nervously spitting tobacco juice onto the road. He scratched his beard but couldn't put his finger on why he had become so apprehensive. *Well, we'll have to wait 'til Richard returns,* he speculated.

As soon as Gallagher pulled up, with Bessie towing the empty furniture wagon, old man Cunningham climbed painfully down from his buckboard and shouted, "Gallagher! We need to talk!"

"Oh, hello Cunningham. So, what can I do for ya?" said Richard as his throat inadvertently tightened up.

Cunningham approached and put a hand on the young man's shoulder. "Yee've got to do the right thing, man. Do the right thing."

"Don't know what you're talking about," said Richard, trying not to sound alarmed.

"'Tis Charlotte. She's with child and says it's youse what's done it."

Richard's brow shot upwards and his hair bristled as he tried to parse what he'd just heard. "What!" he shouted. "Me! Nay, nay, you've got it wrong. 'Twasn't me, I swear."

Woolson, who had edged closer to the door to take in the confrontation, became alarmed. *What the devil! Can this be true? I don't think Cunningham is the type to make frivolous accusations. Oh my God. And he's just gotten engaged! Poor Maria.*

Richard kept protesting his innocence but Cunningham was having none of it. "If ye won't do the right thing, ye'll regret it till your dying day."

"I swear Mr. Cunningham, I had naught to do with this," said the perspiring Richard. *How can this be happening to me?* he wondered, now in a panic. *If this gets out I'll be ruined in this town.* "Nay, I'm not the one you should be looking at," he said as firmly as he could.

"Is that your final word?"

"Aye, 'tis. I'm innocent."

"Curse you Gallagher. Ye'll rue this deed, you scoundrel." Cunningham turned, remounted his buckboard, and left trailing a swirling cloud of dust.

Richard pivoted to see Woolson glaring at him from within the shop, disappointment splayed across his face. "Rozzie," he shouted. "You don't believe any of this, do you?"

Woolson remained silent but his thoughts were jumping rapidly around in his brain. He firmly believed people didn't just go around falsely accusing other people. Not in this town. They were mostly god-fearing people, and the boy did once date the girl, but that was before he took up with Maria. *Could he have seen her recently enough? She's probably beginning to show and can't hide the truth any longer. He's a passionate lad, this much I know.*

"Rozzie, you of all people have to believe me. I did not lay down with that girl!"

"Why would she name you?"

"I don't know! She has to be shielding the father for some reason. Lord knows, she gave me plenty of opportunity, but I swear on my mother's grave, I never lay down with her!"

Woolson's features softened as hints of sympathy invaded his features. He turned his attention to the aftermath of the accusation. "This'll be all over town before nightfall. What are you going to do?"

"Right after I get cleaned up and have dinner I'm going over to Sherwood's to explain. Maria will believe me. 'Twasn't me, I swear!"

When Richard finally pulled up to the Sherwood home, it was nearly dark and all seemed still. He rapped on the door but got no answer. He kept rapping steadily and loudly until a neighbor lady poked her head out a window and hollered, "They've gone away!"

"Gone where?" Richard shouted back.

"I think to Turin, where they used to live. They left after that Cunningham man came by."

"That son of a bitch," Gallagher muttered as he hopped back on the carriage. His hard lashing took his anger out on Bessie on the way back to Woolson's. "They've left for Turin, Rozzie. Oh, God! She heard the rumor from Cunningham and believes it," he said choking back a sob.

Woolson was puffing on his pipe, his brow furrowed in thought. "Well my boy, first you've got to confront the situation down at the Settlement. When that's resolved you can decide what to do about the Sherwoods."

On the next morning, Richard hurried over to St. James, hoping to talk with Aunt Nancy. "It was she, after all, who tried to hook me up with that girl. Perhaps she'll believe me," he hoped.

"Hello, Gallagher," said Nancy in cold greeting to the forlorn Richard. She was the only one who spoke to him. "Gotten into a mess, eh?"

"Aunt Nancy, you've got to believe me. I did nothing wasn't proper with that girl."

"Have to admit, I was surprised when I heard the news."

"'T'wasn't me," Richard said emphatically. "Why is she blaming me?"

"Well, maybe 'cause you're a better catch than those other boys she's run with."

"Will you help me, Nancy? My fiancée's left town. My reputation is in ruins. Please."

Aunt Nancy leaned back to take closer measure of the man and admitted she could see only the bearing of innocence, if such things could be thus determined. "I haven't always approved of that girl's behavior. And she was spied coming outa' the barn with that Monahan boy. I'll try to get to the bottom of it," she said.

Although not much relieved, he went into church to pray, today more plaintively than ever. *If anybody can find out the truth, it's Aunt Nancy,* he thought between whispered Our Fathers and Hail Marys.

Nancy Walsh, when back on her home turf, sent word for Charlotte Cunningham to come for a visit. "What's this story I been hearin'?" she asked in her singsong voice.

Charlotte buried her head in her hands and began sobbing. "I'm in a mess and don't know how to get out."

"Why Gallagher? Ya know lots of people are doubtin' yer story."

"I know, I know," the girl replied as she shook her head back and forth. "I know."

"Ye'd best tell me the truth before this goes any futher."

"'Twasn't my idea," she blurted. "The fella who done it is married! He said we couldn't tell the truth or he'd be run outa town on a rail."

"Do ya think Gallagher'll fare any better?"

"But at least he's single. And I liked him a lot."

"Ya have to tell who the father is."

"I can't, I can't." Charlotte repeated as her voice trailed off in a whisper. "I can't."

"If that's yer choice, ye'll have to go to Utica to the home for unweds. But before ya go, ye'll have to confess Gallagher ain't the one who done it." Nancy thereupon got a sheet of paper and pen and dictated to Charlotte what needed to be said. The young girl, hesitatingly at first, finally did as directed, even while her tears fell silently on the paper and splotched some of the ink. When finally finished, she sat bolt upright, as if a great burden had been lifted from her soul.

"Who'll take me?" she asked.

"I'll arrange it. But first I must show this to your Da. Wait here 'till I return." Aunt Nancy took the letter to Dennis Cunningham, packed a bag for her, took a few dollars from her father, wrote a note for the girl to present at the home in Utica, and finally arranged for the girl's transportation.

"What'll ye do now?" Woolson asked Richard after Nancy brought him the news.

"I'm going to get Maria," he resolutely said. Early the next morning he urged Bessie on to Turin. When he arrived, he asked at the first house where he might find the visitors from Champion. Soon he was knocking on the proper door. A livid William Sherwood answered with cocked fist at the ready to defend his sister's honor.

Richard raised a hand palm up and announced, "You have to hear me out, Sherwood. Here, read this letter."

William Sherwood was hesitant at first but finally took the confession and carefully read it. He noted Nancy Walsh's witnessing signature at the bottom and grunted. He was disappointed because he thought this union had finally been sundered by the scandal. He was ready to believe the worst about this Irishman but would now be forced to reconsider.

Maria was standing in the parlor archway off the entrance hall, eavesdropping on the conversation. She rushed out and into the arms of her fiancé. "Oh, Richard, I knew it couldn't be true," she said through tears of joy.

"I'll bring her back tomorrow," said Sherwood.

"Nay, she'll be coming with me now, as soon as she gathers her things." Maria rushed up to her room to pack and they were soon on their way back to Champion. The lovers, with arms interlocked, sat as close together as physically possible. "I'll never leave your side again," she vowed. And Richard sat up straighter as a broad smile covered his face.

CHAPTER 8

On the first Sunday of June in 1841, Richard Gallagher, along with his rehabilitated reputation, stood in line at St. James Church with Maria Sherwood, waiting to be wed. Several couples lined the main aisle, some to be married, while others had children to be baptized, and a few were prepared to make their First Communion. George and Alice O'Leary stood alongside Richard and Maria as best man and matron of honor as Father Gibson consecrated the marriage vows.

William Sherwood had mellowed considerably and offered the first toast at the couple's reception at Brown's Hotel. He admitted he had reservations at first but now believed Richard would make a fine husband for his sister. "I welcome this man into our family," he said to a chorus of "Here, here."

"We can't really afford a honeymoon, but Rozzie told me to take a couple of days off. I thought we could go to Watertown." Maria was happy with whatever Richard decided so the couple boarded the stage for a two-day honeymoon at the White House Hotel in that growing city.

As he lay in bed beside his bride, basking in the glow of his first encounter with lovemaking, Richard murmured, "We'll take a real honeymoon one day."

"I'll hold you to that, my dear," Maria purred. "I hope it will be as lovely as this one."

The couple returned to Champion and took up residence in the Woolson household as the book of Richard and Maria Gallagher's life opened to its first chapter.

***

"Where's the baby?" Woolson asked with a wink at the couple's first wedding anniversary party. It was a question on Richard's mind as well.

"We're working on it, Rozzie," Richard said with a wink. Only the absence of a pregnancy dampened the Gallagher's happiness. Maria's condition was not due to lack of frequent and vigorous lovemaking-of this the couple was sure.

Children were expected and appeared in profusion in most households throughout the village, just not at the Gallagher's. Those who knew the couple well could see doubts had crept into Maria's mind as she worried about being barren.

As a distraction from her childbearing woes, Maria frequently strolled across the Black River Bridge and up State Street to go shopping. She was often joined by Ann Woolson or met up with Alice O'Leary, as they viewed the latest fashions in the windows of Seth Hooker's clothing and dry-goods store. They marveled at the horse drawn buggies parading back and forth along the street, mixed with the occasional wagon toting products to and from the docks on Water Street. The activity only reaffirmed Maria's faith in Richard's notion that the village's prospects were indeed rosy. The humming factories sang songs of prosperity as lumber, iron, and barrels of potash shipped up river on their torturous journey over the partially completed Black River Canal to connect with the Erie, where some would go south to New York while the others went westward to Buffalo, and across the Great Lakes to bustling centers such as Detroit or Chicago.

"Once the Black River Canal is completed, our goods will reach markets even faster," Richard said. Although the water-way had been under construction for only four years, Maria could not observe all this activity without agreeing with her husband that Carthage had nothing but a bright future ahead.

"You know," Richard said to Woolson at the start of their third year of association, "I think it's time for me to strike out on my own." His senior partner, who anticipated just such a move, agreed. Richard's plan to set up a factory on the Carthage riverbank sounded good to Rozzie. "I've an idea for using waterpower to drive the machinery," said Gallagher.

Richard commenced work to set up shop on the banks of Guyot Island, one of several that dotted the Black River. He chose what he thought to be an ideal spot next to the nail factory. The preparations included carving out a flume and installing waterwheels to power the woodworking machines. It was an ambitious undertaking, one destined to be the first water-powered cabinetmaking shop on the Black River, and it soon opened to great civic fanfare six months later.

The belts, levers and gears looked immensely complicated to Maria, but Gallagher's workers soon mastered the operation. Without having to supply manpower in the form of treadles or cranks, the cabinetmakers could methodically move from stage to stage in the manufacturing process with minimal loss of time. "We'll be able to increase production in no time," Richard proudly announced.

Unfortunately, in his eagerness to make his mark as a forward thinking and progressive innovator, Gallagher had failed to take into account the mercurial nature of the Black River. The river's inability to produce a consistent flow year round was problematic, and this became depressingly clear when the flume ran dry. Richard's dream shop was forced to close before its first anniversary had passed.

Undaunted by the failure, a scarred but impenitent Gallagher moved his cabinetmaking to a building on State Street, leaving his partnership with Woolson to strike out on his own. He viewed this setback as temporary and it only spurred his drive for financial independence. Maria could see the fire in her husband, a man driven to making his way up the business ladder. And she proudly basked in its glow.

When he heard the news, Richard gave prayerful thanks Maria was finally pregnant. Now that his family would be growing along with his business, Gallagher bought a two-story house on North Mechanic Street, a short walk from his State Street shop. It had ample room for the children he expected to sire and the apprentices he needed to hire.

"What's wrong? What's wrong Lovey?" Richard asked one evening when awakened by Maria's anguished sobs.

"I don't know," cried Maria. "I have these terrible pains in my abdomen!"

Richard rose with a start, hurriedly dressed and ran up the street to Dr. Eli West's residence, two blocks away. He banged on the door and shouted, "You've got to come," when the doctor finally answered.

West grabbed his coat and bag and followed Richard as fast as his short legs allowed. "Where's your buggy?" the older man hollered as he struggled to keep up.

"There wasn't time," Richard breathlessly shot back.

When the pair arrived at the Mechanic Street residence, they found Maria had fainted from the pain. "Oh, my God," Richard exclaimed, "is she dead?"

"Get me some water," West ordered as Richard ran off to do the doctor's bidding.

When he returned, the physician made a cold compress to place on Maria's forehead. She was soon revived but he could see her three-month pregnancy had miscarried. "I'm sorry," Dr. West said. "You try to get some rest now."

Richard choked back a sob as he looked down at the ashen and sweating Maria. "It's all right, Lovey. As long as you're safe, that's all that counts."

Maria's sobs, although quieter, continued nonetheless. She had failed her man and that plagued her more than anything else she could think of. The woman was barely five feet tall and weighed only a pound over seven stone. "She'll have a hard time delivering your children," said Dr. West in somber tones as Gallagher showed him the door.

"Worry not, Lovey," Richard said, as he tried his best to reassure his despondent wife. "The Lord will provide."

Although her faith was strong, Maria wasn't as sure as her husband of any forthcoming providential assistance. She vowed to keep those worries to herself.

Gallagher's immediate family did not expand as expected and, as the years wore on, Maria suffered one miscarriage after another-totaling three in their first five years of marriage. The couple was depressed over the prospect that children might never grace their household. They went to services whenever a visiting priest came by, and they prayed fervently for divine intervention in this cause, getting down on their knees each evening before climbing into bed.

Miraculously, in their sixth year of marriage, Maria carried to term with her fourth pregnancy and a girl they named Harriet was born. "She's a tiny one," said Dr. West, "but I think she'll be alright." Richard, overcome with joy, threw a party at Brown's Hotel for all his friends. The Walsh brothers, O'Leary, and several of the town's other businessmen joined in the celebration. A piano player was hired and Richard didn't mind that the Squire led the singing or that several of the attendees got roaring drunk. For his own part, he got tipsy after three beers, more than he had consumed at one sitting since he first tasted the alcoholic drink.

After the party concluded, he weaved a path home while humming an Irish ditty he hadn't sung since he was a child. Awakened by her husband's stumbles up the steps, Maria pretended to be asleep. In the morning when he came down to breakfast, Maria smiled and said nothing.

Now that the parenting milestone had been reached, Gallagher turned his attention to satisfying his entrepreneurial bent. With his prominence on the increase he was becoming the envy of many associates. With his capital accumulating, he began seriously considering expanding into the retail end of the furniture business.

"I've got to have my own store," he said to Maria. "Selling to order is too slow. With a store I could build an inventory and sell furniture on the spot."

Maria simply smiled. She was confident her husband could succeed at whatever he attempted, and stood ready to support him however she could. "If it's a store he wants, a store he'll have," she said with resolve.

Chapter 9

"I've a young cousin back home," Richard mentioned to George O'Leary when the subject of the Ireland came up. "His letters tell me Erin's worse than when we left, if you can imagine. He's asking for help to leave."

"Aye," his friend responded, in a tone that affirmed this was hardly news to him. "We'll have to raise some money to send over." And the pair of emerging community leaders convened a meeting of their confreres at Walsh's Hall to gather funds for their destitute brethren in the homeland.

O'Leary was called Squire because of his erudite manner-which often manifested itself in speech and song. It was a title he carried with pride even though in the "Auld Sod," it designated a man of means, a landlord, or a person in position of authority. In Carthage, however, the honorific was given half in jest and meant to recognize O'Leary's climb to prominence in the community. No one observing the Squire's stout frame, ruddy face, and the shock of cinnamon hair poking out from under his ubiquitous tam could help but think of an oversized leprechaun. He had come to Carthage only a year before Gallagher and had prospered as a shoe and boot maker. He loved the law and continually studied on his own, poring over the many books he had acquired on the subject. As a result of his legal insights, he had been appointed a peace justice. The Squire's increasing wealth allowed him to dabble in real estate, and that only further elevated his status in the community.

When the year 1847 began in Carthage, even the most pessimistic in the Irish community did not expect the deluge of appeals appearing in letters from home. And when they thought conditions could get no worse, even more bad news arrived. The largest crop failure ever was upon them and pestilence, starvation and death marched across the landscape like the Four Horsemen of the Apocalypse. "Those English bastards want to see our people die!" said O'Leary. "They're exporting grain all over the Empire but none to Ireland!"

"Aye," said Gallagher. "Look at the newspaper. The priests are even asking our farmers to take some of the children."

Although both men agreed to lead the local fundraising effort, Richard hatched a more direct plan. "What do you think of sending for my cousin John?" he asked Maria over breakfast one morning. "I've been thinking on this for some time." Cousin John Gallagher, not unlike hundreds of thousands of others, was truly in desperate straits. He was married with an infant child and his pleas to Richard had become more and more plaintive.

"It would be good to help your cousin emigrate, Richard. He'd be a big help to you in your new furniture emporium."

Maria's enthusiasm was infectious, and Richard added, "Aye, it would be good for both of us." There was nothing more important to the businessman than getting double the value out of a single investment. By this act, he satisfied both his need to be charitable and to get help for his business.

Money was sent and cousin John booked passage for his family, quite coincidentally on the very same *Exmouth Castle,* the brig the Gallagher family had taken twenty-two years before. Thus on the 25th of April 1847, John, along with his wife and son, boarded ship in Londonderry, along with 238 other passengers and eleven crew. The family was overwhelmed and eternally grateful to Richard for the opportunity to escape the hunger and poverty that had reached epic proportions in their homeland.

Their euphoria was short lived however, for three days into the voyage a great storm arose as the passengers huddled in their compartment below deck. It wasn't long before the savage winds had torn the *Exmouth's* aged sheets from their masts, and the ship was tossed to the mercy of the waves.

Unbeknownst to the hapless voyagers, Captain Isaac Booth had made a fatal navigation error. He mistook a light he saw to be on the Island of Tory, which lay off the northwest coast of Ireland. He realized his mistake too late, and try as he might no maneuver without the aid of sails could save his ship. The vessel ran aground at the isle of Orsay, off the Rhinns of Islay. The tempest relentlessly dashed the hull of the *Exmouth* against the rocks, snapping its masts and sending them crashing onto the deck, blocking passageways and trapping the panic-stricken passengers below.

The Gallagher family screamed along with their fellow prisoners, a din that grew louder even than the gales raging above them. But no matter how hard they clawed and pushed, they couldn't dislodge the heavy beams that held them captive. Soon seawater rushed in through the smashed, storm-tossed hull and the engulfed throng fell silent. The wreckage was swept out to sea by the tide.

Three sailors barely escaped with their lives, and spent the night on the rocks being lashed by wind and rain. Their physical ordeal was further compounded by the anguish they felt for not having saved any of the others in their charge. When day broke and the storm dissipated, they found a farmhouse on the island and related the grisly tale. Days later a total of twenty bodies washed ashore, but John Gallagher, wife Ann and son Thomas were not among them.

"Did you hear about the shipwreck?" asked the Squire after popping in to visit Gallagher's cabinet shop a week later. "I've just seen the sheets about a boat called *The Exmouth Castle* running aground off Ireland. Only three sailors survived."

Richard turned white as he tried to speak. But the words, like the passengers on the fateful vessel, were trapped in his nether regions. Finally he said in a hoarse voice, "*The Exmouth Castle*, you say?"

"Aye, do you know it?"

Richard nodded, turned and abruptly left the shop through the back door, leaving the puzzled O'Leary and his speechless apprentices in his wake.

The news laid a heavy pall upon Richard as he grimly related what he'd heard to Maria. No matter how much he tried to hide his feelings or how hard the tearful Maria tried to console him, he grieved and wept profusely. He avoided contact with friends until he could effectively mask his remorse for he hated to let anyone see him in this state. He blamed himself over and over saying to Maria, "If only I hadn't sent passage, at least they'd still be alive. 'Tis my fault," he repeated again and again.

On his next visit to St. James Parish, Maria told Father Gibson her husband was in need of the priest's counsel. The cleric advised him that keeping the faith was the best he could do under the circumstances. But the words offered Richard no consolation. "Why would God let this happen?" he angrily said to the priest.

"God works in mysterious ways," the priest responded. "These events try men's souls. You mustn't give in to despair. That is the worst sin of all."

The aggrieved Richard refused communion and stopped his daily praying. *This is not God working in any mysterious way,* he thought.

Maria tried her best to sooth her husband's remorse, but it was three weeks before he returned from the depths of depression to his former devout ways. "I don't know what God wants of me," he said. "I just don't know."

Three months after the tragedy, Maria became pregnant with their second child. Richard vowed if it was a boy, they would name him after his departed cousin John. "I don't know, dear," Maria said, "I wouldn't want him to be a constant reminder of this tragedy for you." But Richard was resolute, and after little John was born, whenever his father was bouncing the baby on his knee, he felt a tear well up and trickle down his cheek.

As life returned to normal for Gallagher, he decided the Mechanic Street house had outlived its utility for his growing family. "I think the dam has burst and we'll be having many children," he said. "I've purchased a lot on outer State Street. 'Tis the best part of town and it's time we built a proper house." After acquiring the land in a transaction with the Le Ray agent P. S. Stewart, Richard contracted with the French-born millwright Arnold Galleciez to build him a large three-story home on the new lot.

"It will be a house befitting a man of your stature," the craftsman said while showing Richard the plans he had drawn up. "You are successful businessman, so you've a right to live it up." Galleciez knew how to play to the vanity of his clients and also knew Richard would enjoy the accolade. Gallagher did not disappoint him.

When the new home was completed six months later, Richard stood in front of the house with his arm around Maria, admiring the new abode. The four massive white rectangular columns stood as sentries on a porch running the width of the house. The brickwork ran up the whole three stories, an uncommon and expensive detail. The first floor windows measured six feet high, with the second and third level treatments reduced proportionately. It was one of the most impressive mansions in the village.

Richard Gallagher had arrived at the top of the social ladder after years of hard work, and he could not be faulted for proudly basking in the moment. He furnished his new house with the finest pieces his shop could produce, and items beyond his workmen's ken were imported from New York.

The third floor of the home housed their live-in servant, Mary Murray, Mrs. Mary McManus, the recently widowed nanny with her two children, and two German apprentice cabinetmakers. Mrs. M's husband had been a good friend of Richard's and so it was he who suggested that she come live with them.

"I so enjoy having Mrs. McManus with us," said Maria, who was the first to acknowledge she wasn't much of a cook. "She's good company and she knows how to make those Irish dishes you enjoy so much." In her formative years, Maria's family had servants and she was encouraged to gain an appreciation for the finer things in life such as literature and music. Cooking didn't make her list of finer things.

The State Street property spanned three acres, which allowed Richard to put in a garden and a hen house on the rear of the lot. Fresh vegetables and eggs would be available in season to feed his growing family. He also set aside a large picnic area, which he called Gallagher's Grove, and which he intended to make available for civic gatherings on various national holidays.

Gallagher was now ready to proceed with his plan to expand his business, and cut out the middleman, by opening his own retail furniture store. After eleven years of expansion his furniture making reputation was at its apex, and the high regard for his work had spread to neighboring towns.

"I've a proposition from Horace Hooker about partnering in building a block in the heart of the business district," Richard told Maria. Hooker was a prominent businessman who had an interest in several other stores. "He's a good man to be associated with."

When the ten thousand sq. ft. emporium was finished, Richard hung a sign out front that simply read *Gallagher's Furniture Store*. He had his craftsmen fabricate a large chair for his marquee and his newspaper advertisements advised potential customers to look for the "Big Chair." The building was initially christened the Hooker & Gallagher Block. His long term plan was to buy out Hooker's interest and make the building The Gallagher Block. The construction featured a brick facade for the first floor with clapboard facing on the two floors above. It was the first building in Carthage to incorporate such a design.

Yes siree! Richard proudly said as he stood in front of his new store. *This is how a proper business block should be built!*

CHAPTER 10

"They thought it was going to be like Paree," said Farrel Neary when the St. James trustees gathered at Gallagher's new house. The men took seats at his expansive oak dining room table for their monthly meeting to discuss how they could leverage their increased membership rolls into greater attention from the recently established Diocese of Albany.

As one of the early settlers of the area, Neary knew what he was talking about. "The Frenchies were sold a bill of goods," he said, "But the weather here ain't like old Paree." He chuckled a bit as he accentuated his pronunciation of the French capital. What he was referring to was the newcomers' discovery that the Castorland Settlement, although on the same latitude, didn't provide the immigrants with weather like that experienced in Paris. Indeed, the North Country winters proved harsh and unbearable to them.

"The weather wasn't the only problem," added Ed Galvin. He recounted how they expected to find the same luxuries here as they had in Paris. Thus, the ultimate disappointment for the Franks turned on the dearth of amenities available in more civilized settings. "Why, there were no balls to attend, and no large mansions to host them." This condition led most royalists to seize upon the tender of amnesty offered at the conclusion of the bloodletting French Revolution. The Castorland Settlement's immigrants didn't have to think twice as all but one family hastened aboard ships to return home. The Irish, who succeeded the French as the dominant ethnic group in St. James parish, enjoyed bragging about how they came from hardier stock, and given their ascendency, felt it was time for them to exert more pressure on the newly appointed Bishop John McCloskey.

"Not all of them were like that," interrupted Henry Haberer, the only man on the seven-member board who wasn't Irish. "My wife's French, and she has adapted to this climate quite well."

"Well, the French are pretty much gone, and we've got to serve the interests of our parish," said Gallagher. "French or Irish don't matter," he said, impatient to get to the core of the problem. "What we need is a permanent priest."

The St. James census was growing, not only because of continuing Irish immigration, but also on account of the large families they begat. "Thanks to their blessed fecundity," as historian Father Talbot Smith wrote, the Irish population was growing faster than any other segment. Fifty years had passed since the French founders of the village of Long Falls first appeared in 1798 and all but a few had departed. It was time the Albany Diocese took note of this change.

The majority Irish saw themselves as the neglected children of the Church, and chafed under the paternalistic attitudes the Catholic clergy vigorously maintained. "We trustees are supposed to decide how the parish should be run and our spiritual needs met," Gallagher affirmed, referring to the laws of New York State governing the establishment of religious societies. "And we will decide," he added with a thump of his fist on the table. The discussion was prompted by a resolution that Gallagher write another letter to the bishop reinforcing their demands. "Ya tell him we need our own priest," they said in unison.

"The bishop don't care much for trustees' opinion," said Patrick Walsh. "Eed be happy to be rid of us all together."

"Well, we'll have to see about that," Gallagher said as the motion was seconded and passed. Gallagher would write the bishop to again express the trustees' wishes in no uncertain terms.

"On another matter, I have to mention your Saturday night brawls are getting us a bad name." This subject had occupied Richard's mind for some time, and although it wasn't a church matter per se, he felt it influenced their appeals to Albany. "The bishop can use this as an excuse for not listening to us. I know you need to let off a little steam after a hard week, but I'm tired of hearing how we Irish are naught but a bunch of brawling drunks." The lecture was delivered in a voice rising in anger and brought color to Richard's cheeks.

Carthage proved no exception when it came to the clustering of like ethnicities and having the actions of a few mold the public's perception of an entire group. The Irish reputation for exaggerated intemperance and pugnacious behavior was widely bandied about town, and Gallagher resented it. But for that one instance during the celebration of his first child's birth, he was quite temperate by Irish standards. "I'm tired of hearing it. Can't you people do something about this?" he said to his audience, most of whom lived in the Settlement.

"Yee're too thin skinned, Richard," said Patrick Walsh, a man who came to these meetings with a bit of John Barleycorn on his breath, and who felt obliged to defend the Settlement's activities. "Pay it no mind, I say."

"One of these days it'll go too far. You'll see."

The meeting came to a close on that sour note. Richard grunted as he rose from the table, his chair growling as it scraped across the hardwood floor. One would not be in error to say he was displeased for he took pride in selling ideas and getting his way. He was offended at being lumped into that general Irish characterization, and became even more so when he saw no resolve to change. He had avoided socializing at the Settlement since he first met the woman who became his wife. And some in the community resented his absence. "They think I'm some sort of snob," he said to Maria as he climbed into bed. "But I don't want to be tied in with them. Certainly not in that way."

"Pay it no heed," said Maria. "Just get a good night's rest."

"You don't know what they're saying about me. I haven't told you they call me a lace curtain Irishman just because I don't like what goes on down there. What really get's my goat is them calling me 'uppity.' They justify it by saying I should have married an Irish lass. But they don't have the nerve to say it to my face."

"There's a bit of envy in those remarks," Maria wisely observed. And it was true that Gallagher's wealth gave his detractors pause in initiating direct challenges. Hence the snipers delivered their derogations out of earshot, so Richard only heard them second-hand, usually in an exaggerated form.

"They can think what they like," the aggrieved Richard continued. "There's a fool born every minute and every one of them lives. They can go to the devil for all I care."

Maria sighed because in a candid moment she had admitted to Alice O'Leary that her husband was no longer an "easy" man. Over the years, as his confidence grew in harmony with increased business success, his youthful shyness gave way to assertive leadership. "Oh, he can be stubborn," she said, "But he means well and prides himself on his reputation as an honest man. And that is much more important to him, and to me."

Despite friction with his countrymen, Gallagher's staunch Catholic faith became the glue that held together his willingness to champion St. James' spiritual and temporal needs. He could not allow petty grievances to deter his mission of remedying the infrequency of church services... or increasing sales for his business.

The bishop's antipathy for the authority of the trustees was very troubling to Gallagher. His responses to Richard's letters showed he barely tolerated idea of laymen running Church affairs. It was a disgrace they didn't have Sunday Mass more often Richard groused. "We should at least have a priest for the sacraments of baptism and matrimony. And a Christian burial isn't something that can wait on a priest's schedule. Why, we've got couples getting married in the Protestant Church, or worse, by a justice of the peace. We're driving people out of the Church, I tell you. I guess the bishop knows more about keeping holy the Sabbath than I do."

Had the trustees thought about it, they might have understood that the Catholic bishops' objections to these laws were rooted in a residual fear of the Protestant Reformation. The lawmakers of early America were committed to the principle of keeping religious associations at arm's length from any centralized religious authority. They marked up State laws with their version of Martin Luther's Ninety-Five Theses.

Gallagher, of course, eagerly embraced the notion of laymen running their own parish affairs, something they never had a chance to do in the old country. "If it's good enough for the Protestants, it ought to be good enough for us!" he often said. And everyone agreed.

These laws headed New York Archbishop John "Dagger" Hughes' list to be repealed, and he encouraged his up and coming Irish parishioners to become politically active so they could further this objective. All clergy, most especially Bishop McCloskey, also embraced this view.

Thus when the bishop of Albany announced in 1849 that the Rev. Mr. Michael Power would reside in Carthage as pastor of St. James, it seemed he had finally acceded to their demands. In fact he did hope the appointment would put an end to their pesky protests.

Gallagher, in a show of *noblesse oblige*, given there was no parish manse, invited the priest to board with his family. As it turned out, he resided there infrequently because, as parishioners soon learned, the assignment of a pastor for Carthage didn't mean what they assumed. The frequency of services remained unchanged.

"We still get Masses just like before," parishioners began complaining to Gallagher.

Squire O'Leary endorsed these complaints. "We're but one parish out of twelve in this impossibly large mission."

Regardless of the priest's nominal residency in Carthage, the schedule of services at St. James satisfied no one. A favorite phrase everyone adopted to justify their complaint was, "We can draw 400 people to Mass on any given Sunday, while other missions are lucky to produce a quarter of that number."

In spite of their discontent, the people grew to love Father Power and placed no blame on him for the paucity of services. Instead, they reserved their opprobrium for the bishop. "It seems St. James is just another pawn on his huge chessboard," Gallagher observed.

Conditions remained the same for three more years, even into the pastorate of Father Roche who succeeded Father Power. The new priest wasn't enamored with the idea of living with the Gallagher's growing family so he bought a small residence that stood on a lot behind the church. By making his residence the *de facto* parish manse, he augmented the false sense of importance of having a resident pastor. This did little to assuage the growing resentment with the situation.

"Poor old Father Roche is showing his age," Richard noted after eighteen months of the pastor's tenure. Indeed, each time he returned from a mission trek, he was bent over like a question mark and walking with difficulty. The years of serving a wide mission area had turned the older man into a beaten figure and, after just two years in the St. James harness, he notified the bishop his health mandated a move to a smaller parish. The mission circuit, traversed in all kinds of weather over streams and rutted roads, would test a much younger man. Therefore, in the spring of 1855, it came to pass a vacancy for the pastorate of St. James loomed anew.

James Walsh introduced a motion at the next trustee meeting to again have the board officially petition the bishop for a priest to exclusively serve St. James. "Now's the chance to get our own priest, ain't it?"

Gallagher listened patiently, although somewhat hesitantly, to all expressed opinions. He had, of course, regularly put the proposition to the bishop, who left no doubt he didn't think Gallagher or the trustees had any say in the matter. Richard's face grew long as he contemplated the bishop's past recalcitrance. He was hesitant to mount another futile initiative. Finally, he warily put aside past disappointments and agreed to lead an effort to press the issue once again.

"I've received a letter notifying me of a certain priest's availability," Patrick Walsh informed Gallagher.

"Aye, I got one too."

"He's a fellow who was an apprentice in O'Leary's shop before he went off to become a priest," Patrick continued. "I remember him as a pious chap, but one who kept pretty much to himself."

When Aunt Nancy heard about it she asked, "You don't mean 'Pockey,' do ya?" That unkind pejorative had been given to a young Settlement boy because of a childhood bout with smallpox. The lad later became a priest and Nancy was sure it was him as no other local had taken religious vows.

The news a former resident might be coming home to minister to them spread across the parish. Convinced this candidate was the answer to their prayers, many rushed to jump on the bandwagon requesting this priest's appointment. The swelling enthusiasm lessened Richard's concerns so he put aside his past reservations to pen yet another request to Bishop McCloskey.

Gallagher was surprised when another Settlement denizen popped into his store to begin interrogating him about this latest development. "I hear ya asked the bishop to send a certain priest here. I don't think ya wanna do that."

A surprised Gallagher looked into the intense eyes of the man who he believed was a brother of the priest in question. He fleetingly wondered if he had made a mistake in joining the undertaking to get this priest assigned to Carthage.

"He's sued me, don'cha know? Yer askin' for trouble with that one."

"Thanks for the warning," said Gallagher, "but the letter's gone off already."

"Too bad," the visitor said. "Too bad," he said again as he turned and left.

Gallagher was a bit alarmed and sent word to the other trustees to report what the subject priest's brother had said. "What do you boys think about this?" he asked.

Patrick Walsh was the first to respond. "They been fightin' since I can remember. Pay no attention, I say."

The other Settlement trustees agreed it was a family issue and had no impact on their affairs, so it was decided to do nothing. "We'll let it take its course then," said Gallagher.

But was this what Gallagher had in mind when he agreed to blaze a trail for the bishop to dispatch this particular priest to Carthage? And would the new pastor for St. James be able to impartially minister to his former townspeople and their neighbors?

Maria Gallagher, as one familiar with the literature of the day, might have cautioned her husband to heed Edgar Allen Poe's admonition in the *Tale of the Monkey's Paw*- "Be careful what you wish for."

CHAPTER 11

"Here's another letter from Carthage, Your Excellency," Vicar General John Conroy said as he placed Gallagher's latest missive on his superior's desk. His three hundred pound frame cast an ominous shadow over the head of the Albany Diocese. Bishop McCloskey sighed as he leaned over the sheet of paper set before him. His experience had taught him to not expect good news in communications from church trustees. "They want a priest of their own," said Conroy, whose alcohol-tinged breath McCloskey chose to ignore.

"Doesn't everyone?" an irritated McCloskey retorted.

Exasperation lined the bishop's thin face as he released an even deeper sigh. He paused, looked up at the chandeliered ceiling, placing the forefinger of his right hand to his temple while his palm embraced his jaw. This pensive pose was familiar to his aide for he knew the bishop was known to never act on impulse. The meditation continued, along with fitful rummaging of his slender body in the oversized chair. Finally he looked at the letter and declared as calmly and firmly as his voice allowed, "I cannot be dictated to by these insubordinate trustees."

Despite his frail bearing and soft speech, the prelate guarded his hard-won reputation as an intractable champion of his Church's positions. His dogmatic attitude was acquired during his tenure as vicar general to the bishop of New York, John "Dagger" Hughes. His superior was brash and aggressive and had acquired his famous eponym because of his habit of affixing a miniature scimitar-like cross next to his signature. Of course no one called him "Dagger" to his face, but his clerical minions, with the marked exception of McCloskey, hardly avoided its use when discussing his policies. McCloskey, although cut from a different swatch of clerical cloth, wholeheartedly adopted Hughes' stridency on issues as grave as the trustee dispute.

When McCloskey ascended to the new bishopric in Albany, he became the frequent subject of discussion by priests assigned to his diocese. Rumors, and even folk legends, circulated about adversities he'd overcome on his journey up the hierarchal chain. During his forty-five years of life, he had acquired a reputation as a pious, contemplative person. His orders were delivered with a ring of authority that seemed alien to his delicate physique. It had not escaped him that virtually no one felt him fit for this important office except Bishop Hughes and the pope in Rome. This perception drove him to command the respect, if not admiration, of all those in his charge. "He expects nothing less from others than he is willing to give of himself," said his loyal aide, Father Conroy. "We all should be as dedicated and obedient to the laws of the Church as is our bishop."

That evening at dinner, with McCloskey confined to bed with a cold, a young deacon asked, "Could the Vicar General tell us how His Excellency made the decision to enter the priesthood? I've heard stories of a miraculous event." The beet-faced Conroy looked up from his wine-pouring chore, ever-willing to regale an audience with all that he had learned. An historian by avocation, he had actually compiled a dossier with the intent of writing a history of the diocese or perhaps a biography of McCloskey after he himself retired.

Conroy began a recitation that would trace McCloskey's life from the time he was born in 1810, through the tragic loss of his father at age ten, and his spiritual journey to a religious vocation that finally culminated in his position as Bishop of Albany.

The bishop had descended from Irish farming stock, just as did his pesky trustee nemesis, Gallagher. McCloskey was not forthcoming about his background, considering it immodest to discuss. Filling in the blanks of his past was left to associates such as Conroy. "His parents came from County Derry in Northern Ireland way back in 1808," the chronicler began. "His mother Elizabeth gave birth to him two years after arrival in America. His Excellency's da prized education, as do most of our people, and, because of his own learning soon found white-collar employment as a clerk with HB (Hezekiah Beers) Pierrepont. The firm was busy amassing a fortune in real estate and distilling gin. 'Tis best not to mention this last part to the bishop. It's clear his father became a good friend of the owner, and when the British threatened to invade New York during the War of 1812, the elder McClosky distinguished himself by taking charge of building the defensive fortifications in lower Manhattan. Mr. Pierrepont applauded him for showing such initiative and held him in even greater esteem from that point onward."

Conroy could see his audience was entranced, and paused for another sip of wine to savor the moment. "Misfortune befell the McCloskey family in 1820, when the bishop's da, only forty-five at the time, became deathly ill. The illness puzzled the doctors, which they called 'fever' or 'paralysis.' Six weeks later the Lord took him. His Excellency never forgot the Jesuit, Father Reynaud, who gave the family great comfort by staying with his father until the bitter end. There came a time when he actually considered joining that order as a way of returning the favor. But I'm getting ahead of myself.

"Our bishop was ten at the time, and was not the healthiest of boys. Although no one mentioned it in his presence, he knew in his heart that many feared he might never reach adulthood. Nonetheless, he was enrolled at Thomas Brady's Latin School where the headmaster took an interest in him. In fact, Brady soon recognized our bishop as his brightest student and judged him a budding prospect for the legal profession. He told Mrs. McCloskey that he'd make her son the 'ornament of the New York Bar.'

"However," Conroy continued, "Mrs. McCloskey was undecided as to her son's education. She was fortunate that her husband left her better off than most who found themselves in similar predicaments. Although Headmaster Brady continued to counsel law school, a prominent lawyer friend of the family, a Mr. Riker, adamantly disagreed, saying, 'There are more young lawyers starving than are making a living honestly.' He suggested enrolling him at Mt. St. Mary's College in Emmitsburg, Maryland where it was thought the mountain air would be beneficial to his health."

It was quite normal, for those financially able, to send a boy to college as early as age eleven, where he would enroll in preparatory courses to ready himself for a full academic program.

"After the father's death, Mrs. McClosky moved the family to a farm in Bedford, Westchester County, a property that abutted the estate of John Jay, the first chief justice of the Supreme Court."

Conroy never failed to cite this circumstance because it demonstrated the family had more significant means than McCloskey ever admitted.

"His Excellency excelled at his studies, graduating college at age fifteen, while placing near the top of his class. However, he returned home, undecided about his future pursuits. His ma told him not to worry as God would show him the way."

Thanks to Conroy's attentiveness, the wine flowed generously, making his listeners anxious to have him continue.

"The bishop loved teaching, and perhaps that was what he was meant to do. But his old schoolmaster Mr. Brady was still pressing the case for law school. Meanwhile, Mrs. McCloskey, unbeknownst to her son, had made application with some friends for a position at a New York counting house. But fate intervened that summer when he suffered an accident that altered the course of his life."

Always at the ready to take on tasks that might disprove his assumed frailty, the young McCloskey noticed a farmhand had left an ox-team and wagonload of logs unattended, and saw a chance to prove his manhood.

"It was a foolhardy thing to do, but at that age boys do foolhardy things," Conroy continued. "The boy saw the idle team as an opportunity so he hopped aboard the dray to finish the chore by driving the team to its intended destination. It didn't turn out well, I'm afraid. The team lurched and overturned the load of logs, with His Excellency partially buried underneath. It wasn't a pleasant experience for the oxen either, for the cart's tongue and yoke flipped the beasts over on their backs, still hitched to the wagon. But for the incessant lowing of the oxen, the unconscious boy might have perished on the spot. Farmhands found him with his legs sticking out from under the pile of logs."

Conroy's expression could easily have passed for the same look of consternation that the family and farmhands must have had, for the boy was unconscious and seemed on the point of death.

"He was brought inside comatose, only regaining his senses several days later. Alas, upon awakening he found himself to be blind but luckily it was a condition that proved temporary. He remembered nothing after the cart overturned, and suffered a lengthy and rather painful illness."

The incident was no doubt a contributory cause of McCloskey's lifelong lack of robustness. But he considered the accident a stroke of good fortune because the accounting job became available while he was *hors de combat* and he never had to seriously consider it. Also, it was during his recovery that he decided on a religious vocation, no doubt an "Act of Providence," he often insisted. Divine intervention or not, the studious boy had to admit he never would have been happy as an accountant.

"After His Excellency finished his tenure at Emmitsburg, a struggle began between St. Mary's President Dr. Purcell and Bishop Dubois, the head of the New York Diocese at the time. Dr. Purcell thought his prize student could best use his talents by teaching other seminarians, while the bishop believed he should return to New York to fulfill his obligation to his native diocese. The bishop ruled against St. Mary's and his charge was ordained to the priesthood in New York City in January 1834."

Not many anticipated a long tenure for the newly ordained cleric. His congenital frailty concerned both his family and the diocese. But despite his history he vowed to defy the actuarial tables.

"Because of his academic aptitude, Father McCloskey was appointed vice-president of the new seminary college at Nyack on the Hudson-some thirty miles north of the city. The work required for the establishment of such a facility was quite arduous and as some feared, much too taxing for his constitution."

In fact, his former guardian and family friend, the aforementioned Mr. Riker, took note of the stressful situation and wrote to the bishop saying, "You are killing that boy up there in Nyack. He is too delicate for the climate and the duties of the place. Why not let him go to Europe to recruit his health? It will cost the diocese nothing; his mother will bear all the expenses." Ailing clergy often went to Europe to regain their health. The material wherewithal available to consider this option was another testament to the family's financial means.

"Bishop Dubois was not disposed to the European idea, so Father McCloskey wrote him and said: 'If you will allow me to act on the advice of Bishop Kenrick, I shall go to Philadelphia and consult him.' This request posed a dilemma for Bishop Dubois because Kenrick was well-known and respected as one with first-hand knowledge of the benefits of study in Rome."

Finally, when he could find no further reason to deny the trip to Philadelphia, Bishop Dubois acceded: "Very well, my child, you can go to Philadelphia," he said to McCloskey. "Your health needs a change, and I shall be glad to approve of anything that benefits it."

Dubois' reluctant acquiescence to the European trip proved to be more practical than magnanimous. He later wrote, "I was the less inclined to deny him, as his weak constitution is not likely to render him very useful and may be improved by spending some time in Italy. He appears more inclined to a sedentary, studious life than to an active one, and I am afraid he may thereby give the last stroke to his already broken constitution." Dubois intentions were clear: *He's not going to last much longer so he may as well die outside my jurisdiction.*

A portrait of the young McCloskey rendered at the time reveals sharp but delicate features, a broad, high forehead, and a boyish, ovate face whose outline navigates downward to a smallish chin. The eyes are intense and inquisitive, set in a head that seems placed over a body too small for the clothing that surrounds it. Indeed, he presented a picture of ill health.

"I was one of those who saw him off as he boarded the packet ship *Erie* in 1834 for his trip abroad", Conroy continued. "We were a somber group indeed, thinking it the last time we would ever see him, alive or dead."

Once upon the sea, however, the salt air proved beneficial and the priest began regaining his strength and color. The improvement continued in his Roman years at the Pontifical Gregorian University and University of Sapienza. It was there McCloskey made many friends who would serve him well, if indeed he lived to fulfill a career in the Church.

"Shortly after he arrived in Rome, Father McCloskey was informed that the Nyack seminary had burned to the ground. He tried to influence its rebuilding from there but his efforts proved unsuccessful. His letters emphasized his conviction that our diocese needed to train locally born priests who would be more acceptable to our American congregations. He felt, as do I, that foreign clergy do not understand our American born parishioners."

To turn that belief into reality, McCloskey felt a seminary within the New York Diocese was mandated, but the objections were formidable and the reconstruction was denied. In a letter to Bishop Dubois, the implacably committed McCloskey heatedly singled out the objections of the trustees for his disdain.

> But for my part I would rather see the whole establishment at the bottom of the Tappan Zee than see it under the control of lay trustees.

"After receiving his doctorate, our bishop returned to New York City where he came face to face with the trustee problem. A spat had arisen at St. Joseph's in Manhattan and the trustees informed the bishop they did not care for the priest he had sent to replace one they dearly loved. The problem became so intractable the bishop was forced to place the church under an interdict.* A peace was finally brokered and Bishop Dubois appointed Father McCloskey as pastor."

The academically inclined McCloskey was abruptly immersed in the rough and tumble world of parish politics, a role he neither desired, was trained for, nor well-suited to fill. And it was a cold reception that greeted the American-trained priest at St. Joseph's. The mostly immigrant parishioners resented that the bishop had imposed him over the will of the people.

To his credit, Father McCloskey eventually won over the majority of the congregation even though a ringleader of the rebellion, Patrick Casserly vowed he would never allow a child of his to bend a knee before an American priest.

After Bishop Hughes was appointed head of the diocese, the thirty-four year-old Father McCloskey became Bishop McCloskey, Vicar General of the New York Diocese, and heir apparent to Hughes' chair.

Archbishop Hughes was well known as a fierce opponent of the "evil" trustee system and a very aggressive apostle of the Church. In Hughes' opinion, the trustee system governing church societies had overstepped its bounds and had long outlived its utility. On January 30, 1844, he wrote a scathing letter to the trustees of the church in Albany that left no room for doubt as to his position.

> It is enough for me to express in brief terms my decided opinion that sooner or later the trustee system as it has existed, will destroy or will be destroyed by the Catholic religion.

"Four years later the Church realized its membership had grown so rapidly it had to subdivide the huge New York See.* It was decided to mark out dioceses for Albany and Buffalo, and in the spring of 1847 Bishop McCloskey was sent to take his seat in the State Capital, and that's why we are all here," Conroy concluded.

Heads turned as a pale and sniffling McCloskey unexpectedly appeared in the dining room and took the vacant seat at the head of the table. "What about the priest Clarke?" McCloskey asked, brusquely changing the subject and mood of the conversation.

Conroy was caught off guard but after a short pause said, "Well, he certainly knows the area. What's the hurt to send him there? Perchance it would quiet the natives."

"Perhaps, and perhaps not-we shall see," the bishop replied as he rose with a weak flourish signaling it was time for the session to be concluded. "Let us all pray before retiring," he suggested, "and seek guidance from Our Lord in all our decisions."

"Well," said Conroy to the remaining clerics after the bishop left, "there's a bit of wine left. Let's not let it go to waste."

CHAPTER 12

The Rev. Mr. Michael Edward Clarke paid rapt attention as Father Thebaud, the visiting priest, imparted the latest diocesan rumors. The transient cleric had arrived to St. John's Church in Utica from Carthage where he had learned St. James was looking for a new pastor. "Father Roche can't do it anymore," he said, "so they'll be looking for a younger man."

When Clarke expressed interest in the job, Father Thebaud was surprised at the parish assistant's interest. "Do you think you've enough experience to handle such a large territory?"

"I've been waiting for just such an opportunity. Do you know I used to live up there? My brother has a farm there at the Irish Settlement. I should fit right in. I'm used to living on the edge of that wilderness."

Thebaud didn't know Clarke's history and wondered aloud how it was he had come to reside in Carthage. "My family came from Dublin where I was born in the year 1818. We emigrated via Liverpool to New York when I was but nine." The elder Clarke, including his wife and seven children, eventually made their way to Carthage and took up residence in the Irish Settlement.

In recounting his personal history, the priest consciously left out some details that those who knew him better would have happily supplied. Clarke avoided talking about his humble beginnings, including his farming background. Although he had grown to be a strong young adult, he saw no future in pulling weeds in the hot sun amid the odor of horse manure. He fancied himself an intellectual and often neglected his chores.

"Go feed the chickens and gather the eggs," his da had instructed. Instead, the boy might be found with his nose in a book or racing around the countryside on one of the farm's horses. The elder Clarke gave tongue-clucking disapproval but finally conceded, "The boy don't like farmin'."

"So, for a time, I looked into plying one of the available trades but none satisfied me," Clarke continued. He skimmed by the fact that he'd actually apprenticed at O'Leary's shoe factory where the Squire had noticed the lad was always "plotting his next move like in a chess game."

It was also no secret he held the accumulation of wealth in great store. "He's worse than a Scotsman," his father had often said, largely because of the boy's stinginess and how he hoarded whatever money came his way.

"One of the bothersome things I encountered in Carthage was all the matchmaking that went on," Clarke continued. "Why do people think every young man has to have a wife?" Those who were closer to him thought it strange the good-looking Clarke showed no interest in the ladies. Any overtures by well-meaning matchmakers, including a few forward eligible women themselves, were rebuffed by red-faced stammering and went for naught. Michael looked the other way when encountering the ladies. He also took great offense at being called "Pockey," a cruel pejorative about his facial disfigurement uttered by his unchristian neighbors.

After seven years at the cobbler's trade, his intellectual restlessness asserted itself. He knew his career as a tradesman, like many of the boots he repaired, had simply worn out. He began using more and more of his free time reading or in deep thought. Although a manual trade wasn't normally expected to prepare a man for the priesthood, Clarke announced he had a vision that religious life was his true calling. This was the first anyone had heard he was experiencing spiritual revelations.

When in such a mood, as he was today with the inquisitive Father Thebaud, he liked to point out he was one of Notre Dame du Lac's first students when it opened. "I went out to Indiana and studied there under the Holy Cross Fathers for three years. But the school wasn't able to offer degrees as yet so I transferred to Regiopolis College in Kingston, Ontario. It was much closer to home and allowed me to complete my seminary studies.

"Money was in short supply so I had to work to support myself." The resourceful and more experienced Clarke defrayed expenses by tutoring undergraduates. Those who could afford his fees necessarily came from the upper classes, presenting an opportunity to ingratiate himself with well-to-do boys who might be useful to him in the future. It was a trait he developed during his shoemaking days in Carthage. When he first contemplated an ecclesiastic vocation, he consulted with the missionary pastor from Watertown, Father McFarland, who served the St. James parish as a visiting priest. McFarland was happy to counsel the lad due mainly to dire shortage of priests in the New York diocese.

The friendship continued via an exchange of letters well into his college days. When his studies at Regiopolis neared their end, Clarke wrote McFarland and asked for a recommendation to Bishop McCloskey, head of the three-year-old Albany Diocese. The bishop welcomed the entreaty, because he was happy to add another priest to his large and needy diocese. Clarke was ordained by McCloskey in August of 1850 and became a member of his stable of diocesan priests.

Now, five years later, even though he had ordained him, the bishop knew Clarke no better than any of his other priests. He had met with him on only two or three unmemorable occasions. But the reports received from his brother clergy, restrained by the code of conduct to not criticize, indicated Clarke was a pious and meditative man. Those few who knew him a bit better saw a stubborn streak that was summoned whenever his temper flared, a trait that became more and more obvious as his tenure advanced.

Back home in Carthage, as soon as word of his ordination became news, his brother John Clarke, the man who had warned trustee Richard Gallagher, wrote the bishop to alert him about Michael's litigious nature, which had flared up all too often even before he embarked on his career as a priest.

> Having seen the notice that my brother Michael Clarke has been ordained to the holy Priesthood, while now engaged in an unjust lawsuit against me and Mr. [Vincent] Le Ray de Chaumont, I thought best to make you acquainted with the circumstances, so that you can judge whether he has acted worthy of the high honor bestowed upon [him]...

Clarke's brother only got "notice" of the ordination, not an invitation to the ceremony, to which family members would normally be honored to attend. But something was "rotten in Denmark," and the brothers were now estranged. Father Clarke's beef with his sibling and Vincent Le Ray concerned money he said he was owed. A glance at the court calendar showed aggrieved parties, lay or religious, were quite disposed to seek redress in civil court, and Clarke was no exception. Underneath the studious and pious exterior lurked a Shylock who was inclined to exact every last penny due him-even at the expense of the unfavorable notoriety a churchman received by going to court.

"Two months after my consecration," Father Michael continued," I was assigned as assistant pastor at St. Paul's Church in Oswego, New York, one of many congregations with a history of trustee disputes with Bishop Hughes. The problems dated back well before the Albany Diocese was established."

Father Thebaud nodded knowingly as such situations were not foreign to him. Indeed they were all too common.

"I couldn't believe the situation I was thrust into at St. Paul's." Indeed the place was smoldering from a civil suit brought by a layman seeking court damages for being deposed from his trustee position. Bishop McCloskey at the time was "Dagger" John's vicar general and was given the task of answering the aggrieved man's written complaints. McCloskey journeyed to Oswego in an attempt to smooth over the troubled waters but the parishioner was unmollified. He demanded to know what charges Bishop Hughes had placed against him. And what justification Pastor Kenny had to denounce him from the altar with 'hard language'. Bishop McCloskey's response was a classic rebuke of the trustee system and left no doubt, if anyone entertained such, where he stood on the issue."

> The course which you and your associates have pursued, and which you seem determined to persevere in is wholly at variance with the discipline of the Catholic Church, and with your duties as professing to be members of that Church, and believe me, my dear Sir, unless you listen to the teachings of our holy faith, and submit in obedience to the laws of your Church, you will only be daily invoking upon your head fresh calamities.

There was no doubt that "calamities" was meant to be temporal in nature because he went further to threaten spiritual punishment.

> ... the Church will not set itself up against the law, but it will within its own pale, inforce its own discipline, and they who will not abide by it, must, if they continue obstinate, be severed from her communion, and from the participation of those Sacraments which she can only dispense to her faithful and dutiful children.

"I enjoyed reading that letter," Clarke recalled, cracking a smile from ear to ear. The priest was learning how to deal with disputes of this nature, should he encounter them in the future. Pastor Kenny's denouncement of the Church's enemies from the pulpit, without mentioning them by name, he felt, was a stroke of genius.

Clarke's baptism in the festering trustee dispute of Oswego helped form and harden his opinions, and it reinforced where the Church stood on these matters. In fact the young priest even looked forward to going head to head with some of these apostates. "I encouraged my Pastor Kenny to crack down on them. You must step on their necks," I told him.

"After nine months at St. Paul's, I was transferred to Father McFarland at St. John's here in Utica." It sounded as if his former mentor had requested him but in fact Clarke lobbied hard for the job. He was unconcerned that the forsaken Oswego parish might resent his leaving after such a short tenure.

Thus, in the summer of 1851, Clarke went off to an assistant pastorate in Utica, the position he currently occupied. He soon was busy with his usual duties of saying Mass, dispensing the sacraments, visiting the sick, instructing the children... and making important friends.

"I've enjoyed my time here," he said, "but all good things must come to an end." He was ready to abandon his uneventful four years, during which time the parish experienced no obvious discord.

"So, how was your European tour?" Thebaud asked.

He had heard of Clarke's continental sojourn from which he had recently returned. Rumors traveled the missionary circuit that the priest had befriended a very wealthy and influential parishioner by the name of Nicholas Devereux. All the clergy knew the story of Devereux's fabled generosity. Shortly after the fifteen-year-old immigrant arrived in New York in 1806, he reportedly had dropped one-third of his total fortune of three gold coins into the collection basket at St. Peter's Church. The story, which had become a legend throughout the diocese, claimed the sexton thought it a mistake and offered to return the offering, but Devereux said no. "I want to give thanks for my safe arrival to America." The young man subsequently prospered as he became involved in manufacturing, banking, insurance, and railroading. Churchmen frequently claimed his rise to prominence and wealth was due to his initial generosity.

"I was taken ill and needed a rest," Clarke continued.

As luck would have it, Devereux was planning a European vacation for his family that summer in 1854. Two months before Devereux's boat was scheduled to sail, Clarke suggested to his pastor he be given leave to take a health cure to Europe (just as McCloskey had done some twenty years before)... with the Devereux family.

"My pastor thought it a good idea, so off we went." That McFarland acquiesced was curious on its face, Thebaud wondered, given the persistent shortage of priests. But then, perhaps Clarke really was sick.

Devereux was extremely happy to have "a priest of his own" for his family trip. He could schedule a Mass every day if he wanted, which was a luxury few but the royalty of Europe could enjoy. The prosperous parishioner was willing to pay all of Clarke's expenses-travel, meals, and lodging-for the privilege of having a priest at his family's disposal.

The group embarked on what became an eight month journey-touring continental capitals and famous cathedrals along the way to their ultimate destination... Rome.

A highlight of the trip for Clarke was the visit to Notre Dame Cathedral in Paris, which was still undergoing extensive renovations because of the vandalism perpetrated during the French Revolution. "I never imagined it in such a state of disrepair," Devereux had exclaimed as he viewed the remains of broken statuary littering the grounds.

"They've only been at the renovation for nine years," Clarke advised. "And it's estimated it will take another fifteen years or so to fix all the damage those apostates caused sixty years ago." His pious benefactor shook his head for it was unfathomable that people could desecrate such a holy place. The stopover served, on a more positive note, for the priest to recall his days at the cathedral's namesake College back in America, and the three enjoyable years he spent there.

By the time the troupe arrived in Rome, Clarke's health had been rehabilitated. He was thrilled to be invited to sit in on his patron's papal audience with Pope Pius IX-one that had been arranged by Bishop McCloskey for the influential and generous member of his diocese. The bishop had many powerful friends in Rome and was more than happy to facilitate the meeting, for which he knew Devereux would be ever grateful. "It was a wonderful experience to meet the pope," Clarke exulted, "and wouldn't have been possible without Devereux's kindness and generosity."

The party returned to Utica in April of 1855 with Clarke appearing hale and hearty. After hearing the gossip about the availability of the Carthage position, Clarke began his letter writing campaign. He wrote to each of the St. James trustees and to his bishop, attaching an endorsement from his current pastor, Father McFarland. He was ready for a parish of his own.

Would this move be all that he thought it would be? The scheming Clarke might have recalled the biblical admonition...*And Jesus said to them, "A prophet is not without honor, except in his hometown and among his relatives and in his own household."*

Chapter 13

Jimmie Walsh, as did most farmers on their Saturday visits to downtown Carthage, window shopped and chatted with shopkeepers. "Do ya think the bishop gonna' act on our petition and give us Father Clarke?" he asked when he entered Gallagher's store.

"If it suits him," Gallagher replied. He had brushed aside his gnawing doubts about the shoemaker turned priest. If this had been a business transaction he would have weighed the plusses and minuses and decided whether the risk was worth taking. Father Roche was leaving and they had no one else on the horizon to take his place. This became the sole criteria for the decision.

There was one question Gallagher wanted to ask, had the euphoria in Carthage permitted him to pose it: Why does McFarland endorse this priest's transfer given the bishop's claim of a general shortage of clergy in the diocese? Anyone who knew Clarke well, understood why the ambitious priest would desire the St. James position, but those who didn't should have wondered about this more penetrating and unasked question. His pastor in Utica never mentioned his rationale in any of the correspondence that was exchanged. If Clarke had worn out his welcome in Utica, a supposition that was within the realm of possibility, the situation should have borne closer scrutiny. But the Carthage folk worried they might end up with no priest at all, so the opportunity to get a "priest of their own" caused them to ignore the need for due diligence.

Gallagher knew the shoemaker turned priest only by name and reputation. Whenever he had visited Squire O'Leary's shop, Clarke never sought to introduce himself, which might have meant Gallagher wasn't important enough. O'Leary, who, other than his Settlement acquaintances, probably knew him best, tendered a qualified endorsement. "We need a priest," said the Squire, "and maybe this fellow will fill the bill."

"A bird in hand..." said Jimmie Walsh.

Because of his advanced education and extensive travels, Clarke had accumulated a storehouse of personal pride. He had met the pope, after all, and this alone would make him superior to any and all in Carthage. If you added in the slights he endured as a youth, he seemed justified in adopting this position. In any event, the important people in Carthage were the intellectually superior Protestants. They would be the ones to cultivate if and when it became necessary.

Gallagher was committed to remedy the infrequency of services at his church, and because of the enthusiasm of his fellow trustees, embraced Clarke's appointment. That the bishop decided to accede to the wishes of the St. James trustees, given his past reluctance to even countenance their authority, surprised everyone, not the least of whom was Gallagher himself.

Two months later, on Friday July 20, 1855, without fanfare, Father Clarke arrived to take up his new pastorate. Although he had visited the year before for his father's funeral, he still hadn't gotten over how much the town had grown in the twelve years since he left. While riding in the buggy that was delivering him from the stage depot to his brother's farm at the Settlement, he drew himself up straight to affect the demeanor of a returning hero. He was, after all, coming to save the endangered Carthage Catholics from the scourges of Protestantism.

The St. James trustees had notice he was coming of course, but did not know the exact date or time. Word of his arrival didn't spread until he had taken up residence with his elder brother William at his old homestead in the Irish Settlement.

"You've a big job ahead of you," his bachelor brother William remarked. "Doesn't it bother you the mission spans such a wide area? Why, its got to have a radius of over thirty miles as the crow flies."

"This is what I've been working and waiting for," Michael replied. "It's much more than the Utica assistantship could ever offer. And I'll be my own boss here."

***

"I see he's arrived," Patrick Walsh said. "Perhaps we should call on him." All the trustees were duly informed and they agreed to meet with the new pastor at the Settlement on the next day.

"I'll come down and meet you there," Gallagher told Patrick Walsh. In their deliberations before the visit, they decided they should advise Clarke of the availability of the house vacated by Father Roche, which could become his parochial house.

After the perfunctory amenities concluded, the subject of a pastoral residence was brought up. Clarke surprisingly demurred, with his head tilted back just enough so his eyes appeared to look down at his guests. "Truthfully, I don't think that house is suitable," he said slowly in a voice just above a whisper.

His visitors strained to hear, and after this pronouncement had sunk in Gallagher asked, "Have you looked it over?"

"I saw it when I was here last year. I think we need to build a proper manse for the future," he continued in an affected, low, slow cadence.

The delegation's simultaneously raised eyebrows betrayed bewilderment, not the least because the suggested residence sat on land adjoining the church property. They viewed the little house a proper residence, one good enough for former pastor Roche, and should have been good enough for the new one. Gallagher could feel the hairs shiver on the back of his neck, a reaction that usually signaled caution. *I hope this isn't the herald of some future difficulty with this man*. But he kept his worries to himself.

After more discussion about scheduling services and Sunday school for the children, the trustees returned to the problem of the priest's residence. Clarke would not be dissuaded from having a new manse built on the expansive three-acre church lot. "One of my first acts will be to set up a committee for gathering subscriptions for the new parish residence," he said to the surprised group. "When the requisite amount of money is raised we'll discuss the matter further." The priest, looking rather smug, stood to signal the meeting was concluded.

"Rather imperious, don't you think?" Gallagher said after the delegation was outside. "And too high and mighty for my taste."

"I di'not know why he di'not like that house," said Patrick Walsh, a man whose words always betrayed his emotions.

"It's certainly a proper house," echoed his brother James.

After a period of dark silence, Gallagher said, "There is no old stocking that doesn't find an old boot." He occasionally resorted to his repertoire of old Irish sayings with which his cohorts were familiar.

Patrick added rather seriously, "It's odd that 'eed rather be five miles down the road from the church instead of right next door, don'cha think?"

Gallagher agreed but said, "Let's give him the reins and see how it goes from here."

On the next day, forty-eight hours after arriving, Father Clarke celebrated Sunday Mass to an overflow assembly at St. James. "Ah, look at the crowd we have today," a smiling Richard Gallagher said to Maria as they walked arm in arm into St. James.

The seasonably warm July day only served to augment the festive atmosphere. The ladies, dressed in their Sunday best, with ribbons on their straw hats fluttering in the gentle breeze, promenaded into the church two by two. Some of the men claimed they could smell the corn ripening in nearby fields, and it was a good omen, one that signified bumper crops to come.

Richard nodded to everyone as he and his family waltzed in to take their seats in the family's subscribed pew # 34. And all nodded their approval in return for they credited Gallagher's leadership with making this day possible-a priest of their very own. Maria beamed proudly for it was her husband who led the drive for this banner day. Triumphs that augmented the practice of her faith were to be celebrated and remembered.

The service was conducted smoothly, and Clarke remarked during his homily that he was pleased to be returning home. "I've waited for this day for a long time," said the smiling priest.

The congregation's infectious enthusiasm could not be contained and the wood framed structure reverberated with each robust rendition of prayers and hymns. After Mass the celebrant recessed to the church entrance to shake hands with each parishioner as they left. Gallagher lingered in the vestibule, waiting until the crowd had thinned before he approached the priest. "My family and I especially enjoyed the homily and the singing, and I am pleased we could make possible your return."

"Thank you for your help and support," said Clarke as he continued grinning broadly, embracing the convivial spirit that had infected the entire congregation. The parishioners went home happy in the knowledge this vexsome problem of having a priest of their own had at last been put behind them.

On Monday morning, Father Clarke counted out the collection the ushers had put in a small canvas pouch and given him after Mass. He mounted his buggy and drove up to State Street where he opened an account at the Bank of Carthage. "Not a bad start," he thought as he counted out $40 and change to the teller. He then turned his attention to mapping out the lengthy itinerary for his missionary rounds.

Before he could leave town, as he had signaled to the trustees, he would set up a building committee for the new parish house. "I'll be happy to chair it," Richard Gallagher said, and Clarke agreed but made himself the treasurer. Richard, ever the persuasive salesman, immediately went about soliciting subscriptions and nearly everyone he met would hear his sales pitch. The parish house account would soon begin to swell.

On Thursday morning, Clarke hitched up his horse and buggy and started on his way to visit churches in his mission. His first stop was at Copenhagen only eight miles away, a trip that took him an hour and a half. Although his horse, if pressed, could make eight miles in an hour on these rugged roads, he knew it was best to walk his steed up hills so as not to damage the animal's tendons. Caring for horses was a valuable skill he learned on the farm, and his horse received the care it required to ensure he wouldn't be stranded out in the wilderness, with refuge unavailable for miles around.

While walking his horse, Clarke used the time to pray-sometimes quite loudly-for he had no concern about being overheard in the desolate countryside. At other times he had conversations with his favorite saints, one of whom was Christopher, the patron of travelers. "Keep me safe on this journey," he often implored.

On the ensuing Sunday he shuttled between Copenhagen, Pinckney, and Montague to say Mass at all three of those churches. Bells, if churches had them, announced his arrival and people happily dropped whatever they were doing to come to Mass.

Clarke spent most of his time introducing himself to parishioners and conversing with trustees about building or repairing their churches. He was particularly interested in acquiring land and deeds, all the while partaking of one or another parishioners' hospitality, which most felt privileged to provide. The priest was an engaging conversationalist, and his flock was impressed with, and respectful of, his educational background, which was obvious from his manner and speech.

After sufficiently ministering to these parishes, he ventured on to Harrisburg, and thence to Belfort. He stayed an average of three days at each stop, usually insinuating himself into the homes of the wealthiest parishioner, who most often was also a trustee of the church. The Belfort congregation, which was primarily made up of Alsatian French immigrants, was most happy to see him when they learned Clarke spoke passable French. He said Mass, gave communion, and talked incessantly to trustees about financial matters.

The peripatetic preacher still had a fair distance to go so he hitched his trap and headed north over rough roads to Lewisburg, a four-hour ride give or take depending on the weather. He took care to dodge the stumps still littering the roadway where large trees once stood. He had lots of time to say his prayers and talk aloud to break the loneliness. He said his rosary every day, practiced sermons, and mentally went over plans for his new parish house. Every minute was to be used in furthering his mission and he often marveled at how disciplined his thinking was.

When he arrived at Lewisburg, his first stop was at the home of the burly and prosperous Mr. Fuller, the founder of the town. It didn't take Clarke long to win the man over and mentioned he was disposed to stay an extra night with him, "to give us a chance to get to know one another better." As usual, he said Mass, gave communion, and took up a collection before heading to Gouverneur. From there he went to Rossie, on over to Redwood, and down to Sterlingville where he chatted with Mr. Sterling, the town's namesake, about getting title to the land for a church. This, the man promised to deliver.

After a journey that had taken him almost four weeks to complete, Clarke finally returned home to Carthage. The trip covered nearly 200 miles-over burbling streams and rutted trails, many of which hardly merited being called a road. This was an auspicious start for the new pastor, and he was brimming with pride over his success. And most importantly, a tidy sum had been collected from those priest-starved congregations.

Meanwhile the people of St. James wondered aloud where the "priest of their own" was, and many voiced their concerns directly to Gallagher. They came to his store from all corners of the village saying, "This wasn't what we expected. No Sunday Mass in the last month!" Richard listened patiently but had no ready answer. He would, he said, seek one at the next opportunity.

As promised, on the following Sunday after Mass, Gallagher asked Father Clarke, "Where have you been? We've missed you."

The priest looked surprised and said, "I've been on a mission for the Lord. The people of Gouverneur need a priest as much as the people of Carthage."

"But this wasn't our understanding when we requested your appointment here."

"Be patient my son," Clarke said, a bit condescendingly to a man who was nearly a year older than he. "All things in good time."

Clarke seemed totally oblivious to the fact he had just brushed off the most important man in his parish. As good as he was at making influential friends, he now demonstrated an equal and opposite capability for making enemies. Had anyone dared ask, he would have revealed that he considered Gallagher a man who was subject to his authority just like everyone else. The priest saw no better way to ingratiate himself with Bishop McCloskey than by bringing to heel the man who continually wrote complaints to the diocese. People like him should be brought to heel and given to understand the hierarchical order. Yes, even the man who had facilitated his appointment to St. James.

The priest went merrily along believing in his own mind that he was doing a superb job-and wouldn't be reticent to report such to his superior. Just a year and eight days in the St. James harness Clarke penned a letter to McCloskey in which he enthusiastically reminded his bishop of the progress he was making.

> July 28, 1856… Everything goes on prosperously here. I have a number of deeds for you, and among these I have the deed of Belfort Church, which you are aware was a source of a great deal of trouble to you. A few kind words from me to Mr. Stewart prevailed and I have the deed as you wished to have it drawn.
>
> I visited Rossie as you wished me to do, and I got the deed of all the land we want and one hundred dollars from Mr. Parish towards the Church. I will be able to accomplish this without incurring a debt.

Clarke, like a preening peacock, felt the need to display his feathers. He had, after all, worked very hard for a year, and modesty would not further his goals. He mentioned how he had even used the prominent Methodist elder, attorney and land agent Patrick Somerville Stewart to assist him. This did not surprise Vicar General Conroy for he had heard of the priest's ability to make important friends, as noted with Nicholas Devereux. Religious persuasion was not part of Clarke's equation if the person could serve a useful purpose.

Clarke went on to tell the bishop of his plans to build churches at Sterlingville and Lewisburg and how he was busy procuring land for two other places of worship, actively paying off debts, and painting and repairing buildings. He closed his letter with a few self-congratulatory pats on the back for his work, essentially giving himself an A on his report card. As he did so, however, he had a few short-lived pangs of concern he might have crossed the boundaries of pride, but chose to ignore them.

> … I can assure you that I feel myself truly happy in discharging my duties faithfully, and the fruit so abundant that I cannot but behold it. I do not know what trouble is, it never approaches me. I tell my people to only seek to please God, and they will be enabled to practice what their religion requires of them.
>
> May I have a share in your prayers, and believe me to be always your most obedient child in Xto [Christ]…

Nowhere in the letter is there mention of Carthage, his largest parish and where he was pastor in residence. It was as if the place didn't exist. Could this be a precursor of trouble on the horizon? Was Clarke deceiving the trustees, himself, the bishop, or all three?

Had they been consulted, the people of St. James parish might have given their pastor a different grade. There was naught for them to do but bide their time, lament their misfortune, and wait to see if their spiritual needs would ever be satisfied to their level of expectation.

Chapter 14

Bishop McCloskey smiled as he looked over Father Clarke's letter. His hope this appointment would dissipate the complaints from Carthage was reinforced. Alas, Richard Gallagher would soon disabuse him of that belief. The grumbling at St. James was rising steadily like the headwaters of the Black River in spring. And they soon took voice as most parishioners felt no better off spiritually than before the new pastor arrived.

The priest had not only crossed swords with Gallagher, but with other prominent and influential people like Squire O'Leary, his former master craftsman. These people must now bend their wills to his. He didn't have any problems with his parishioners out in the missions, most of whom were happy to see him and showered him with affection and hospitality.

The Carthaginians, in addition to wanting a priest of their own, had high hopes for their town's continued growth. Why, their church might even need to be expanded if the growth continued apace. These expectations underlay Gallagher's determined insistence the diocese was treating them unfairly. He sent McCloskey a letter in July of 1857, just two years after Clarke's arrival to emphasize the village's prospects as proof of their need for a priest to be there, at the very least, on two Sundays a month.

Gallagher's impatience was augmented by his arrival at the top of the town's ladder of success. He had been elected a village trustee and became accustomed to people listening to his opinions.

> ... we of Carthage do want a priest to ourselves and until we have such we will be in the back ground... We are receiving the benefits of our Publick works, as you will see in the articles I mark in one of our county papers. Our Catholic

> population is increasing in this village by the erection of large tanneries & other improvements... I also send you a county paper to show the benefits which we are beginning to derive from our Black River & Canal Improvement.

The town fathers seemed either unconcerned or oblivious to the Erie Canal's experience. That waterway was being obsolesced by the fast encroaching railroads, which deflected settlers to the more abundant agricultural lands in the south and west. Carthage was continuing to grow, but the pace had slackened considerably. Gallagher's expectations might have been more realistic if seen by more objective eyes. The mercurial Black River that Gallagher touted so highly was commercially navigable for only 42 miles southeast to High Falls. And the fast encroaching railroads had already begun to erode that small advantage. During winter months the river froze over and canal shipping had to be suspended, reducing its usefulness to recreation and harvesting ice.

The much touted Canal had only been completed in 1855, thirty long years after the Erie began operations. Although the waterway gave villagers great expectations as the engine to drive Carthage's continued growth, it was proving to be a day late and more than a dollar short.

In its favor, Carthage's saw mills were kept busy because of the huge supplies of hardwoods from nearby forests. The spruce used for making potash was also plentiful. Ore from the north was available for their single blast furnace to make pig iron. Farmers along the river provided cowhides for their tanneries.

"Why, there's no going but up," said Gallagher. "As our markets expand, the more we'll sell, and the more our businesses will grow." But he and other optimists had turned a blind eye to the invading railroads, already competing with the Canal for speed to market, year round availability, and cost of delivery. And no thought was given to the readily available spruce being an exhaustible resource.

The town fathers still hoped the Canal would go all the way north to Ogdensburg as originally proposed. The St. Lawrence River would give their goods access to transoceanic shipping. Alas, that idea had come too late and was too costly, so the waterway terminated in Carthage. The sad, unrecognized fact was that this engineering feat had been rendered obsolete well before its completion.

Optimism still reigned in Carthage, however, and steamboat captain George Sweet partnered with two other investors to incorporate the Carthage, Lowville and New York Boat Line. Gallagher was ready to continue investing in local businesses, putting money where his mouth was. He had become a man of means and even though blind to the onrushing reality of more efficient methods of transportation, participated in bankrolling the boat line.

Gallagher had to smile whenever he passed by the bustling docks at Water Street. The hub-hub of activity made it easy to ignore the handwriting writ large on the proverbial wall that this mode of transportation was in the twilight of its life. Nonetheless, the boat company plowed ahead, constructing six steamships in the first year of operation. These boats were soon towing barges up the Black River portion of the canal to the first lock at High Falls. Pulled along towpaths by mules or oxen, the boats would pass through the many locks on their way to journey's end. It certainly made economic sense to the ever-optimistic Gallagher.

Most observers were taken in by the hustle and bustle of activity at the Carthage docks. However, as often proved to be the case, activity on the surface masked an underlying story. Carthage's movers and shakers had not even considered that the final chapter might not chronicle anything but a history of continued growth and prosperity.

Despite the lack of enthusiasm by local Canal supporters, serious railroad conversations finally came to Carthage in 1857. There was talk of routing a spur of the recently completed Hudson River & Lake Erie Railroad to pass through the village. This would certainly have negatively impacted the boat-based business model, but those developments always took longer and cost more than planned. One only had to look at the twenty-seven long years the Black River Canal had taken from inception to completion. The railroad idea, should it have come to fruition, would actually have dealt a death blow to the canal but also have been a boon to Carthage's manufacturing base. Discussions of a Carthage to Ogdensburg railroad had taken the place of the canal extension and Gallagher was asked if he was interested in becoming a stockholder and director. He was giving the idea serious consideration.

The furniture mogul was always on the lookout for ways to expand locally. The undertaking profession was proving to be quite profitable-an odd coupling, one might think, but a quite expedient one. Cabinetmakers made the caskets so it seemed practical for them to become morticians and complete the job. The undertaker's task wasn't very complicated because the relatively unknown process of embalming wasn't considered. Once a casket was fabricated, all that remained was to line the box, wash and dress the corpse. The deceased would be buried within two days to avoid any decomposition problems. Gallagher had become a prominent player in the local undertaking game.

Although business was foremost in Gallagher's mind, the problems at St. James were not far behind. As the man in charge of the parochial house building fund, even though Father Clarke was nominally the treasurer, he collected and deposited the monies and maintained control of the bank account. Gallagher proudly informed Bishop McCloskey in his letter of July 29, 1857 that his committee had already raised a goodly sum in subscriptions.

> There is near $800 paid in & on interest. The balance should be collected & more with it if the House would only Start

> [his emphasis]. And all I can see in the way is a want of time on the part of our priest to attend to it, as he is engaged in seeing to the erection of several small chapels on the mission.
>
> Our Sunday School also wants the vigilant eye of a pastor, as the people, or a portion of them want constant urging to do their duty to their children.
>
> It is the intention to have Mass here twice now a month but we sometimes have but once on account of Duty on the outborders of the mission, which arrangement will never permit the Carthage Church to go ahead. Will your Grace give us a trial?

The trustee was piqued that the "small" chapels Clarke was building took precedence over the large church at home. He inferred Clarke was behaving this way only to vex him because the priest had taken great dislike to the way he was running the board of trustees. For his part, he saw nothing in his behavior warranting such an attitude.

The issue of where a proper priest's house should be built became the sorest point of contention between Clarke and an increasing number of his parishioners. The problem was a sore spot with the trustees. "Did you hear he wants to build a barn and put some animals on the property?" said Jimmie Walsh. The thought of turning the church property into a farm was repugnant to nearly everyone. Even the farmers saw it as despoiling the acreage. "What's next," asked Walsh, "little piggies runnin' around on the lawn?"

"That'll be the day," said Gallagher.

Reportedly, Clarke responded to these complaints with a tart, "These people need to learn they must obey the dictates of the Church." He then initiated a series of sermons which displayed his displeasure with the trustees' resistance to his plans. He chafed at Gallagher's reluctance to turn over the building funds, and hinted the monies were not safe in his hands. "If these people do not yield to the Church, I will have no recourse but to consider other sites for the parish house," he said. Although careful not to name names, everybody knew he was talking about Gallagher, and on occasion the Walsh brothers.

Contentiousness was on the rise and the more frequently the manse project was discussed the more polarized people became. "In this matter I am sure the people of the outlying missions appreciate the efforts of their priest more than those abiding here," Clarke trumpeted. He was obviously displeased as his jawbone tightened with each hurled taunt. He hammered the theme that the money wasn't safe out of his hands, a contention greeted with suspicious murmuring from the pews.

As he sat through the priest's verbal assault, Gallagher's ears slowly turned bright red. His reputation was being besmirched and he could not let this go unchallenged. Maria could see from the tensing muscles in Richard's jaw that her husband was becoming aroused to the point of outburst. She put a hand on her husband's thigh, gently stroking and hoping to restrain his mounting anger. She whispered, "Now, now dear, please don't make a scene." Although rarely ever cross with her, she knew he had a temper and would angrily berate people whom he thought had cheated or lied to him. He had become increasingly stern with customers who failed to pay their bills, or employees who shirked their duties.

Because of his wife's urging Richard restrained himself and held his tongue, although he could not suppress an audible grunt or two. But outside the confines of the church, anyone within earshot would know his feelings.

The dispute that had taken root early in Clarke's tenure was now being exacerbated by the priest's assertion the building fund could be used outside the St. James parish. This prospect prompted Gallagher to pen yet another letter to the bishop, this time with language leaving no doubt that the escalating parish passions were reaching the boiling point.

I have as I informed you continued to swell our subscription list at the urgent solicitation of the Priest, until we have together an amount equal to our most sanguine expectations of the priest & more. I am accused of dishonesty, in fact & intent.

Now all I can say is that I am perfectly willing to submit all to our building committee and have always done to everyone interested in our welfare until we were threatened from the Alter that our money would go to Antwerp or some other place to build or buy a priest's House.

Nor have I refused to exhibit the accounts at any time, but did refuse to let them out of my hands, after I was publickly and shamefully attacked from the Alter of God. I have done so for my own protection. I could do nothing less.

I trust I have a good reputation to sustain. At any rate I defy a living man to say that I ever took a dollar wrongfully from him & why should I cheat the House of God. I will submit it to any Priest who has ever known me, but this is all to destroy me, to put me out of the way in church matters & also in my business, it appears to be intended for both.

So far as I can learn, this man Haber used to work for me, is now on his own account. He & a man by the name of Kenna are the principals & in fact the only men who would sustain the priest in the course he is taking at present. Our people were all in favour of buying the House that Father Roche built from the beginning & the very best men in our Church will hold up both hands for it & say with one voice if it is bought now, it will be paid for unto the last farthing within ninety days. Those are facts, no guess work about it. It can be had for a very low figure, say $1150 or $1100. Several hundred less than cost.

The committee met this evening at Mr. Stuerts [Stewart] office for the purpose of consultation. We met there because the fact is, the priest has made a confident of him. We consulted with him in regard to the matter. He is altogether in favour of buying Father Roche's House as all of the committee, the two Mr. Walshes, James & Patrick, Mr.

> Farrell Neary & myself. Mr. Kenna is not really in favour of it.
>
> Your Grace may think my conduct a strange contrast between the present & the past but I was strongly urged to press his coming here, at the time by himself, which I have his letters to show & will do if necessary in his own words for at least six months & what is my thanks, you will determine.
>
> I think that Mr. Clark does not want a House here at present. I think he finds it far pleasanter where he is 5 miles in the country. We see him but seldom.

The bishop did not need an interpreter to see Gallagher did not trust his pastor. Had he also listened to the whispers of the St. James parishioners, it would have been obvious that they too didn't trust their priest.

One of the claims Gallagher made in his note was that the majority, both trustees and parishioners, stood on his side. Clarke had succeeded in winning over only two of the seven board members. When Gallagher mentions trustee Haberer's name, he not only shortens it, but allows he only vaguely remembers he was formerly in his employ. This was his way of dismissing his enemy's importance.

Ever the consummate businessman, Gallagher insists he is a diligent guardian of the people's money. He was a man especially adept with numbers and had built a reputation for fiscal conservatism and honest business dealings. He took great umbrage at attempts to sully this hard-earned reputation. Although this argument held little sway with his bishop, it resonated with fellow parishioners because, reputation aside, they also shared his dedication to fiscal conservatism.

Patrick Somerville Stewart, the respected lawyer and long-time Le Ray land agent, in whose office the building committee met, was someone whom Clarke had already adopted as a friend. Gallagher felt a need to emphasize he had to be persuaded to take the lead role in sponsoring the Clarke appointment. Several others in the parish, and even Clarke himself, had urged the recommendation upon him. And he was loath to take sole responsibility for this looming disaster.

Gallagher often mentioned that Clarke wasn't fooling him. He knew the priest was ingratiating himself with people he could use to advantage. Haberer the undertaker and Kenna the farmer may have gone over to the pastor's side, but they formed a definite minority. Galvin, the seventh trustee who was normally on the fence, was ready to come down on Gallagher's side. Of this he was sure.

The battle was heating up and the rhetoric escalating. Many in the parish wondered aloud how hot it would have to get before an explosion occurred.

Chapter 15

"We're going to have to be extra careful with this one," Mrs. McManus cautioned Richard. Only two years had passed since Maria gave birth to her fourth child, a girl they had named Mary. The midwife could not hide her concerns over this latest pregnancy. Each of the previous births produced healthy children but had proved difficult for the mother, and the midwife. Mrs. M affected an assertive posture with hands on hips as she said to Richard, "I'm not looking forward to going through that again."

"What choice do we have, really?" replied the expectant father. Large families had long been the order of the day in pioneering communities like Carthage. The census rolls bulged with up to twelve children in a household, Protestant and Catholic alike. The Gallaghers followed the dictates of their religion, gallantly trying to live up to the bargain they made with Church and God. Maria certainly knew what was expected and was doing her best to produce a large family, and did so without complaint.

She also did her part in church. Her petite stature notwithstanding, the devout convert gradually assumed a more vocal role in the women's activities of St. James parish. She was, as some of the other ladies whispered, affirming the old axiom that converts sang loudest in church. Active in the ladies Altar & Rosary Society from the first, Maria was its president and treasurer, a position granted her by former pastor Father Power. Intelligence, persistence and persuasiveness, qualities that had originally attracted Richard to his mate, were on display for all to see. The vivacious Maria threw herself into the Society's support activities with a steady hand and attentiveness to detail that made her husband proud. She made sure the priest's vestments were in good repair, the communion hosts properly baked, and the ciborium filled and ready for distribution of the holy viaticum to the faithful-whenever the priest showed up, that is. She also led other women in their weekly novenas at the church, using the silver rosary beads her husband had imported from Rome and blessed by the bishop of New York.

"I so love the Church," Maria often remarked to the other women in her society. "And I feel we ladies are doing so much good for the parish." Of course Richard was very pleased Maria had so completely adopted his faith. To the casual observer she actually seemed more devout than her husband, and if he noticed he did not resent it in the least.

In discharging her treasurer's duties, Maria collected donations for the purchase of necessities such as candles, incense, and cloth with which to make albs for the priest and cassocks for the altar boys. Like her husband, she was meticulous in her accounting and honest to a fault. It was thus she was taken by surprise when Father Clarke abruptly asked her to turn over the society funds to him. The shock caused her mouth to form a tiny oval as she audibly sucked in her breath. "Why, Father, is there some problem I'm not aware of?" She intimately knew, of course, her husband's many concerns about this priest's coveting of parish funds. The flustered Maria stammered and said the first thing that came to mind, "Why, I'll have to go to the bank, Father."

When Richard arrived home that evening, he found a nervous Maria, handkerchief in hand, pacing the parlor floor. After some delicate prodding, she related her encounter with Pastor Clarke whereupon her husband exploded, "You'll do no such thing! You must definitely to keep the money under your control! Finances are the responsibility of the trustees."

"I believe Father, it is my duty to keep charge of the funds," Maria said firmly the next time she encountered Clarke.

The rebuffed priest's face froze, and when finally he spoke, the words came forth cold and menacing. "Just like your husband! Disobedient to the end!"

Maria shuddered, wondering how a priest could be so mean-spirited. When she reported her latest brush with the agitated Clarke to Richard, she added sorrowfully, "I think I should resign."

"You'll do no such thing!" he roared indignantly. "The priest serves at our pleasure. We will decide these matters!" According to their charter, the trustees had the power to choose their priest, manage the finances, and schedule services. And, no matter how much the Church hierarchy protested, the trustees firmly believed they rightly had such authority. "He thinks he's above the law, so we'll have to educate him about that," Richard said.

The next Sunday that Father Clarke was in residence, he renewed his war of innuendo from the pulpit of St. James Church. During his sermon the priest fired several more salvoes at certain unnamed members of his parish as he shouted, "There are those among us who would do the work of Satan. A prominent member of this congregation has stepped between me and the altar, advising another parishioner not to render an offering that was due."

Warming to the task, he mentioned how unappreciated his good works were and went on to decry the "falsehoods and hypocrisy" exhibited by those anonymous persons. "Parish moneys are unsafe in their hands," he repeated, to the murmurs of several of the congregants, and to the utter embarrassment of Richard and Maria Gallagher.

After Mass concluded, Clarke abruptly announced, "Members of the Altar & Rosary Society come to the front of the church for a meeting." After the women gathered, the priest said, "I must remove Mrs. Gallagher from her office and appoint a new slate of officers." As Clarke paced back and forth in front of Maria, like a wolf circling a wounded animal, he continued, "A pregnant woman should not be so observable and cannot discharge these duties properly."

The surprised and hurt Maria tried to choke back the tears welling in her eyes. She was inclined to mount a defense but her tongue grew thick and her mouth ran dry. Angry and flustered, she turned abruptly, strode up the aisle and rejoined her husband waiting at the rear of the church.

When Richard saw the look of mortification on Maria's tear-stained face, he guessed what had happened. With the blood pounding in his ears, every instinct impelled him to rush to his wife's defense. He leaned forward like a bull ready to charge but the Walsh brothers alertly restrained him. Maria shrank in horror, upset she had unwittingly become the cause of yet another church dispute. "Let us not do anythin' that we'll hafta regret later," Jimmie Walsh said.

Gallagher slowly regained his senses, and turning on his heels muttered, "We'd better get out of here before I commit assault and battery on an exalted member of the clergy." Maria took Richard's arm and with heads held high they strode from the church. "It used to take a lot more than that to get you so angry," Maria whispered.

"I've taken it all my life and I won't be taking it anymore," he responded firmly.

The news of what transpired was soon circulating among the congregation outside the church. A lot of grumbling ensued, especially from Aunt Nancy who was always quick to defend women from the many injustices she felt patriarchical institutions heaped upon them. "You poor dear," she said to Maria. "His day's a'comin'," she added ominously.

The priest had not come to the front of the church to greet parishioners, a practice he had abandoned once his excoriating sermons began. He went directly to the rectory, divested his garments, mounted his waiting buggy and left for home. Only then would a smug smile crease his lips.

Back at the church Aunt Nancy continued her invective against the priest. "The best way to keep loyalty in a priest's heart is to keep money in his purse," she said, making sure everyone heard her words. There was no concealing her anger causing some to whisper that her comments were more than a bit intemperate. They tsk, tsked their disapproval, adding she was not behaving like a lady.

"If you've a mind to write to the bishop, I won't discourage you," Richard said while patting Maria's arm in consolation as they walked to their carriage. "You know the priest is doing this just to get back at me."

Maria remained silent, still dazed over what had happened to her and the altercation that nearly followed. "Write the bishop?!" she said in astonishment. Her nose wrinkled at the thought and her eyes searched for some sign of verification.

"I mean it. This insult will not go unpunished if I have anything to say about it."

After agonizing over the turn of events for the next two days, the aggrieved Maria sat down at the escritoire Richard had made with his own hands, to draft a letter to the bishop. She knew it was not common for females to write letters to men other than immediate family, much less to a bishop. After all, women were not considered persons in many quarters, a position often abetted by the widely rumored dictums of Thomas Aquinas. The revered saint of the Roman Church had reportedly stated it was doubtful women even had souls. He was also said to believe the conception of a woman was due to a defect in a male's seed, a freak of nature.

Whether these statements attributed to Aquinas were actually true or not, the standing of women in the Church and society in general was often thought to be misogynistic at best. One needed only to look at government forms for verification. The Federal Census of 1850 was the first that even recorded female members of a household by name. Many thought the change was a nod in the direction of the fledgling women's movement started by Elizabeth Stanton and Lucretia Mott. The inaugural women's rights convention, held in Seneca Falls, New York just ten years before, may have influenced this change but no one knew for sure. Aunt Nancy, who had gone to great lengths to attend the conference, believed this change was due to their efforts. With this meeting, the battle for women's suffrage had been joined although no evidence other than the census had been noticed. Women, like children, were supposed to be seen but not heard, both in the Church and in society.

Maria's face was radiating warmth two days later as she took out a piece of parchment, picked up a quill, dipped it into the inkwell. She had decided to do as Richard suggested and leaned over the paper to begin writing. Her hand was surprisingly steady, given her unease. She would recount what had happened in church the previous Sunday.

> Most Reverend Bishop McCloskey,
>
> I hope you will not frown on me as a woman for addressing Your Grace.
>
> The Rev. Mr. Clarke attacked my husband from the altar without naming him, probably for fear of legal consequences. He accused my husband of falsehoods and insinuated that the money for the planned parochial house was not safe in his hands.
>
> My husband has not spared his time nor his money in the promotion of St. James Church. He is the one who gathers the children for catechism on Sundays even when there is no Mass. But now that is vetoed by the pastor on the reason that they were not securing the church afterwards. 'The key was left in the door,' he claimed but no such event has occurred. He also claims that the children are making a playhouse of the church but this is not true. There are always pious adults there to supervise the children after their lessons and to pray and say the rosary.
>
> A few weeks ago a woman of the congregation died. Her bereaved son told my husband that Father Clarke wanted three dollars for celebrating the requiem and two dollars for choirmaster Mr. Haberer to sing it. My husband advised him to give the offering to the priest but not to the choirmaster because he had not requested him. For this our priest accused Mr. Gallagher of 'stepping between him and the altar.'

> It is our most heartfelt desire to have everything pertaining to Catholicity advance and prosper, to see the Priest and people united and happy, a state of things which I fear is not in a very rapid progress at present.
>
> Now the whole end aim of this persecution seems to be a desire, a secret determination to crowd my husband and myself out of the church, to bring disgrace and ruin upon our inoffending family, and to gratify some secret malice or purpose. I tell you sir that no amount of ill treatment from Father Michael Clarke will destroy my faith in the one Holy Church of God.

Maria decided it was well past time to inform the bishop that many parishioners were upset about the unavailability or unwillingness of the priest to render the sacraments. When finished she slowly read over what she had written, and her face glowed with satisfaction. She was astonished at the letter's legibility as she blew her hot breath over the parchment. She fleetingly had second thoughts about sending these words to the bishop, but Richard, who had appeared behind her without notice, offered reassurance. "From what I can see, 'tis a good letter, Lovey," he said as he put his arm around her, his face brimming with satisfaction.

Maria wasn't the only one questioning Pastor Clarke's behavior. Other's said he had become increasingly inflexible and unpredictable-performing his duties only when it suited him. As could have been foreseen by the diocese, had they cared to notice, Parishioners now had to choose sides in the dispute, a development that boded no good conclusion.

Undertaker Haberer had sided with the priest even though Gallagher had played a role in Haberer initially coming to Carthage. He had hired him as a cabinetmaker back in 1850 when he also became the St. James choirmaster for the first time. But the man had stayed less than a year because of his inability to obtain suitable housing. He had returned to Utica, his place of origin.

After Haberer left, St. James was without a choir leader so Gallagher placed an advertisement in the *Freeman's Journal* in New York City for a cabinetmaker/choirmaster. He would try again to slay two pigeons with the same shot by getting both a craftsman and someone to lead the singing at church. At the time virtually all choirmasters were of German ancestry so a few wondered why Gallagher cast his net via the popular Irish *Journal*. But the newspaper was widely distributed throughout the northeast and also read by other ethnicities.

Haberer found his return to Utica economically infeasible for the cabinetmaker situation had not improved since Gallagher was forced to leave those many years before. When the *Journal* informed him the choirmaster's job was still open, returned to his former haunts in the latter part of 1852. He did not return to Gallagher's shop, however, and opted instead to open a funeral parlor in competition with his former boss. He soon resumed the choirmaster's job, assisted by his Alsatian born wife Juliana, an accomplished vocalist in her own right. Not only did undertaker Haberer provide coffins but he and his wife also sang at the funeral Masses, for a fee, of course.

When Clarke first arrived at Carthage, it didn't take him long to sense the cool relationship between Haberer and Gallagher. Always ready to exploit such situations, the priest added Haberer to his list of favored friends. He cultivated his loyalty by insisting parishioners retain him for funerals and weddings. As we saw from Maria's letter, those services were rendered even though many had neither requested nor could afford them. With the skirmish more clearly defined, Haberer easily chose the side of his beneficent priest.

Clarke, not surprisingly, appointed the choirmaster's wife Juliana to replace Maria as head of the Altar & Rosary Society. Mrs. Haberer readily accepted the commission and Maria resigned from the group.

The seeds of animosity had been sown and fertilized, and it now remained to be seen how long it took before they bore their bitter harvest.

Chapter 16

"No sir," Gallagher said when the subject of the priest and his desire to control all parish funds arose. He was chatting with a group gathered on the corner of State and Mechanic Streets. Still smarting over Maria's dismissal from her Altar & Rosary Society post, he took the opportunity to vent about the priest's money-coveting ways. "A good beginning is half the work and that man has done none of it. The shoemaker will have to walk on water before he sees one dime of the subscription."

"That'll be a good trick," said Anthony Walsh, a shoemaker himself. "I di'not think he can make shoes ta do that!"

The building fund, from Father Clarke's point of view, belonged under his control and when the fund had reached the tidy sum of $1,200, it became all the more imperative that it be turned over to him.

Tales of the juicy scandal were scattering across town like dandelion seeds in the wind, and people discussed it on street corners, in bars and parlors, whether in polite company or not. The dispute was on everyone's mind now and this caused the acrimony to reach new lows. Some parishioners began referring to Clarke in more pejorative terms than "shoemaker priest." In the worst case, he was called "that bastard priest." Aunt Nancy continued with her favorite reference, Pockey.

Clarke's spies helped keep him up to date with fresh intelligence at every opportunity. "What are they saying now?" he would anxiously ask.

"Gallagher and the Walsh brothers keep calling you "that shoemaker priest," Haberer reported.

Clarke's face turned beet-red before darkening and muttering, "They'll pay for this. I know Gallagher has sent another letter to the bishop. Why His Eminence pays any attention to him I don't understand. He continues to go over my head and must be made to pay for this."

"What should we do?" asked Haberer.

"One thing my loyal parishioners can do is not patronize the businesses of these apostates. They will soon realize there are consequences for their actions."

On another front, Clarke received a letter from his bishop asking him to send a few dollars to the needy Father McNulty in Watertown. McCloskey had made a habit of suggesting his better situated clergymen send funds to support other less well off priests. As Clarke pored over the letter, his mood became less and less charitable. His thoughts actually bordered on insubordination. *The bishop has a much larger purse than I have to draw upon. If he tried to get money from my flock he would see how hard I have to work for it. I can't support the Watertown priest too. Why can't McNulty make do as I have?*

The letter also asked the pastor to respond to Gallagher's latest allegations. With but a small amount of scheming, Clarke saw an opening to strike yet another blow against his nemesis.

> … I am sorry to say that I fear we cannot help Rev. Mr. McNulty, being that Mr. Gallagher has not given us any return as yet, nor much sign of it, he is very stiff and impertinent, he is not afraid to say in public that if you do not answer his latest letter, that he will refer it to the Archbishop ["Dagger" John Hughes in New York]. He does not believe in Ecclesiastical Aristocracy. I have not provoked him, nor neither have I said anything to him, but I prayed for his conversion, I hope that you will show him that he has no right to dictate to your priest concerning the stipend of his Masses nor his Choir, nor to keep the Book containing the names of those who paid their money, and also the money since the last of May. I am sorry that I have been so easy with him but I thought all for the best, and done all for the best.

Clarke could not help but smile smugly when he read the letter over before sealing the envelope. Yes, it was the stiff and impertinent Gallagher's fault he couldn't spare a few dollars for the impecunious McNulty. He was sure his blaming of his adversary would find a receptive ear with his bishop, although perhaps not quite as much with Father Conroy. The bishop's aide thought Clarke may have prayed for his adversary, but to say there was no provocation had to be considered an exaggeration at best.

When word got back to Gallagher about the priest's claim, as it usually did, he answered with a bit of dark humor: "He couldn't have prayed for me because he didn't ask for any payment." Despite the downward turn the dispute had taken, this bit of levity tickled many of his cohorts.

A few wondered aloud if Gallagher might have underestimated their adversary. "Aye, that man's a shrewd one, I'll say that," James Walsh said as he sat around the open fire at the Settlement, sipping Irish whiskey. "His brother tried to warn us but we thought 'twas jist a family squabble."

"I di'not know why Gallagher thinks he could git anywhere with the archbishop," said Patrick.

Most Catholics across the State had heard Archbishop Hughes' dictum: "They will bend their knees and their backs to the Church."

Because of all the detrimental chatter, even Gallagher wondered if things had not gone too far. It was then he decided to ask for an audience with Bishop McCloskey. "I have been maligned at every turn," he wrote. "I must see Your Excellency to let you understand that I am the wronged party." His letters hadn't done any good so he felt a face to face meeting might make him listen to reason. When the appointment was reluctantly granted by the chancery, Gallagher quickly embarked on the arduous trek to Albany.

Of course, "going over his head" yet again to the bishop enraged Clarke even more. This additional affront to his pastoral authority was one more insult Gallagher would have to pay for, the priest said.

Although tired when he finally arrived at the doorstep of the bishop's residence, Gallagher couldn't help but be impressed by its grandeur. He blew a soft whistle as he eyed the three-story brick edifice with its marble colonnades and half-dozen steps leading up to the tall, ornate double doors. *Pretty impressive,* he thought as he instinctively compared it to the house he had recently built on upper State Street. He estimated the doors to be twelve feet high, and the large oval plate glass windows, inlaid with stained glass cherubs, were an expensive touch he hadn't thought of. *Now this is a proper parochial house,* he thought.

He pulled on the knob that was attached to a wire causing a bell to tinkle inside the foyer. Shortly thereafter a young deacon appeared, opened the door and ushered Gallagher inside, all the while nervously exchanging the required, perfunctory pleasantries. He knew who this visitor was for his reputation had preceded him. While leading him to an anteroom he continued to make small talk. "And how was your trip, sir?"

"It was fine," came the curt reply.

"Nice weather we're having."

"Yes, 'tis."

Gallagher obviously wasn't in the mood for chitchat, and the deacon could say nothing to smooth his furrowed brow. The issues he brought with him seemed as heavy as Sisyphus' stone, and he hoped having rolled it this far he wouldn't have to take it back home with him.

Gallagher was offered one of the plush chairs to await a summons from his bishop. "Is there anything I can get you?" asked the solicitous deacon. "Tea, perhaps?"

"Nay," said Richard, "I'll be needing naught other than to see the bishop." With that, and a slight bow, the deacon disappeared.

The furniture maker's practiced eye took in the ornate red upholstery and drapery framing the large windows. *Didn't get these chairs from me,* he observed, and wondered with whom the bishop had contracted for these opulent appointments. *Not from Haberer either. He couldn't craft furniture as nice as this.*

Finally, after being kept waiting for nearly an hour, he was ushered into the large office where McCloskey held court. The bishop, imperiously dressed in red cape and cap, was seated behind his enormous mahogany desk, one that made him look even more diminutive than he actually was. His corpulent coadjutor, Father Conroy, stood at his right side-looking like a papal Swiss Guard, sans armor and lance.

McCloskey rose, came around to the front of his desk and extended his right hand, palm down with fingers curled inward. It reminded Gallagher of the way a genteel woman offered her hand at a social function. He hesitated but genuflected with his left knee, took the proffered limb in his hand and dutifully kissed the bishop's ring. It was an old custom meant to convey a profession of obedience and reverence, something Gallagher, it goes without saying, hesitated giving. When he arose, all three men took seats and the meeting officially began.

McCloskey spoke first by gently reminding Gallagher, yet again, of his role in the affair. "It is my recollection, Mr. Gallagher, you are the one who implored me to assign Father Clarke to Carthage. So, what are these complaints I've been hearing?"

This ploy did not sit well with Gallagher, who believed the bishop knew the complaints intimately and should be addressing Clarke's assault on his character-the reason he had come this distance. He became further agitated as McCloskey talked on, circling the Church wagons, closing clerical ranks, defending his priest, and reminding him of his required submission to his authority. "Tragedy awaits those who speak ill of a priest," he intoned.

"And what befalls the priest who speaks ill of me?" Gallagher shot back in a rising voice. The bishop stiffened visibly and Conroy's eyebrows arched appreciably.

The man is impertinent, Conroy mused with a tinge of admiration as he took closer measure of this self-assured Irishman.

Gallagher soon brought up the issue of the application and control of the building fund, which evoked a sour expression from McCloskey, one betraying impatience and distaste for this subject.

"A local matter," he replied tartly. "It is not in my purview to dictate to your priest or to the trustees on such a small matter." The bishop's unmistakable condescension galled Gallagher but he awaited his turn. "I am the overseer of a large geographical territory with many more problems than a trifling fund that amounts to $1200," he continued. "What should happen if everyone brought such matters to my attention? There would be no time to do God's work."

McCloskey was a man of letters and a practiced orator who took every opportunity to preface his responses with the casual interjection that Gallagher was "responsible" for Clarke's appointment, should exhibit Christian charity and work to smooth things over so as to forestall any cause for complaint.

Seeing Clarke made the victim when he felt so deeply aggrieved, only served to further aggravate Gallagher. His facial expressions could not suppress his annoyance as it flashed in anger. McCloskey, seeing he had rattled his adversary, pressed his advantage. He peppered his foe with popular platitudes about believing in "divine providence," "having faith," and ended each declaration with "don't you see my son?"

No matter how many times Gallagher tried to explain his role in the matter, the bishop was deaf to his pleas. The visitor grew weary of the debate, and with McCloskey's incessant harping on his responsibility for Clarke's appointment.

"Well," said the bishop as he stood abruptly to indicate the meeting was concluded, "I believe we've discussed these issues thoroughly. I would like to leave you with one final precept of our beloved Church: Those who disobey Her and do not bow in obedience will reap untold misery. There is no salvation outside the Church. Take my words to heart and go in peace, my son." He smiled triumphantly as he came round to the front of the desk and again offered his hand to Gallagher. Instead of a kiss of fealty, the aggrieved man shook the bishop's hand, resisting the temptation to give it an O'Leary style squeeze. Vicar General Conroy was left to escort the unmollified Gallagher to the front door.

The bishop's coadjutor tried to strike a conciliatory tone while walking Gallagher out. "These are difficult times," Conroy said with a sigh. "There are so many parishes, so many problems, and so few priests."

Richard only nodded because he felt further conversation was useless. *If I couldn't make my point with the bishop, why the hell should I bother with his aide?*

Riding in the stagecoach on the last leg of his journey home, the rebuffed supplicant could not stop rehashing the meeting over and over in his mind. Usually, when traveling, Gallagher played the role of voluble salesman, exchanging stories with fellow travelers while deftly inserting a word or two about his fine furniture. "If you ever have need of some quality pieces, here's my card," he often said. But today he was so distressed about his encounter with the diocese of Albany he totally ignored his fellow passengers. He couldn't muster the energy for his usual jocularity as the Church dispute had overruled his business concerns. His dour face, accompanied by an occasional involuntary grunt when a particularly offensive thought crossed his mind, invited no conversation either.

One thought that kept returning to Gallagher was the bishop's threat of "untold misery." *Was the hell was that, the threat of some kind of hex being placed upon us?* He then admonished himself, over and over, for not having said this or that, or not having made this or that point. And the stagecoach monotonously rambled and rumbled on towards Carthage.

The journey, along with the self-flagellation, had taken a heavy toll on Richard's mind and body. By the time he finally arrived home he looked haggard and worn. A worried Maria asked what had happened at his meeting. "I need a hot bath and a good night's sleep, so it'll have to wait 'til morning, Lovey." The servant was instructed to heat the water as he dragged his weary body up the stairs.

The next morning a much refreshed Richard sat at breakfast ready to discuss his trip with his concerned Maria. As his recitation of events gathered steam, his anger returned. "I'll be needing to write a letter to the bishop, the one I was composing on the trip home, while it's still fresh in my mind," he said.

"Is it a good idea to write when you are so angry," Maria gently asked.

"I know, Lovey," he responded glumly. "But these damn clergy have been provoking me no end. I don't know how much more I can take. He's even threatened me with some "untold misery."

"What on earth does that mean?"

"I don't know, I don't know." And after his last sip of coffee, Richard went to his writing desk and removed a sheaf of paper.

As he composed his thoughts anew, he continued his involuntarily grumbling, much to Maria's concern. "Please, dear," she cautioned, "don't write anything you'll be sorry for." Richard ignored her with a wave of his left hand and with continued drawing bold strokes across the page with his quill pen. He intended to inform the bishop that his smooth arguments had neither redressed his grievances nor closed the subject.

Rev & Dear Bishop

As my visit to the Episcopal Palace a short time Since seemed to be a failure in regard to the application of the moneys raised for a priests house here, and as Your Grace declines to act in the matter, and also to censure me for the part I have taken etc. in getting Mr. Clark here, and that I should have been the last one to appear before Your Grace with complaint etc. I feel keenly the rebuke and as a man, & I hope a Christian, I feel in duty bound to vindicate the reputation of myself & Family, which I trust is not so low as represented by this person who I once thought better of, we are exposed to the vilest attack, and compared to Judas with the thirty pieces of silver at every station in this wide mission, it seems to be his whole aim. The crimes I am charged with are horrible to think of, and the worst of all there's not the least shadow of truth in one of them. I call my God to witness what I say to be strictly true, to show Your Grace I was not alone in requesting Mr. Clarke to be sent here in the first place. I find four of his letters of that time & I have several more in my possession. After noticing their contents, I request Your Grace to return them to me. Nothing but the wickedest personal abuse would have indused me to the present course. I know of but one way to get redress and that is to appeal to our [Arch]Bishop if this fails the Law of the land will protect private character, this is the last extremity.

Yours truly in Christ
Richard Gallagher

PS. The letters are numbered, they are just as they came to me with the names erased.

Gallagher had ignored Maria's admonition for restraint, and couldn't resist calling the bishop's residence an *Episcopal Palace.* He wanted his adversary to understand his antipathy for the dictatorial orientation of the Church and its hierarchy. To him it was little different from European aristocracy, which he inherently despised. And his complimentary closing phrase "Yours truly in Christ," one normally used by the clergy, was Gallagher's way of returning the bishop's condescension in kind.

“The Church is just like a monarchy,” he said to Maria. “Hell, even Garibaldi said the pope is the ‘Papal King.’ The cardinals call themselves princes, and they have their archbishop-barons, bishop-dukes, and priest-knights. The bishop doesn’t understand what we put up with here to live out in the middle of the forest. He used to head up a college for Christ’s sake. His head’s in the clouds.”

Maria only nodded. She was loath to admonish her husband, which might only encourage him to amplify his tirade against her beloved Church.

"What irritates me most is the bishop singling me out for sole credit for the priest's appointment." Everyone now knew this bothered him almost as much as the charge of dishonesty leveled by Clarke. He felt the blame for this appointment gone awry should be shared among all those who got him into this mess in the first place. “If he's going to fault me, he's going to have to fault a hell of a lot of people, including that goddamn shoemaker priest,” he growled.

Maria automatically cringed when her husband cursed the priest. "Oh dear, I hate to see you speak this way."

Even some of his friends, who witnessed his increasingly foul moods, began avoiding the topic with him. Gallagher was at his worst when he felt unjustly wronged, and this definitely was one of those times.

"It's out in the open now," said Squire O'Leary. The latest exchange between the layman and his bishop clearly demonstrated charges and threats would no longer be veiled or whispered behind closed doors. When he heard of the threat to go to the archbishop in New York if Albany didn't stop this nonsense, O'Leary asked, "How do you figure you'll get sauce for your goose in the big city?" It was a mystery to him why Gallagher ignored Hughes’ well-known antipathy for the trustee system or how far he would go to guard his own priests.

"I've got to protect my name and i'll take them to court if I have to."

"He's behaving like a child," said McCloskey after reading Gallagher's letter. "He doesn't understand how our Church must function." "Dagger" Hughes was a man with a notoriously short fuse and often vented his wrath to complaining parishioners wherever they may abide in his ecclesiastic domain. No cleric could be made to take the fall for a layman, most certainly not a trustee. That was clearly not the way the Church operated, and McCloskey wondered if Gallagher, like the deluded *Don Quixote,* really wanted to tilt at that windmill.

The thought of yet again having another Protestant judge preside over Church matters did trouble McCloskey. He'd seen this tactic used a few times and didn't like it at all. One only had to recall his words to the unrepentant Oswego trustee:

> ... my dear Sir, unless you listen to the teachings of our holy faith, and submit in obedience to the laws of your Church, you will only be daily invoking upon your head fresh calamities.

This was the proverbial Sword of Damocles the Church held over the heads of recalcitrant laymen such as Gallagher.

Not one to sit still while the battle raged around him, Pastor Clarke dipped his pen into the roiling waters to send yet another note to his bishop. He feared his superior might waver in his resolve to admonish his antagonist Gallagher, and felt it necessary to keep prodding him to act as he, in all humility, had done everything humanly possible.

> I consider it necessary for you to interfere for the good of religion and the future peace of the congregation. Should you deem it not necessary for either, I will resign immediately and you may send one more capable to take my place.

Bishop McCloskey was not happy to receive yet another letter from the badlands of Carthage, especially from this troublesome priest. "What does this man not understand?" he said with uncharacteristic exasperation to Conroy. "I laid down the law in no uncertain terms to Gallagher at our last meeting, and Father Clarke knows this. He also knows I can't replace him. I cannot be seen to capitulate to the trustees." And, of course, he didn't have spare priests lying about to send to places such as Carthage.

Conroy could see his superior's irritation with the pesky priest was increasing, and which he thought was overdue.

Of course Clarke knew there was little or no chance of the bishop accepting his disingenuous resignation. The priest seemed oblivious to the jaundiced record he was compiling at the chancery, one that could redound to his disfavor. He demonstrated a cavalier concern about offending the one person who had made it clear on more than one occasion this problem should be resolved without his intervention. Father Conroy, the more practical politician of this clerical trio, understood this very well.

Clarke's brother John had tried to warn the Carthage trustees that his sibling would be relentless in pressing any perceived advantage, even to the point of seeking legal remedies. "The man displays an incredible naiveté," said Conroy. "Even more so than that fellow Gallagher."

Meanwhile, Gallagher gathered a few of the trustees at his home for another meeting. He wanted to go over reports of the bizarre behavior of Pastor Clarke and what steps they might take. Still smarting from the bishop's rebuff, and the innuendoes of the priest from the altar, he brought up the pastor's incessant demands for the money held in his charge.

“I've been thinking on how to maintain our authority in these fiscal matters,” he said as he made a new suggestion. “I think it's time to show him we have authority over the parish's temporal matters. His precious pocketbook is all he cares about. I propose we organize a boycott of the pew rents, which are coming due. He thinks he alone controls the money so we'll send the bloke another message by withholding our subscriptions. That should remind him who really runs things around here."

Grave reservations were voiced about this new tactic, especially by the Walsh brothers. "Di'ya think this wise, Richard?" asked Patrick. "We may be diggin' a hole too deep to climb outa'. 'Tis one thing to push a mule inta the pit, and 'tis another to pull 'im out."

"I'll not be wanting to get this mule out," Richard said with a wry grin. Since Haberer, Galvin, and Kenna had declined the meeting invitation, no serious objection to the proposal was made. The only misgivings concerned how far this action took them versus how far they really wanted to go. The motion was passed by acclimation, and it wasn't long before Haberer brought the news to Clark's ears. To say the priest did not take kindly to this affront to his authority was putting it much too mildly. When his anger subsided he immediately turned his thoughts to counterattack.

The three-year parishioner war with their Church was definitely heating up, and skirmish lines formed with cannon lined up behind them, lobbing charges and countercharges towards enemy lines. Any chance of resolution by more moderate parties was evaporating as fast as the dew on the church lawn under the morning sun.

The combatants were at pains to prove the old Irish adage that *long churning makes bad butter.* Oft times, when the game appeared deadlocked, one of the players came up with a fresh ploy to ignite the conflict anew. The knave Gallagher refused to be stalemated by the Bishop and was pressing his new line of attack. The bystanders awaited the next move for there was no stopping this game now.

Chapter 17

The year 1858 had begun inauspiciously as the Gallagher household buzzed about the lady of the house. Every Gallagher child had come haltingly into the world, so this one was expected to be no different. Nearing full term, Maria was confined to bed by Dr. West, the man most familiar with her previous birthing problems. The solicitous Clark servant girl (no relation to the priest, with or without the e), was at her mistress' beck and call. Maria remembered her own family's descent into near poverty after her father's death, and the menial chores she had to perform. Reaching prominence among the wealthy of Carthage did not induce her to treat her servant in similar fashion.

"No, no, I can do it myself," Maria protested to her servant after stealing out of bed against doctor's orders.

"Now, now, Mum," the girl chided. "We mustn't overdo."

Lying in her big four-poster under enforced rest, Maria reflected on the escalating battle at St. James, a conflict that concerned her far more than her impending delivery. Whenever Richard came to her side, the first thing she asked was, "Anything new, dear? Have you heard from Albany?"

"You needn't worry your pretty little head about it, Lovey," he said. "It'll all come out in the wash."

Two weeks later Maria presented Richard with his third daughter, Isabella. It was another difficult delivery but Dr. West was able to forestall any serious complications. A week later Maria was up and around, her old smiling self.

Meanwhile, Gallagher's rebellion against his priest, which had also swelled significantly, showed no sign of giving a healthy birth. Pastor Clarke, determined to crush his recalcitrant parishioners' rebellion, sought council from anyone with advice on counter-initiatives. A visiting priest, Father Thebaud, said he had seen a similar problem in Syracuse.

"Two years ago," he recalled, "there was a struggle at St. John's Church, where a lawsuit over the sale of the pews went to court. The jury ruled title to the real estate was owned by Bishop McCloskey, who therefore had absolute control of the property. As his agent, the priest had rights to any rental proceeds. So, it seems to me, you can do as you wish here."

"But we don't have title," Clarke said. "The trustees have refused to hand over the deed, just as they refuse to hand over the subscriptions for the parish house."

Thebaud paused to rethink his advice. "Well, that could be a problem, but it seems you controlled the pew rents when rendered in the past so you ought to be able to sue for them."

Clarke smiled at the prospect of another court battle as he said: "Now I know what I must do."

As we saw, the Gallagher family had long subscribed pew #34 in St. James Church, where they took their seats the following Sunday morning. At the conclusion of Mass, Father Clarke asked all those who wished to pay their pew rent to stand. "Piffle," Gallagher muttered as he rose to defiantly stalk out of church. His like-minded cohorts joined him.

After all the dissidents had left, Clarke held an auction for the delinquent pews. He shouted, "Who will bid on Pew number 34?"

"I'll take it," said Joseph Savage, a shoemaker from the Irish Settlement.

It didn't take long for the village crows to broadcast the dark news to Gallagher. In his now usual confrontational tone he replied, "We'll have to see about that!"

Buoyed by his *coup d'état,* Clarke decided to remain at home and have a rare Sunday Mass two weeks in a row. This would be the perfect opportunity to show the people who really controlled matters at St. James.

When Gallagher arrived at church and found his stall occupied, he flew into a rage and proceeded to commandeer his rightful place by physically shoving the Savage family out of his pew. Even Richard's friends were startled and thought the whole affair unseemly.

Hearing the commotion, the priest looked out the vestry door to see what happened. As he began the service, he stewed over how he should respond. By sermon time his brow was dripping sweat as he menacingly jabbed his index finger towards Gallagher and shouted, "How dare you defile the house of God! I have the right to demand the pew rents, and there will be consequences for this sacrilege. The bishop has warned you! You people will bring calamities down upon your heads!"

An uneasy murmuring rose from the gallery as the rapid fire excoriation continued. But the unbowed Gallagher sat stiffly, responding only with a wry smile. He would show the priest he had trifled with the wrong man. The next day he went to the village hall and filed civil suit against Savage for trespass, seeking damages of $25. The fact he had evicted the man from his pew was of little consequence to him.

The town was soon abuzz with anticipation of another airing of the church dispute. When the trial convened, Judge Marcus Bickford peered over his wire-rimmed glasses to see his courtroom packed with spectators. The seating capacity was less than half the size needed to accommodate everyone who stood in line to attend. The citizens of Carthage had been following the Church scandal for three long years and hungered for the latest juicy details.

Bickford, an attorney whose Anglo-Saxon name was aptly derived from a type of battle axe, also was a preacher and pastor of the Disciples Protestant denomination. As a devoted Reformationist, the judge had honed his legal axe for battle with anyone who flaunted the principle of separation of church and state. He dabbed at his neat moustache as he leaned forward, primed to interject himself into the cross-examination of witnesses whenever he felt it necessary. Father Clarke, whom the accused Savage had asked to appear on his behalf, would be the first to come under the scrutiny of Judge Bickford's questioning.

"Where do you get the authority to usurp the trustees?" the judge asked as he mercilessly grilled Clarke about who had control of the pew rents.

The greatly offended Clarke tersely responded, "I get my authority from my bishop. No one has the right to countermand my bishop in Church matters."

"Is that right?" said Bickford. "Well the court will determine that."

Gallagher and the spectators greatly enjoyed this exchange for it was obvious Bickford believed strongly in the independence of the laity from church hierarchy. The pillorying went on for two days and at one point Gallagher's attorney, encouraged by Judge Bickford's position, stood to interject that, "Roman Catholics here are naught but slaves to the bishop and their clergy." Richard could barely conceal his glee as Clarke fumed and the hapless Savage wondered what his priest had gotten him into.

Savage, no matter what his patron Clarke said, didn't fare well in court as Judge Bickford ruled in Gallagher's favor and awarded him $5.31 for damages. Poor Savage, an expendable pawn on Clarke's chessboard, had to pay an additional $8.69 in court costs. He wondered if the pastor might give back his pew subscription.

Of course, Father Clarke was incensed at the verdict. *How can I be blamed for accepting the advice of the Father Thebaud?* He certainly did not feel the bishop could fault him since the decision was no doubt influenced by the Protestant judge.

The priest rushed home to write his bishop about what had transpired at trial. It was yet another letter McCloskey did not enjoy receiving.

> I have delayed longer than I should on account of duty to answer your kind letters, and at present I regret much to have to inform you how Mr. Gallagher continues not only to be obstinate, in not surrendering the money and accounts still in his hands belonging to this church, but he has tried to

form a league in the church to annoy me by not paying Pew Rent. Finding this to be about the time Revd. Father Thebaud was here I asked his advice what would be the best course to pursue. He advised the following plan, to request that all would remain in their pews until their names and the number of each Pew and Pew Rent would be taken.

Accordingly I did so, and I further announced to them that all those who did not answer for their Pews on that occasion, they would be rented to the first applicant. All remained and cheerfully answered to their names, and paid their Pew Rent, but Mr. Gallagher who walked out contemptuously and did not pay his Pew Rent.

Accordingly the Committee and Collectors consulted me how to act in this matter, and we jointly concluded to rent his Pew to another person who paid for it, and on the following Sunday, this man & family came to church, and occupied his Pew. On the same Sunday, Mr. Gallagher came to church, and forced his way into this man's Pew, regardless of any rule or regulation, and his family occupied it for that Sunday. In a few days after he sued this man for his Pew, and yet did not pay his Pew Rent, before a Justice of Peace who is a Protestant Preacher in this village, whom he knew to be an enemy of the Catholic Church and the jury being of the same material with the addition of one bad Catholic, who decided in favour of Mr. Gallagher putting thirteen dollars cost on this poor man.

Whilst in public court he encouraged and insisted his Lawyer ask all the scandalous questions he could think of. Among the questions were these, are not the Catholic Laity tools in the hands of Bishops and Priests, intending to draw odium and disgrace upon the Bishops and Priestly functions and the discipline of the Catholic Church in a crowded Court Room for the space of nearly two days and the greater part of the night.

He has no provocation from me for his rebellious course, in as much as I have not mentioned his name from the Altar on any occasion nor will not until I receive your advice as my Bishop how to act in this matter.

> Now I have given you a precise statement of Mr. Gallagher's conduct and it is for you to determine how to settle this now, for he seems by the present appearance of things, and the bold stand he takes, he is only beginning his troublesome course in this congregation.
>
> I think this man will continue coming to the Church to raise a public disturbance, so on these grounds, I think it best for me not to attend the Church until I hear from you...

The priest, of course, asserted the deck was stacked against him as he was beset by the miscreant Gallagher, a prejudiced Protestant Judge, and a "bad Catholic juror," whom he did not name. This accounting by Clarke only reaffirmed the prevailing anxiety Catholic clergy had that the Protestant Reformation had such a hold in America it could only contribute adversely to the Holy Roman Church's mission.

Clarke's lament that these actions are the product of a fallen away Catholic, heaping "odium" on the clergy and the Church found a receptive, albeit distressed, ear with the bishop, a man everyone knew to be totally committed to restoring discipline among the laity. The priest felt the need to stress his innocence in the affair lest the bishop be disposed to infer the contrary. That Gallagher had gotten "no provocation from me...I have not mentioned his name from the Altar..." was a familiar, if transparent, defense. Although Clarke denounced the perceived miscreants anonymously, he knew the congregation had no doubt to whom he referred. With this artifice, the priest avoided the charge of defamation, which Gallagher was seriously considering seeking to redress in court.

Clarke told his superior, yet again, it was up to him to take action, a suggestion that sorely exasperated McCloskey. When Father Conroy last saw Clarke, he had repeated the admonition that, "His Eminence wants, as any able executive would, local problems solved at the local level and not rising to his attention. It is the parish priest's job to see problems begun at the parish level are resolved at the parish level." His advice made no apparent impact on the priest.

When next he saw Father McFarland, Conroy brought up Clarke and his problems to the Utica pastor. "The man has an obvious flaw. Besides his pugnacious nature, he has a tendency to twist the facts in his favor. I don't understand why he can't recognize that petty arguments continually referred to the bishop, place an unneeded burden on the diocese."

McFarland admitted he might have seen those traits when Clarke was in his charge at Utica. "But we all have flaws," he rationalized. He had not sounded warnings to the Carthage people because, "No one asked my opinion."

"In his eagerness to ingratiate himself with the bishop, he overlooks the fact these troubles only magnify his inability to manage his parish," Conroy added.

This latest letter caused it to be whispered about in the chancery that Clarke was becoming more erratic and difficult to deal with. Conroy would admit, if asked delicately, that this behavior was not unknown with other priests of the day. When the opportunity next presented itself, he mentioned to McCloskey, "His Eminence may ultimately have to intervene in this dispute."

The bishop demurred, uncomfortable at being placed in what for him was an untenable situation. He reaffirmed his position with a voice uncharacteristically rising to a higher pitch. "The trustees will never dictate policy in my diocese. I have no priest to send them and would not if I did."

Vicar General Conroy thought the bishop's continued refusal to directly address the problem had allowed it to fester and might result in an even more intractable problem later on. Thus he felt compelled to press the issue. "Then, what shall we do about this Carthage problem?" he asked.

"Those people have been warned. We shall do what any good priest would do-pray," said McCloskey as he walked away.

Chapter 18

"The bishop thinks I'm the troublemaker," Richard complained the next time the trustees convened.

The Settlement farmers, Neary and the Walsh brothers, listened patiently but feared the dispute had spiraled out of control. "We've gotten in too deep," said Neary. "There's no way out, short of leaving the Church."

"Worry not," said Gallagher. "They need us if they want to have a church in Carthage."

Gallagher felt he was spending much too much time on this squabble, and this didn't please him at all. Although he occasionally protested to the contrary, his cohorts knew he was needed as the leading force in the rebellion, holding them together if only by force of will. He and Maria were the only ones, besides the priest, who had written McCloskey, and although their voices may have represented the general feelings of the parish, they felt isolated. It was easy for the bishop to assume, abetted by Clarke's letters, that it was only the Gallaghers who complained and caused problems.

But gossip, like darts flying through the air at the pub in Brown's Hotel, began hitting targets other than Gallagher, including the faithful long-time trustee Farrel Neary. As a result of the pew trial, Clarke had expanded his cast of culpable parishioners, and Neary found himself labeled as a "bad Catholic." When he heard the pastor claimed he had said the people of the parish controlled all church matters-spiritual as well as temporal-Neary became agitated and aggrieved. He was one of the first to colonize the Irish Settlement back in 1823, and felt his community standing was being unfairly impugned. The wizened and weathered farmer decided to defend himself.

Your Eminence,

I am an old man and for the first time in my life I was on as a witness in a suit between two persons in this

> congregation where our pastor took a very active part. I testified on the trial to the Rules which pews were rented and regulated but to my surprise after the trial I learned that it is reported among the people of this Mission that I swore on the Trial that the Laity had control of temporal & Spiritual matters.
>
> I am a Resident of this Town for the last 35 years and now to be charged with advocating a principle which would control the Clergy of my Church in their Spiritual Duties it is painful to me indeed and more so when I am calumniated by a person who Should give his counsel and advice and not Stir up and Encourage Litigation and Strife amongst his congregation.
>
> I have raised a family of 11 children all now grown up to the age of men & women and now to have their father charged with advocating a heretical Doctrine and to be branded as a perjurer is worse than death and to Sustain my reputation at Least in the Estimation of the Bishop of my dear religion I Enclose the proceedings on the trial which I refer to...

Neary was now sixty-nine years old, a goodly span given that many of his contemporaries had not lived much past forty years. He was tired of the charges and counter-charges about St. James, and he wanted to put an end to it.

The bishop now could clearly see that Gallagher wasn't the only Carthage Catholic who was upset with Father Clarke's actions. He also saw that others felt his disregard for their complaints had become part of the problem. To no one's surprise, Neary received the same party line response: "You have to submit to the authority of your Church and its mediary, your priest." The weary McCloskey refused to acknowledge the case against his beleaguered priest had any merit and continued with his party line support and dire warnings of consequences for disobedience.

Clarke seemed unaffected by the eddies of complaint swirling about him. On May 30, 1858 he again wrote to his bishop extolling his progress in preparing the outlying mission children for confirmation*-a sacramental rite only a bishop may perform.

> I have prepared the children of Redwood & Rossie for confirmation having to help me the Fathers from Montreal. I trust there will be a great many in both places for confirmation ... There are but few if any at Carthage for confirmation but if you see fit you may visit it....

Oddly, although larger than Redwood and Rossie combined, the Carthage congregation didn't have any twelve-year-olds ready for confirmation. The fact that Clarke wasn't even sure about this should have raised a red flag for McCloskey, but it apparently did not.

This admission, when it became known to the St. James congregants, only reinforced their complaint that Clarke was derelict in preparing children in the rubrics of their faith. The Gallagher's were upset their twelve-year-old daughter Harriet was not receiving the sacrament. As Maria had complained in her letter to the bishop, the priest was using false pretexts to refuse holding Sunday school for the youngsters, and the pastor had gone out of his way to veto her husband's attempts to rectify the situation. "I don't understand why the bishop isn't concerned that our priest, who has taken a vow committing him to our spiritual care, is venting his anger on the youngsters," Maria said.

Like the priest, Gallagher had become consumed with what he saw as unseemly behavior and often exclaimed he would be damned before he'd give in.

"Have we gotten in too deep?" Patrick Walsh wondered. "Is there no escapin' this mud hole?" He was not alone in fearing they might go to their eternal judgment without benefit of the sacraments.

"Send something to the bishop," Patrick pleaded. And, after some deliberation, Gallagher decided to forward to

McCloskey the church insurance policy, plus a list of the parish house subscribers-while still keeping control of the money in the bank.

"Patrick, you should know that I've sent the information to the bishop," he said, "but nothing to the priest, nothing! So quit worrying about it."

In his June 13, 1858, transmittal letter to McCloskey, Gallagher said, "I do insist that I be protected from those charges if [proved] false." He was referring, of course, to the numerous accusations made by Clarke-both to the bishop directly and by innuendo from the pulpit.

Many dissenters breathed a sigh of relief when they heard of Gallagher's concession. But Aunt Nancy Walsh was upset. She spit her anger at brother Patrick for revealing his fears. "Ya gotta stand up to the man," she berated. But Patrick refused to argue with his sister because the chunky spitfire had always gotten the better of him and knew that another encounter would be no different.

Tempers and inflammatory rhetoric from parishioners seemed to flag and took a much needed hiatus for the remainder of the year. No more letters made their way to Albany. Since all seemed quiet, McCloskey assumed the squabble had run its course. The temperature drop among the laity did not, however, ameliorate Clarke's capacity for holding a grudge. His tirades continued from the pulpit even though his appearances in Carthage had significantly decreased.

"Do ya think he sees his mission as dividing the parish into two camps?" O'Leary asked Richard.

"Whether it's his intent or not, that's what's happening."

At the Gallagher's New Year's party to usher in 1859, little time was spent on Father Clarke and his frequent absences. The calm was broken when another parishioner, following the example of Farrel Neary, decided he had enough. Arnold Galleciez, the one who had built Gallagher's house on upper State Street, was born in Goux-Doub, France. He was known as a scrappy fellow, or so those who dealt with him had said. His family had arrived in Carthage only ten years before and all faithfully attended St. James Church.

Content to be a bystander while others took the fight to the bishop, he was aroused to act when he felt the personal sting of Clarke's interference with his family. He wrote Bishop McCloskey on January 7, 1859, in his native language, which the bishop, an accomplished linguist, had no trouble reading. Despite his annoyance at receiving yet another complaint about his priest, the bishop could not help but admire Galleciez's fine script. It signaled a cultured upbringing, something McCloskey appreciated, even if it came from a complaining layman.

Taking care to address McCloskey respectfully, Galleciez launched into his assessment of the situation.

> Lord Bishop of Albany,
>
> I address you on the subject of my congregation at Carthage. Permit me to give you a little information about the position in which we find ourselves, and at the same time, to give you some news about the conduct of the Reverend Mr. Clarke.
>
> I tell you that we are quite disheartened by the situation at present. I tell you also that it is a scandal for our religion to see a man behave as he does. To begin with, he has put out the principle men of our church. He has put them out by abusing them publicly, by blaming them for deeds, which all the people know are false.
>
> For me, more than a month has passed since I last attended the church at Carthage. The reason is that when I did go I heard nothing but bickering and wrangling. His sermons heaped blame on the congregation, abused them, threatened them, even made them hear that they were worse than thieves. I was shocked to hear the pastor preach such things, and I stopped attending the services.
>
> The disputes began in this way. When Father Clarke came to Carthage, he flattered the people by promising them

this and that. He would build a parsonage. First he named his officers to collect money. They accumulated, I think, $1100 in the space of a year or a year-and-a-half.

The leading men of our congregation felt that we had enough to start with, and that when the people saw what we could do they would give more. We laid this idea before the pastor, but he hemmed and he hawed. He said that we ought to buy a ready-built house.

He sent his committeemen to see if such a house were for sale. They reported that there was one for sale, but he was no longer satisfied. After that, someone proposed that they buy Reverend Mr. Roche's house, but this did not please him, because of a grudge against him [Roche].

After all were done we let him have his own way. He continued until he had money in his pocket, wherefrom we do not know. Now he speaks of it [the parsonage] no longer. I tell you, my Lord that he looks for nothing but to create trouble and disorder wherever he can.

The other day I found myself at the home of a man named Guyot. There came in a poor man who worked for him to ask him for 12 dollars to have his infant baptized. He said that he had to go as far as Constableville [over 30 miles away] to have the child baptized. "It has been three times that I have brought him to Father Clarke. He never has the time to baptize him." Another poor man who has a big family of 7 or 8 children was telling me on Thursday of last week I brought my infant to be baptized, but Father Clarke said to me, Have you any money. I answered him, no, but I will pay you shortly. The Pastor answered keep your child until you have money to pay me.

There is [your] Christianity. The name of this man is Maloney. My Lord, if the time permitted, I could cite more, but I think that you will be satisfied that Father Clarke does not suit us at all, and that our religion is not prospering in Carthage as it ought to prosper.

Please believe me, my Lord, that we are not infidels, indeed not. All of the people in our congregation are ready to do all for the good of our church, and pay as much as possible.

All that we need is a good priest: A devoted priest who will preach the Gospel rather than divide the people one against the other. He looks upon his congregation as if we were chattel, brutalizing, abusing and threatening. All that he knows how to do is to flatter himself. In that he is not lacking. He tells how this one and that one likes him, the great wonders he has performed, that is the most of his sermon on Sunday.

Now, my Lord, you see our condition. You see how our religion prospers in Carthage. Our salvation is in your hands. It is up to you to see if Father Clarke is good for us.

Your devoted servant,
Arnold Galleciez

McCloskey grimaced when finished reading Galleciez's missive, even his observant aide Conroy wondered if his superior had a fleeting moment when he regretted letting this errant priest go too far. In the end, loss of face might pale in comparison to a full-scale rebellion.

"How much further can, or should, we go in backing up this priest?" Conroy finally asked.

The bishop pondered the question for a long minute before deciding, yet again, that giving in would do more harm than good. He, not unlike Cato the Elder, who concluded every speech with the famous *Cathago delenda est,* responded to his aide that, "The trustee system must be destroyed."

CHAPTER 19

As the year progressed, the winds of change began briskly sweeping across the American stage. Despite the abundance of fodder for the local gossip mill the church squabble provided, Carthaginians had to make room for unfolding national news. Groups gathered on the corners of State Street to discuss world events which seemed to demand more attention than ever before. Eight years of stringing telegraph lines across the national landscape had caused America to shrink appreciably. After a steamship docked in New York, the latest dispatches were sent to the nearest telegraph station, transposed into Morse code, and sent over wires to various newspapers. It was all happening much faster than anyone previously thought possible. And because of this new invention, news quickly traveled by wire as far west as St. Louis-even though from that point they had to rely on the Pony Express to take the reports on to San Francisco.

Carthage, true to its experience with railroads, also lagged behind this new technology. Acquiring telegraphy had not even been seriously discussed in Carthage. Village residents depended on mail coaches to keep up with the world's latest news. Residents anxiously crowded the bookstore and post office where they could get a peek at the many newspapers and magazines that made their way to the village. In addition to *Harpers Weekly*, they could choose from *Frank Leslie's Illustrated News, The New York Ledger, The New York Mercury, The Utica Herald, The Utica Telegraph,* and *Leslies Budget of Fun.* Gallagher subscribed to *Harpers, The Ledger,* and the previously mentioned *Freeman's Journal.*

One item in the *New York Ledger* that caught Gallagher's eye was the announcement of a planned daredevil feat by the Great Blondin at Niagara Falls. The French rope-walker had been on tour in the States for nearly eight years and audaciously claimed he would walk across Niagara Falls on a tightrope. The news reminded Richard of the proper honeymoon he had long ago promised Maria. Could this be another two for one deal, the kind that Richard really liked?

It had been nearly sixty years since Aaron Burr's daughter Theodosia had chosen Niagara Falls as her honeymoon destination. It had since become a popular spot for many newlyweds. Richard thought this would be a perfect time to get away. When he arrived home that evening proposed the idea to Maria. She eagerly agreed.

The news became the talk of the town when Carthaginians heard of the Blondin crossing. When apprised of Gallagher's plans, O'Leary mentioned he and Alice might like to go along. "The missus has never seen the Falls so this might be a good opportunity for her too. For sure there'll be a big crowd so we better get hotel accommodations." He offered to take care of the arrangements since he had visited the place some twenty years prior. He had made friends with the manager of the Cataract House and would write to see if they had rooms available.

"Is there nowhere that you don't have connections?" Gallagher asked.

The event was scheduled for Thursday, June 30, some three weeks hence. Maria admitted she had actually forgotten Richard's promise of a "proper honeymoon" made eighteen years before. He was so busy expanding his business and accumulating wealth that he had stopped taking pleasure trips. "This will be splendid," Maria said with surprise when Richard proposed the trip. "We could both do with a week away. Perhaps we can forget this nasty church business for a while."

Maria threw herself into excited preparation for the trip. A proper trousseau was required so she and Alice O'Leary went to see their dressmaker, Mrs. Coyle, where each ordered two dresses in the latest fashion.

Richard also busied himself with planning the trip. "We'll take the stage to Watertown where we'll board the train to Buffalo. From there we'll take the train up to Niagara Falls," he told his wife in a voice that could not mask his enthusiasm. And it filled Maria with anticipation because she hadn't seen her husband this excited about anything in a very long time.

Thousands of others across the eastern seaboard, including railroad barons, steamship captains, and merchandise vendors also saw Blondin's feat, not only as great entertainment but also as a splendid money making opportunity. The usual assortment of con men who plied their skills wherever unsuspecting crowds gathered, also took note. Interest in the spectacle offered an unprecedented occasion for a variety of opportunists to turn a coin or two.

The Gallaghers and O'Learys boarded the early stage for Watertown two days before Blondin's planned feat. The sunny weather was cooperative, making the bumpy journey tolerable, if not quite pleasant. The group gave up trying to make small talk as the carriage rocked them from side to side, bounced them up and down, and occasionally pitched them abruptly forward. The Squire was all for making the best of it. "'Tis the finest time of the year in the North Country," he shouted, and all happily agreed.

Once on the train, the foursome welcomed the change to the quieter and smoother ride. Rail travel gave them the opportunity to have frequent, animated conversation. Before Richard had a chance to bring it up, Maria said talking about the problems of St. James was off limits. "We're here to enjoy ourselves so please don't bring up any unpleasant subjects." Alice O'Leary seconded the motion.

"What do you think of this Blondin fellow?" O'Leary interjected.

"I read that his idea of traversing the Falls at Niagara came to him in a dream one evening after a night of drinking," said Richard, who had absorbed everything written about the stunt in the papers and magazines. "There's a lot of competition in this adventure business, and he thinks crossing the Falls will give him the boost in fame that will set him apart from his rivals."

"In a dream!" both ladies replied in astonishment. Maria and Alice gave great credence to dream dissection and analysis. They had attended a visiting "professor's" dream lecture at Walsh's Hall, and were impressed by his theories. "We don't pay enough attention to our dreams," Maria said, leaning forward a bit earnestly. "Why, Shakespeare's plays are full of dreams, and they usually foretell the future."

Richard wrinkled his nose, rolled his eyes, and thought, *Poppycock,* but wisely kept it to himself.

When at last they finally arrived at Niagara Falls, the party checked into the Cataract House, a short walk downriver from Goat Island. Many of the rooms offered a gorgeous view of the scene from which the hotel derived its name.

Unsurprisingly, to Gallagher, the manager remembered O'Leary and was happy to see him. The notion that the Irishman was an unforgettable character who left an indelible impression wherever he went was reinforced as the pair exchanged jovial greetings. "Are you still singing those old ballads from home?" his countryman from Cork asked.

A beaming O'Leary grinned as Gallagher declared, "Try and stop him!"

It was late in the day and the troupe was tired from the hours of travel so they decided to retire immediately after a modest dinner in the hotel dining room. "There's something about this natural wonder," said Maria as she gazed out the window at the Falls. "It just excites me so."

Richard came over to stand by Maria's side and put his arm around her waist. He drew her close, causing Maria to murmur, "Why, Richard, I do believe you are getting amorous." There was no audible answer but a passionate kiss soon followed. Maria was taken by surprise, because since their last child had come two years before, Richard's ardor had cooled considerably.

"You've had such a hard time birthing that I didn't want you to go through that again," he explained. Of course, contraception, what little was available or known to the couple, was out of the question. All religions banned such practices and their Church's position was understood by all its members. Maria, her heart quickening, would admit in a more candid moment that she didn't look forward to another pregnancy. But this new venue with its breathtaking view had a magical effect on the couple. Richard's kisses grew longer, deeper, and more sensual. It was only a moment before her eager lover deftly freed the dozen buttons on the back of her dress while their lips were still locked in passion.

The object of his affection quivered in anticipation. "Oh, Richard," she moaned as he picked her up and carried her to the bed.

A long time had passed since he had been this attentive, and their ensuing sinuous, rhythmic merging seemed as eager and fresh as on their initial honeymoon. Maria threw caution to the wind, giving herself to her paramour completely and without reservation. When she finally caught her breath, she couldn't help but reflect on their first coupling at the White House in Watertown those many years ago. "Remember our first honeymoon?" she coquettishly asked.

"How could I forget?" her lover responded.

Their energies spent, the pair lay their heads back on the pillows as Richard whispered, "I do love you, Maria Sherwood."

"And I you, Richard Gallagher. Is this what you had in mind for a proper honeymoon?" she teased.

As Maria lay there reminiscing and basking in its afterglow, she realized how much she had missed their love making. She took her husband's palm in hers and they made small talk as Richard's eyes slowly glistened anew. He again gently glided his hands over Maria's firm body saying, "You know, you are just as slim and pretty as when we first met." It was a minor exaggeration, and an excusable one, given the man was so filled with love and anticipation. Before long they both became aroused anew and threw themselves into an encore of lovemaking, just as vigorously as they did the first time. At last the exhausted couple lay back silently and, unmindful of the roar of the Falls, were soon fast asleep.

In the morning, when they awoke from their much needed rest, they lay next to each other holding hands. They smiled and talked about how lucky they were to have met those many years ago. "We've Woolson to thank for that," said Richard as Maria laughed at the memory of those early years. Her voice had such a romantic effect on him that his thoughts returned to romance. But this time, Maria gently and firmly pushed him away.

"It's getting late," she admonished. "We're going to be here a week, after all! What will people think? We'd best get ready for breakfast."

It was after ten o'clock when they finally descended the steps to the dining room. The O'Learys had been seated at their table for some time, enjoying their third cup of coffee. "Well, here's the happy and smiling couple!" the Squire boomed. Richard blushed as everyone in the dining room turned to look, thinking they would see a pair of young newlyweds instead of the middle-aged, blushing couple who sheepishly slid into chairs at O'Leary's table.

"Good morning," the blushing Maria said as cheerily as she could under the circumstances. Alice gave her friend a wink along with a knowing smile.

"I was walking around earlier. You're not going to believe the crowd that's out there already, and the event isn't until tomorrow," O'Leary said, changing the subject. The group had a leisurely breakfast and left the hotel to blend in with the gathering throng. They spent the day sightseeing in anticipation of the coming event, even taking a ride on the *Maid of the Mist* up close to the Falls. They didn't even mind the two hour wait in line for tickets.

Richard's ardor was far from spent and that evening he repeated his amorous advances with a willing Maria. "Why Richard," she exclaimed, "I do believe the Falls have reinvigorated you!"

"They haven't treated you badly either," he smiled. "In fact, I don't think a week here will be enough."

On the day of Blondin's scheduled crossing, Gallagher asked O'Leary if he had found a good observation spot.

"White's Pleasure Garden's got a good view and is charging a quarter for admission," said the Squire. "They've got tables and drinks." The two couples then sauntered down to White's where Richard gave the ticket taker a silver dollar for the group's entry fee.

"They say there are 25,000 here today," O'Leary exclaimed. Indeed, for a mile downstream from the cataract the banks were black with people, on both sides. Mingling among them were vendors of every stripe, selling souvenirs such as pennants, hats, and sweat cloths. They also sold drinks such as buckshot whiskey for a dollar and tartaric lemonade at a quarter a glass. People filing in to sit at White's tables groused about being hoodwinked by one or another of the sharpies. "They charged me a dollar for a lousy glass of lemonade," one man complained.

The comment made O'Leary chuckle and caused him to caution his friends. "Believe you me you had better watch your wallet. There's many a blackleg in this crowd."

The mood, despite the infiltration of conmen and unscrupulous vendors, was festive and there was great anticipation, along with a concomitant amount of apprehension. Blondin's forthcoming attempt caused many to wager he would fail and plunge into the gorge below. "I have to admit I am skeptical of this venture," said Richard. "Why, just look at that rope," he added, pointing to the enormous length of hemp stretching across the gorge. "I'm sure he won't make it."

Gallagher was prompted to give a synopsis of what he had learned from all the reading he did about Blondin's career. "The ropedancer, as such performers were popularly called, had come to America in 1851 as a member of the famous Ravel troupe. He was headquartered at Niblo's Garden in

New York City, but the group also performed at various cities along the East coast.

"Blondin is a born showman, always looking for spectacular ways to attract attention." Richard continued, his voice rising enthusiastically as he warmed to his storytelling. "He never could resist a risky stunt. Why, one night, when he wasn't even scheduled to perform, and didn't have his costume on, he saw a group of actors getting ready to put on a mock military battle. The dozen 'soldiers', outfitted with military caps, were milling about waiting for their cue to perform. Their rifles were upright with bayonets fixed, extending well above their plumed hats." Gallagher gesticulated for effect, raising his arm to demonstrate how tall those "soldiers" were. "This Blondin fellow approached, took a few steps and somersaulted right over the top of them! The actors were as surprised as the people in the bleachers when he cleared their bayonets with ease." Richard was obviously as impressed as everyone in the Garden that night, all of whom shouted and applauded approval. "And now they're calling him the *Monarch of the Cable*."

"Look there, isn't that Almont Barnes?" interrupted a surprised Alice O'Leary.

"'Tis, 'tis," said the Squire. "Hey Almont," he shouted. "What're you doing here?" Barnes was startled that someone in this throng actually recognized him, and he hastened over to the roped off area to see who had called out.

After greeting everyone, he mentioned he was here as the editor and publisher of the *Black River Budget*, Carthage's new weekly newspaper. He was on his way to attend press briefings being held in a tent near Blondin's departure point.

"I'll tell you what I've learned so far, if you're interested," said the newspaperman. Of course, everyone was eager to know the details, so he began relating his insider's knowledge of the crossing attempt. "They say the main rope is woven manila fiber, a bit over three inches thick." He formed a circle with his hands, touching his thumbs and fingers for effect.

"They say it stretches across the gorge for about 1,300 ft. and where it sags in the middle it's 160 ft. above the water. They have nearly 40,000 ft. of smaller diameter ropes just to steady the main cable." The ladies oohed and aahed as Barnes reeled off the statistics. From where they sat, they could see the dazzling tangle of cables stretched across the gorge, the magnitude of which awed them.

"How on earth did they ever get the cable across?" asked Maria. It was a question that puzzled everyone, for they couldn't even imagine how they went about it.

"They say it was a show in itself just to watch Blondin use his acrobatic skills to string it. Well, I've got to be off," said Barnes. "He's going to make his first attempt at 2 o'clock."

The young waiter who appeared to take drink orders offered to pick up where Barnes left off. "You know," he said, "Blondin really didn't want the final placement of the tightrope where it is because he didn't think it offered enough of a challenge. He wanted to cross right above the falls between Terrapin Point and Table Rock, but the landowners vetoed that idea." Requiring no prompting to continue, the youth added, "It's going to be unbelievable. Where he wanted to fasten his cable," as he pointed up river to the roaring Falls, "would've been a real test. Many experts said crossing at that point wasn't possible. Why, the air turbulence and fog above the Falls would have increased the chances of his slipping." Everyone looked up river at the mist rising over the cascading water and nodded their heads in agreement. "No doubt it would have been much more perilous-quite possibly fatal."

The waiter anxiously related other statistics including how much the rope sloped, the one foot drop every ten feet, allowing only forty feet of level section in the middle. All heads simultaneously swiveled towards the cable to verify this fact. Many believed the cable too flimsy to hold Blondin, and others said he just wouldn't be able to make it across. Given Blondin's size, at 5′8″ and weighing 142 lbs., there should not have been cause for concern, but the vast majority of onlookers were not conversant with the actual details of the attempt.

"The lad's excited," said Richard after the waiter left to fetch their drinks. "I wonder if Barnes knows all of that."

"I imagine this is something we'll remember for the rest of our lives," said Maria.

After listening to the flood of data and the resident skepticism about the attempt, the ladies began showing genuine concern. "What if he does fall?" asked Maria in a slightly quivering voice. Alice's brow puckered with concern in concert with Maria's unease.

"Don't worry ladies," said O'Leary, "I think he knows what he's doing." But secretly he had his doubts, as did the majority of spectators lining the gorge.

CHAPTER 20

The Gallaghers bid Squire and Alice goodbye as their friends boarded the train for home, two days after Blondin's first crossing. "You young folks enjoy your honeymoon, the Squire said with an impish wink."

The Niagara Falls adventure was the talk of the town in Carthage and many awaited the vacationers' return to hear of the crossing first-hand. And who better to give it than Squire George O'Leary.

The Gallaghers arrived home just before sundown on July 5. They had spent a glorious Fourth at the Falls-complete with the largest fireworks display they'd ever seen, and additional ropewalking by the now world famous *Monarch of the Cable*.

Almont Barnes had prepared an article about the Niagara Falls adventure for Thursday's *Budget*, and it quoted Squire O'Leary extensively. The reporter visited Gallagher at his store to ask if he would like to add anything before the print deadline. "You want to tell us about your honeymoon?" he teased.

The red-faced Gallagher replied, "O'Leary's told you all you need to know. I'll be surprised if he doesn't write a poem about it."

O'Leary, of course, was more than happy to be quoted in the local paper, even consenting to make a public appearance on Friday evening at Walsh's Hall to recount the adventure. The 40 by 80 foot auditorium was on the third floor above John T. Walsh's [no relation to the trustee Walsh brothers] grocery store. The venue often hosted a variety of performances, with as many as 250 people in attendance. Traveling orators promoting temperance or abolition, orchestras, stage plays, and lecturers on a wide variety of subjects, including dream analysis, had performed there. The fees charged allowed Walsh to turn a modest profit on his Hall.

On this occasion, however, the use of the auditorium was donated for O'Leary's recitation. The irrepressible bon vivant had never met a speaker's dais he didn't like and was delighted to have the opportunity to strut before an audience.

Gallagher, although he said he'd attend, declined the opportunity to speak. "The Squire will do a good enough job," he said. "It would be unwise to try to follow his act."

After the large crowd was seated, the Tammy-topped Squire, looking as if ready for a political rally, began by hushing the assembly. "You'll want to hear this!" he boomed and the crowd fell silent with anticipation. He launched his oration by describing the size and makeup of the mass of people gathered at the Falls. "They lined the shores of the Niagara River below the cataract, some 25,000 strong!" he said, and the crowd signified its amazement with audible oohs and aahs, including an occasional whistle or two. He rattled off the statistics he had committed to his renowned memory-which included the size, length, and weight of the rope. "Many people wagered as to the success or failure of the feat," he said.

"How did you bet, Squire?" a voice in the audience shouted.

"If I'd have bet," he admitted, "I might have gone against. It was truly a sight to take your breath away. When he stepped out on that rope, everybody stopped breathing, I among them. Lordy, it was a feat to behold."

The Squire, encouraged by the enthusiastic audience, continued with a blow-by-blow description of the crossing. "They said it was to go off at two o'clock but it wasn't until five that he began. It was truly breathtaking. This Blondin fellow showed neither fear nor trepidation. He started out from the American side, from a place they call Prospect Park, using a thirty-foot balancing pole that was weighted with lead to come in at forty pounds. It was like a carnival with flags, bunting, and streamers on both sides of the gorge. A brass band struck up *On the Other Side of Jordan* as Blondin took his first steps. It gives me the shivers to think of it, and to make matters worse, after about 100 ft., he stopped and lay down on his back on the rope!" The Carthage assembly, just as did the crowd at the Falls, let out a gasp.

"And that wasn't all," O'Leary continued. "He went to the middle, unwrapped a length of twine from around his waist, motioned to a boat below, the *Maid of the Mist* I think it was, to come under the cable. He lowered the twine and a crewman tied a bottle of wine to it. Blondin hauled it up, and drank it while sitting on the rope!" The Carthaginians roared just as did the Niagara crowd. The Squire didn't know Blondin was a teetotaler and the "wine" was non-fermented grape juice. This information also cast doubt on the original story that Blondin had gotten the idea of crossing Niagara in a dream after a night of heavy drinking.

"So how much did he get for this feat?" someone asked.

"Don't know," said the Squire, "but it must've been a goodly sum because they were charging admission and passing the hat." It was revealed, again after the fact, only 1,000 out of the 4,000 people at White's Pleasure Garden actually paid the 25¢ admission. As a result, Blondin's cut was only $250. Also, much of the money collected from passing the hat never found its way back to the performer, and he actually received the paltry total of $600 for risking his life in a never before attempted feat of daring do.

"Those Blacklegs had a field day," orator O'Leary continued and he mentioned a few of the villainies perpetrated against the unsuspecting crowd. He regaled his audience with additional details including the railroad cars parked on the suspension bridge, giving passengers a ringside seat to the crossing, and boats on the Niagara River so overloaded they came perilously close to sinking.

The audience was much amused and shuddered in disbelief of it all. Some said the Squire's recitation made them feel they were actually right there watching the spectacle. It was a *tour de force* for O'Leary, something that provided conversation on the streets of Carthage for the remainder of the summer.

As the season turned to fall, reports of the Great Blondin's crossings continued to pour in. Each time the performer ventured out on the cable he came up with a stunt that topped the previous one. He once made a trip covered in a cloth sack, followed by another pushing a wheelbarrow, and one with his terrified manager on his back. The papers eagerly reported every detail of these exploits.

***

"**W**hat do you think of this Garibaldi fellow?" O'Leary was seeking Gallagher's opinion about the news reports coming out of Italy. The papers trumpeted that Italians, led by Giuseppe Garibaldi, were bent on driving the occupying Austrians out of Milan. Both men had read the *New York Times* reports of how the Garibaldi led Piedmontese were on the march in Italy. Members of the Western press were there to report the fighting and give the details to their readers. As always, the body counts, cannon lost, and who was gaining the upper hand depended largely on which side's dispatches dominated the reporting.

The *Times* correspondent on the scene openly lamented the “fog of war” and his subsequent inability to get the true picture. He couldn't trust the local reportage, he said, but did manage to give an account of a personal sighting of the impressive Garibaldi at the Milanese City Hall, where his arrival was greeted with shouts of *“viva Garibaldi.”* The tall commander, elegantly dressed in a green Sardinian uniform, “wore a look of resolution” and was greeted with huzzas wherever he went. When inquiring of other soldiers about their feelings towards Garibaldi, the reporter said they spoke in admiration of his battlefield accomplishments but disdained his politics. “He is a *democratico,*” they said, and it was obvious that such ideology was not respected by many of the troops.

Despite the reservations held by Italians, Americans in general and Carthaginians in particular were captivated by Garibaldi's campaign. Although their Church struggle was on an infinitesimally smaller scale, St. James dissidents exhibited great regard for the emerging Italian hero, identifying with his struggles against Rome. Some even thought the events taking place in Italy might affect the papacy, and by proxy their own struggle.

"Maybe he'll knock some sense into the Church," said Gallagher. He was taken with the rebellious Italian, not only because of his stance against the pope, but also because his tall, lean physical stature was similar to his own.

Although initially ecstatic over the election of Pius IX, Garibaldi had become disenchanted and reportedly was quoted as saying "priests are the scourge of Italy." This caused Gallagher to remark, "They're a scourge here too." The Carthage renegades were looking for support anyplace they might find it, even as far away as Italy. And they needed all they could get for the Church, as Garibaldi knew so well, was indeed a formidable foe. "Maybe we'll have to mount a campaign like Garibaldi's," Gallagher said to parishioners gathered at the church on the following Sunday.

Would the St. James people actually have to wage a war against their Church? And what dimensions would such a war take? Only time would tell.

CHAPTER 21

"Well, dear," Maria said two months after the Niagara Falls trip, "I'm pregnant."

Normally her husband would greet such news with elation but this time he had mixed emotions. He was happy on the one hand while very concerned on the other. "Will you be alright?" he asked in a voice embroidered with concern.

"Oh, you needn't worry about me," Maria said brightly. Her smile was a bit forced because she would turn forty-one before the baby arrived and thought it too late in life to be having children. She kept her concerns to herself, but in the depths of her soul she rued the passion that had gotten the better of her at Niagara. But, when she reflected on their time at the Falls, in spite of the unsought consequences, a smile would cross her face. She then dutifully admonished herself for reveling in carnal pleasure and resolved to put her trust in God that everything would be alright.

As the remaining months slipped by and dawn broke on the year 1860, Gallagher was poised to have one of the best years of his life-save his problems with the Church that is. Dr. Eli West, the Democratic Party head, had watched as Gallagher's leadership qualities emerged. He had first asked him to run for a seat on the village board of trustees six years before and Richard won the one year term. He won another last year and West felt it was time for him to take the village's helm. "How would you like to be president this time around?" the party chairman asked.

"Do you think they are ready for the likes of me?" a mildly surprised Gallagher replied.

"Of course," West said with a confident smile. "Based on what I can see, you're not only a well-respected citizen, but also a born leader."

But the furniture proprietor had one major concern. "You know these damn Know Nothings are still making lots of noise. They don't like us Catholics very much."

"The Know Nothing's have had their day," said West. "They've been having trouble recruiting people ever since the last election."

Indeed, the party seemed to have reached a pinnacle of prominence in the election of 1856. The easily aroused anti-papists, opposing the candidacy of the rumored Catholic, Col. John Freemont, attracted a large number of people to their cause. It mattered not that Freemont vehemently denied the alleged affiliation but his opponents said he was lying. Slavishly true to their belief in the tenets of the Protestant Reformation, they loudly opposed anyone with an "allegiance to the pope," real or imagined. "We don't want a papist president!" they screamed, and newspapers did not hesitate to print these views.

"You've got the Irish vote, that's what'll count," said Dr. West, who at the age of sixty-eight years was still practicing medicine. In fact, Gallagher thought so much of the man he continued to entrust Maria to his care. The doctor owned considerable real estate and dabbled in many other businesses besides medicine. West's "bedside manner" put his ailing patients at ease and was at least as effective as the pills he dispensed, no matter how serious the sickness.

"Anyway, party isn't what decides these elections, it's the man." The village election was scheduled to be held on the first Tuesday in April, three months hence.

On the business side, things were also looking up. "We're doing so well," he said to Maria, "I'm going to expand my advertising to other towns. I think Lowville would be good." He also mentioned his plan to employ sales agents in smaller, more rural areas such as Antwerp and Rossie. Yes, everyone had to agree, he'd come a long way from his impoverished County Westmeath days.

Several of Gallagher's Irish friends were also doing well. John T. Walsh was making his mark with his business block, including the grocery and general store, across the street from Richard's furniture store. George O'Leary continued his climb with his own business block and humming shoe factory, now employing six shoemakers. The boat works was putting the finishing touches on a new steamer that would be christened the Richard Gallagher. The candidate for village president had every reason to be proud, except perhaps for that vexatious priest and his enabling bishop. Amid the hustle and bustle of business success, Richard thought rather optimistically, this might be the year even those St. James problems went away.

The second floor of Gallagher's forty-foot wide business block contained the law offices of George Gilbert and partners Atwood and Stiles. Across the hall was the mortuary viewing room presided over by young James Walsh, Anthony's son. The lad was only twenty-two but already had ten years of undertaking experience. His father's friendship with Gallagher had allowed him to start his mortician's career at the tender age of twelve. In the ensuing years he had developed a reputation for having a refined and sympathetic manner. People often mentioned to Gallagher he was the one they wanted for their dearly departed... and one day for themselves. Wags reportedly said of the juxtaposition of law and undertaking, "On one side of the hall, they drain you of your money and the other your blood."

The third floor of Gallagher's block housed the printing facilities of the defunct *Black River Budget,* which had ceased publication the previous November. Judge Bickford was talking about purchasing the printing equipment and reviving the newspaper. "Almont Barnes couldn't make a go of it, why do you think you can?" Gallagher asked.

"He didn't know how to collect his debts," replied the judge. "I know a thing or two about getting people to pay up," Bickford said with a wink.

It was on Friday afternoon, January 13 that an excited John Walsh came running across the snow covered street to Gallagher's store, his hand trailing a fluttering newssheet.

"Did you hear about the accident?" he shouted to Gallagher as he stamped his boots to rid them of snow.

"What accident would that be?"

"The train. They say our bishop was seriously injured."

"McCloskey?"

"Aye. He was on his way to the City on last Thursday to attend some conference or other, when his train was smashed in the rear by another. They say his car was crumpled up, and they may have to cut off his foot."

"Lord have mercy!" said Gallagher, as his face twisted in genuine concern. "We've had our differences, but I wouldn't wish that on anybody."

"The first reports said no one was hurt. Later they said there were four fatalities. Now they say only a young newlywed woman was killed and the bishop has a serious injury to his foot."

As newsmen slowly gathered and reported the facts, they learned the bishop was headed to a provincial council meeting in New York City when the engine of his train developed a steam pipe leak. They pulled out of the Sing Sing station 17 minutes late, which was quite unusual for the Express train. Later reports said a man riding with the engineer of McCloskey's train passed word to the other train's engineer that they had a problem and "to look out for us." An agent of the Hudson River Road later disputed this and claimed no word of a problem was ever received.

Railroad travel in the United States was but thirty-years removed from the first experimental line. The mechanical devices and precautionary procedures that would give passengers improved safety were slow in evolving. The forty-six railroad lines in operation in New York State reported that 120 people were killed and another 104 seriously injured in a variety of accidents just in the previous fiscal year.

"According to reports McCloskey's stopped express sent a flagman back to the curve to warn any oncoming trains, but the Sing Sing engineer saw only the white flag so, as usual, he only slowed down for the approaching bend in the track," Walsh continued. "Witnesses disputed the speed at which the train was traveling-some said 30 mph, others 25 mph, and the brakeman claimed he hit the brakes when he heard the other train's whistle and was down to 10 mph."

The Express was struck from behind resulting in the complete demolition of the last car, in which Bishop McCloskey was riding. The train had been slowed twice during its journey because of the engine problem and finally stopped dead on the tracks south of the Sing Sing station.

Gallagher decided the St. James trustees should send a note of concern and condolence to their bishop, which he composed. He added the names of each trustee, unconcerned he needed their acquiescence before acting. "Well, they can't possibly object to this," he said as he sealed the envelope and sent it across the street to the post office.

No one was surprised when news reports contradicted themselves. Subsequent editions might even report diametrically opposing details. Two weeks elapsed before an inquiry tried to determine the real cause of the accident. Gallagher followed the developments with great interest and scanned papers and journals for the latest information. In the back of his mind was the thought that this incident could change things in Albany. Would Conroy replace McCloskey? And how would this affect St. James?

At the coroner's inquest, the husband of the woman who was killed gave testimony as to what occurred and revealed why he was uninjured in the crash, a question on everyone's mind. *The New York Times* reported the following:

> *Thos. W. Field,* sworn: Am husband of the lady who was killed by the collision; got on board the express train at Rhinebeck; we had been detained twice before the detention when the catastrophe occurred. At the place of the first detention I asked an officer of the road, whether any train was following us, and he gave me no reply; think we were

> detained each time from ten to fifteen minutes. When we stopped the last time I went to the rear platform of the last car, and saw the flagman a short distance from the train; he loitered along, turned around frequently, and held his flag drooping. I returned to where my wife sat, and while talking to her I heard a whistle. I went back to the platform and asked a man standing there what that was, and he said it was the whistle of an "up' train. I then got off the car and saw the conductor, who asked me for my tickets, and I gave them to him. I remarked to him that we were standing near a curve. He replied that there were plenty of signals. I then got on board the train again to look for seats for myself and wife in a forward car. I could find none unoccupied, and while passing through the second car from the rear I saw some one who I thought was the conductor jump from the train; I then jumped off myself on the river side. After I had jumped off I saw the Sing Sing train coming round the curve. I thought it would certainly stop before it reached our train; but it did not, and in a moment the collision occurred. I should think the Sing Sing train was running at a speed of at least thirty miles the hour - I don't think the flagman had gone more than *200* feet from our train when the collision occurred. [The witness was here asked to identify the flagman, who was sitting in the audience, and did so.] I think that the flagman had plenty of time to reach the curve, by going at a moderate walk. The distance from the place where our train was standing to the curve is about 1,000 feet; am City Surveyor of Brooklyn, and accustomed to estimate distances. I think the Sing Sing train was slackened but little, if any, after it came round the curve. Could not say whether the engine was reversed or not.

The collision, which caused the destruction of McCloskey's carriage, tore his boots from his feet and resulted in his right foot being badly mangled. It took several hours to extricate the prelate from the damaged and frigid railway car. The doctors pondered amputating the foot but the bishop remained so calm during the ordeal it was decided to try standard medical procedures as the first course of treatment.

After a recuperation period lasting several weeks, McCloskey miraculously regained use of his limb, with no lingering harmful effects. "Once again," the prelate proudly announced, "Divine Providence has interceded on my behalf." The railroad company gave the injured cleric a settlement of $5,000, which he immediately turned over to the building fund for the new cathedral he'd been planning. When completed, this edifice would serve as the capstone for his reign as bishop of Albany.

Pastor Clarke wondered if he should go to Albany to express personal concern for the bishop's mishap. He also thought a visit might give him the opportunity to report the further slanders he had endured. The derogations being reported to him by Haberer and Kenna always evoked painful facial contortions. The choirmaster began doubting the wisdom of bearing these tales. He was concerned the problem was reaching depths from which it could never safely rise and became wary of being in the middle between parishioners and priest. He now wanted to extricate himself. On the other hand, he thought the slurs unwarranted and Clarke had every right to take umbrage. But he also occasionally wondered if the Christian dictum to "turn the other cheek," might not be more appropriate.

Clarke's reaction, when looked at in the cool light of theological principles, betrayed an alarming departure from his priestly vows. His persona, as it must have at one time in his clerical career, no longer allowed him to forgive his enemies, a rather well-preached Christian tenet. His response to the derogations had taken quite the opposite tack-threatening to put his foot on their necks. He even cast aspersions on their manhood by saying, "They're no match for the men of Montague." He knew, having lived among them, the rough and tumble Irish of Carthage would find these words highly offensive and indeed, when they heard them, they took great umbrage.

"Yeah, I want to see the day he tries to put his boot on my neck," Gallagher said.

Patrick Walsh had become increasingly alarmed at the escalation of hostilities and tried to soften Gallagher up. "How does this bickering help bring peace to the parish?" he asked.

"The bickering will stop when we get rid of this shoemaker priest."

The insults continued to be exchanged, by priest and dissidents alike, and they served to harden wills on both sides.

"Have you heard he has visions while traveling to the outlying missions?" Aunt Nancy mentioned with a roll of her eyes.

Clarke had confided to a few friends that the apparitions he saw in the early morning fog while out on the mission trail actually spoke to him. "It is extremely euphoric," he vividly recalled.

Gallagher wondered if they knew of this in Albany. But the diocese did know and, although it prompted the shaking of a few heads, the bishop chose to ignore it. "If true," he said, "it is probably due to the man's piety and spirituality. Who are we to judge? The Lord works in mysterious ways."

Clarke decided to bring the festering parish house project to a head. The issue, discussed and arbitrated many times over the previous three years, had shown no signs of being resolved. The priest would not give up his battle over control of the funds, and often mentioned this impasse to members of his outlying churches. His version of the dispute fertilized the imaginations of his agrarian parishioners, which in turn caused their resentment of Carthaginians to grow. "As soon as I control the funds, I'll consider building my parish house right here," he said in sermons at more than one mission. He mentioned Antwerp as a possibility in a letter to McCloskey. The people of Pinckney and Harrisburg were given similar hopes. "If they won't let me have my presbytery at home, I'll shake the dust from my shoes and put it here," he said.

Clarke's words gave his flock in the outlying districts, many of whom also contributed to the fund, a sense of entitlement. They assumed this gave them a right to equal voice in the location of their priest's residence. This surmise became quite popular, despite the disparity in contributions in Carthage's favor. The inequality of parish sizes relative to Carthage was not part of the equation to the outliers'.

The promises, or threats, depending on who was telling the story, always found their way back to Carthage and generated renewed rancor against the priest.

The chess pieces were moving into position for the end game. But who held the upper hand? The players wanted to know.

CHAPTER 22

"Did you hear that?" Maria said as she gently shook her husband from his sound sleep.

Richard Gallagher stirred, rubbed his eyes and sat up in bed. "What? What's going on?"

"I think it's the fire bells," said Maria.

Richard threw off the covers, slid out of the warm bed, and hurried to get dressed.

Indeed, it was the fire bells some five blocks away that had awakened the light-sleeping and six-months-pregnant Maria. It was a cold, crisp Monday morning that greeted Richard when he ran out to the barn to hitch up his carriage to head down to the fire station on Church Street. Still in office as a village trustee on this January 30th, he had a duty to see what was happening to his town. When he arrived at the new engine house, the open barn door signaled the volunteer firemen had already left. He hollered out to the night watchman, "Where's the fire?"

"Down by the river," was the reply.

Gallagher had long been an advocate for modernization of the fire department. A new fire barn, a part of the village hall, had been completed in the past year but the equipment was not updated, much to his concern. The taxpayers had turned down the additional levies required to buy a new pumper and hoses. "You're courting disaster," he warned, adding under his breath, *you stingy Yankee bastards*. The frugally conservative voters carefully went over each and every proposed expenditure before approval or rejection. They had decided the current equipment was sufficient. Fire departments weren't cheap, certainly not as cheap, Gallagher said, as the people who relied upon them.

Gallagher could see the glow of a fire as he headed down State Street. He soon discovered the alarm had gone out because Charlie Smith's stave factory, located on the riverbank, was ablaze. The building, as was common practice for most of the town's businesses, had banked its furnace on Saturday night and locked up for the weekend.

By the time the firemen arrived, the inferno was out of control. They chopped a hole in the ice, dropped a hose into the Black River, and began pumping away. They had been at it for a half-hour by the time Gallagher arrived. The building owner watched sadly as the firemen valiantly fought a losing battle with the blaze.

"Sorry to see this," Gallagher said to Smith.

"Sometime during the night, the fire roared up, overheated the boiler, and ignited the wall behind it. I've got no insurance," Smith lamented. "There's no way they coulda' saved it!"

Richard shook his head as the building crumbled into a heap of charred embers. "This is what they get for being so shortsighted," he said to the gawkers at the scene. "Some people never learn." Smith's loss was estimated at $6,000 to $8,000.

"I repeat," Gallagher said at the next village trustee meeting, "we're setting ourselves up for a catastrophe. Sooner or later we're going to have a really big fire, and we won't be able to do anything about it. The hoses we have are leaking and will soon have to be replaced." The stitched leather tubing they used didn't have a very long life span under the best of circumstances. Many larger towns and cities had converted to steam driven pumpers with larger diameter hoses, some even made of a new material called rubber. A fellow by the name of Goodyear had discovered and refined a unique process called vulcanization some twenty years before and this led to a steady introduction of new products using the material, one of which was fire hoses.

The village's fire engine was a twenty-year-old L. Burton & Co. hand pumper that was purchased for $300. "We need a steam pumper," Gallagher said. "And that 400 barrel cistern we have up the street isn't nearly enough." Many agreed with him, but try as he might, the town fathers still couldn't muster the votes to overcome the objections of the parsimonious populace. The village dithered on, despite dire warnings they were courting disaster.

Maria Gallagher had been depressed after her dismissal as head of the Altar and Rosary Society, but since her second honeymoon and subsequent pregnancy had given it little thought. The bishop hadn't bothered to respond to her letter, not that a reply was expected. Richard told her to put it from her mind. "When we get a new priest, you'll be able to resume your duties as before. But for now, I want you to take your ease until the child comes."

The Gallagher household concerns became focused on the impending birth of Maria's sixth child. Of course, Dr. West was intimately acquainted with the problems each of her deliveries had presented, so he again prescribed complete bed rest. Richard, followed by the fretting Mrs. McManus, insisted the orders be strictly followed. "You must stay in bed," he said to Maria. "And take care what Mary says."

"Now, don't you be doin' that," was Mrs. M's constantly heard to admonishment.

"Oh poo," Maria answered, "I feel fine. I must get up and do something. Dr. West is a fuddy-duddy." For the most part, however, Maria begrudgingly played the role of obedient wife and stayed in bed.

"I had an unsettling dream last night," Maria confided to Alice O'Leary on one of her frequent visits. "I saw an angel! The spirit tried to tell me something, but I couldn't make out what it was. The angel was weeping. It was so sad but she then smiled and fluttered away. What do you suppose it all means?" she asked apprehensively.

"Why, I have no idea. If only Professor Urbanus was here we could ask him. But it certainly sounds like a good omen." Alice was referring to the dream analyst whose lecture both ladies had attended, and in whose opinions they placed great store.

"Well, don't tell anyone about this, especially Richard. He thinks this dream business is a lot of poppycock, although he won't say it to me." Alice promised her lips were sealed.

Dr. West estimated the newest Gallagher child would arrive at the end of March. At the request of Richard, the doctor looked in on the expectant mother every day or two. "She's fine," he reported to his friend afterwards. "Nothing to worry about."

As to the church dispute, Squire O'Leary had finally come down on the renegade side but his support was not overt enough for Richard. "I've got to watch what I say," the Squire rationalized in his defense. "After all, I am peace justice for all the people and have to be seen as impartial."

Richard scoffed as he replied, "I'm a trustee of the village for all the people too." He had hoped to goad his friend into a more active role in the Church battle and continued to rue that the bishop blamed only him for the opposition to Pastor Clarke. "I don't like it," Richard groused. "I think I'm alone in this fight."

Five blocks from the Gallagher residence towards town, on the corner of West and School Streets, was where the lawyer and land agent Patrick Somerville Stewart resided. He and Gallagher had not become close friends, mainly because of their political differences. Stewart was a prominent Whig cum Republican in opposition to staunch Democrat Gallagher. Another impediment that distanced them was the feeling the older man harbored about the very public St. James squabble. "Men of the cloth should be shown more respect," he said more than once. "It's scandalous, an affront to the village."

The short, heavy-set, stern-faced Stewart lived next door to the land office he managed for the Le Ray family. His full set of whiskers, sans mustache, served to exaggerate his severe demeanor. Maria said he reminded her of the Dickens character Scrooge, which amused Richard. The Edinburgh born septuagenarian and long-time resident was one of the first men elected a Town of Wilna supervisor (the township that encompassed Carthage). The Scotsman worked for the Le Ray land company for the past forty-five years, and was so highly regarded he was given full power of attorney over the family's affairs. Stewart, as every man of note in the village did, involved himself in politics as a civic duty.

Back in 1844, Judge Bickford and Stewart hosted New York Governor William H. Seward on his first and only visit to Carthage. Gallagher, although he remembered the event, had not yet arrived on the political scene. Stewart, who was politically well connected throughout the State, had invited the governor to speak at a local political rally. Just before the dignitary arrived, Anthony Walsh's wife Mary delivered a rare set of triplets. The news set the town and the State abuzz and caught Seward's fancy. When he arrived at Carthage he asked to see the newborns. The Walsh family, even though politically opposed to Seward's party, happily obliged. The governor was so taken with the little girls he impetuously suggested they be named Frances, Cornelia, and Harriet, after members of his family. The first two were his daughters and the latter a niece. The Walshes acceded to the governor's wishes and after returning to Albany, Seward sent each of the girls a gold-enclasped bible with a $50 bill tucked inside.

Tragically, Mary Walsh died shortly afterwards from postnatal complications, leaving Anthony to care for seven young children. The burden was too heavy for the shoemaker so with leaden heart he sent the triplets off to St. John's Orphan Asylum in Utica. Cornelia, one of two surviving triplets, had just returned to Carthage to reunite with her family after sixteen years with the Daughters of Charity of St. Vincent DePaul.

Stewart was a devout Protestant elder and trustee at Maria's former church. The man, despite his strong sectarian beliefs, had become friendly with the Rev. Mr. Clarke. On several occasions his work had involved the transfer of outlying property deeds in the Le Ray domain to the Diocese of Albany. This cordial relationship didn't go unnoticed by

Gallagher, and he often wondered if one day he would see Stewart involved in his dispute with Clarke. *The priest has the gift for making useful friends, and bad enemies,* he observed.

The Gallagher household, with five youngsters running about, was alive with the din of activity. Mrs. McManus continually chided the children to "be quiet" mostly because they loved to bang away on the family piano. It had been but a year since the village acquired the competent music teacher Maria rushed to engage. Adelaide Masury was soon giving the children their thrice-weekly piano lessons. Addie, as the children called her, was an accomplished player and vocalist. Although only nineteen years old, the Canadian born musician appeared more mature than her years. Her billowing dresses, with her hair severely pulled back into a schoolmarm bun, only accentuated the appearance of maturity. The girl's parents and siblings were also musicians. Addie had learned to play the piano even before her legs were long enough to reach the pedals.

Nearly every child of John and Mary Masury had a different birthplace-among them, besides Canada, were Boston, Boonville, and Rochester. The family had moved around a lot-starting at Port Borough [Peterborough], Canada and finally, after short stays in the above mentioned locales, landed in Ogdensburg, where the family now resided. Addie was anxious to get out from under her stern taskmaster father's thumb so, when she heard Carthage had no music teacher, she packed her bags to come live with her sister Harriet-the wife of Carthage baker Justus Chase. His bakery was located down the block from Gallagher's store.

"The children just love Addie," Maria said to Richard. "She's not much older than Helen."

"I'm glad she's working out," replied Richard with a smile. He too had noticed the blossoming young lady and added, "She's a pretty lass too."

Maria wasn't sure if she liked this observation, but smiled anyway.

Only six years older than Helen, Addie was readily accepted by the Gallagher brood. Because of Maria's indisposition, she began acting like a surrogate mom to them. Addie was strict and made them practice their scales on the family's upright pianoforte until they got it right. Richard had the instrument shipped in from Utica and placed it in the large parlor to the left of the entrance foyer, directly under the master bedroom. When Addie played after the children's lessons, Maria sent word down how much she enjoyed her music and wished she would continue a bit longer.

Richard occasionally arrived home before Addie took her leave. "My wife really enjoys your playing and singing," he said with an Irish twinkle in his eye. Addie blushed.

With more than three weeks remaining before the anticipated birthing day, Mrs. McManus began thinking Maria would come through this ordeal without any problems. "She's not eating enough," the midwife confided.

Richard promised to try to get his wife to at least sip a bit more soup. He sat alongside her under the canopy of their bed, holding a bowl of broth and blowing softly over the steaming spoon, encouraging Maria to take a few more swallows. "This'll give you more strength," he said with a smile.

"Don't you worry about me," she said weakly, and Richard wasn't overly concerned because he'd been through this five times before.

As requested, Dr. West dropped in every couple of days. He never failed to repeat his oft uttered admonition to "make sure she's well fed and stays in bed." He didn't offer much else. "She'll be ready to deliver in a few weeks," he added. No one was overly concerned with due date precision so they accepted the good doctor's best guess as to the birth date as just that-a guess.

Two weeks later on Wednesday the 14th of March, Richard was at his desk in the back of his store, looking over his latest advertising copy. Carthage had no local paper ever since the

Budget folded, so Gallagher planned to place his ad in the *Lowville Northern Journal,* some sixteen miles to the southeast. He read the copy aloud:

> GREAT BARGAINS - The Largest Stock of CHOICE FURNITURE Of all descriptions ever before offered to the people of Jefferson or Lewis County, At Reduced Prices, And No Mistake! If the good people will only give me a call, I will guarantee to give them Better Bargains than they can get at any other establishment of the kind. Don't forget the place: Gallagher's Block, State Street, Carthage, at the Sign of the Big Chair, and opposite the Baptist Church.

Looks good, he thought, glancing up at the wall clock which read three minutes to ten. Just then a commotion arose in the front of the store and he looked up to see his servant Mary Clark racing up the aisle past the outstretched sofas and chairs.

"You've got to come quick Master Gallagher," she shouted at the top of her lungs. "Mrs. McManus says you've got to come now!" Richard put down the ad copy, turned to his bookkeeper and said he'd be leaving and for him to take care of the place.

"What's happening?" Gallagher asked the servant girl. "Has the baby come?"

"I don't know. Mrs. M sent for the doctor and told me to come fetch you."

Richard grabbed his coat, darted out the back of the store and unhitched his horse from the rail. There was no time to couple the animal to his buggy so, without benefit of a saddle, he mounted his steed and proceeded to ride bareback at a rapid gallop through the alley and up State Street, leaving servant Mary in the distance running up the boardwalk, far behind him.

The house was six blocks east, past Mechanic, Church, School, James, and Clinton Streets. He crossed the last one, called Irish Settlement Road, to arrive at the front porch of his home. He leapt to the ground, didn't bother to tie his mount to the hitching post, and darted up the steps, bolting through the front door. The children and their music teacher were huddled at the bottom of the staircase. They were uncharacteristically hushed, looking anxiously up to the second floor where they heard evidence of frantic activity. Richard brushed by them with barely a glance and tore up the carpeted steps two at a time to the second floor.

Just as he reached the landing, his bedroom door opened and Dr. West came slowly walking out. "What's happened, Doc?" Richard asked anxiously, his voice ragged with concern. Dr. West shook his head but said nothing. "What's happened?" Richard shouted, grabbing the diminutive doctor by the shoulders.

There was a pause as his friend Eli, eyes downcast and holding back what appeared to be a tear, slowly and somberly said, "She's gone."

"What do you mean, she's gone?" a distraught Richard said in a voice that had abruptly gone hollow.

"I'm so sorry, I couldn't stop the bleeding. She's passed away."

Those dreaded words once again penetrated his soul. Richard tried to speak but his throat became constricted as he began convulsively sobbing. He hurried into the room to see Maria lying on the bed in ghastly repose. Ashen though her complexion was, she looked strangely at peace. He went to the bedside and took her still warm hand in his, gently kissing it as the tears streamed down his face on to the lifeless limb. He tried not to look towards the foot of the bed where a large, deep crimson circle had made its way through the bedspread. "Oh God, oh God," he sobbed. "No, no, this cannot be!" His head dropped onto Maria's bosom as he broke into uncontrollable weeping. It was several minutes before he regained control of himself and slowly and reluctantly lifted his head upright.

A baby's cry startled him and he turned to see Mrs. McManus, her face also drenched in tears, standing off in a corner holding a swaddled child. That was the moment he first realized the baby, whom he had forgotten to even ask about, had survived. He rose and approached the midwife whose free-flowing tears had soaked through the baby's wrap. "'Tis a boy," she mumbled as Richard was overcome with conflicting emotions of sorrow and joy.

Gallagher took the baby into his arms, looked down at his new son and whispered, "You've a lot to atone for, boyo."

Chapter 23

Richard Gallagher came slowly down the stairs, cradling the baby in his arms. The bereaved father tried to compose himself, desperate for the words he might use in speaking to his now motherless children. As he scanned their frightened, tear-stained faces, he could see they knew something was terribly amiss. The children had not seen their father cry before, but they noticed the unmistakable traces of tears on his cheeks. As they looked up at him in frightened anticipation, he beckoned them to follow him into the parlor.

"Mama's gone to heaven," he finally said between muffled sobs, and the children began weeping uncontrollably. With the new baby still clutched in one arm, he stretched out the other to draw his brood to his breast. The children wailed in unison, and there was no comforting them. "There, there," Richard said, "Mama wouldn't want you to do that. She's with the angels now."

Adelaide Masury, the music teacher, was standing in the parlor doorway crying silently. Only a year in service to the Gallaghers, she had become as fond of Maria as she had the children. Death was not a stranger to her, but she had never mastered the words to console the bereaved in these circumstances. She decided to slip away and let the family grieve in private.

Dr. West left the residence, mounted his one-horse shay and took the tragic news downtown to Gallagher's funeral parlor. Not long after, young James Walsh appeared at the Gallagher residence. He spoke to Richard in hushed tones, asking what his wishes were about preparations. Gallagher nodded and whispered but one instruction. "Just do what you do, Jimmie." Walsh went back to the cabinet shop and selected a rosewood casket with pink tufted lining, the most expensive one they had in stock. He returned to the Gallagher home with three apprentices, and as Richard watched, the quartet trundled up the steps with the casket on their shoulders. They filed into the bedroom to prepare Maria for burial. Mrs. McManus had already lain out the funeral attire and took care of washing and dressing her departed mistress. When she had finished, the men placed Maria in the casket and summoned Richard to help carry her downstairs. A bier was brought in from the hearse and placed in the spacious parlor where Maria's remains would rest during the wake that would begin that evening.

Maria's funeral was scheduled for two days hence. There would be no embalming, a methodology that morticians only used if the body was to be transported a great distance. The interval between death and burial avoided dealing with any deterioration of the deceased.

As he stood over the casket, looking down at the woman he had loved for nearly twenty years, Richard noticed his wife's rosary was not with her. Servant Mary was sent to fetch it from the nightstand in the master bedroom, and Jimmie Walsh entwined the silver beads between Maria's fingers while Richard looked on. He approved of the casket selection and the way Maria's hair had been arranged. "You've done a good job, Jimmie. She looks as if she's asleep," he said as he turned away.

"Have you thought about the funeral Mass?" Walsh asked.

He hadn't, but said, "I'd like to get Father Power if he can come."

Jimmie said he would immediately dispatch a messenger to the telegraph office in Watertown to send a wire to the priest, now stationed at Wappingers Falls, and scurried off to do so.

Bad news spread rapidly in small towns and that evening a parade of mourners began dropping by the Gallagher house, filling the lower floors to overflowing. Mourners lined the staircase nearly to the second floor landing. The respected businessman and village official was on a first name basis with just about everyone, and except for the priest and a few of his most ardent supporters, most forgot their disagreements over church matters and came by to pay their respects.

Neighbor O'Leary and wife Alice were among the first to call. The Squire couldn't hold back his tears as he hugged Richard. "Aye, so young for the Lord to take her," he murmured.

"Yes, yes," said Richard. Alice was so overcome she was unable to speak.

A visibly distraught Roswell Woolson came in shortly thereafter. "Why, oh why?" was all he could say over and over. Richard put his arm around his old partner's shoulder, saying nothing in return. The silence bespoke all that needed to be said.

Patrick Somerville Stewart was among those who came later that evening, and Richard could see from the old Scot's eyes he was genuinely moved. The man knew about untimely family death from personal experience and could sincerely empathize with Richard. "We are so sorry," he said. "Is there anything I can do?" Gallagher thanked him and said there was nothing but perhaps a prayer. Even a Protestant prayer was welcome under the circumstances.

Finally his fellow church trustees arrived, followed by the Altar and Rosary Society, who gathered everyone in front of the catafalque for a recitation of the rosary. A chorus of Hail Mary's was soon echoing throughout the house rising above the sobbing of the Gallagher children gathered around the banister on the second floor landing.

No one knew where Pastor Clarke was, and no one inquired. He'd been staging a boycott of the Carthage parish, spending most of his time in the outlying missions. Even if in town, many doubted he would consent to perform the service. The dispute's depth of bitterness trumped normal decorum, even in death.

The next morning a messenger returned with the news Father Power was on his way. Richard was pleased because Maria often fondly reminisced about the priest and those days when he boarded with them. "The children must have driven the poor man to distraction," she often remarked. Unmistakable sadness invaded Richard's eyes whenever he thought of those times. So different than these days, he said to himself. And he meant this in more ways than one.

Father Michael Power arrived later that evening and made sure everything would be ready for Mass in church the following morning. At ten o'clock on the funeral day, the priest held a brief prayer service with the family at their home. When the private service concluded, six pallbearers took Maria's encased remains outside to the waiting hearse. They gently slid the casket into the rear of the conveyance, and Jimmie Walsh began smartly urging the pair of jet-black horses slowly towards the church. He had engaged two drummer boys who tapped out a muffled beat in time with the equine footfalls.

The mourners, joined by the mayors of Watertown and Lowville, followed on foot. Officials from other smaller hamlets also appeared to offer their condolences and join the march. Passing carriages took to the curb as people on the street paused and stood quietly while the cortege passed-with men doffing their hats, and women bowing their heads, each placing their right hand over their breasts. The long slow procession, whose silence was broken only by the sound of drums and horses' hooves, lent a further air of solemnity to the proceeding.

As the mourners filed into the church, many women could be seen holding handkerchiefs over their mouths to stifle their sobs. The church was soon packed with mourners, all of whom were distressed to see anyone die "before their time."

Although not of their faith, Adelaide had asked Richard if she could sing the requiem during the high Mass. "Maria would have liked that," he said, and asked Haberer to step aside. The choirmaster, with wife Julia at the organ, usually sang at St. James funerals, but he graciously agreed to yield. With Julia accompanying her, Addie sang the Ave Maria, which French composer Charles Gounod had set to music only the year before.

When Addie finished her emotional rendition, the sobs of mourners could be heard throughout the church. As she looked down from the loft at the Gallagher family, she saw Richard had buried his face in the sleeve of his coat while surrounded by his crying children. She cried too.

At the conclusion of the service, the crowd filed out and gathered at the burial site behind the church.* The gravediggers had worked hard to excavate the tomb as the ground had not totally thawed to the required six-foot depth. Everyone stood by and appropriately muttered "Amen" as Father Power recited the final prayers. Maria's remains were lowered by ropes into the crypt for her eternal rest. Mourners filed by in turn, each picking up a token amount of earth to throw onto the casket. Richard threw the last handful and turned away as the gravediggers proceeded to fill in the void.

On the following day, Richard gave stone carver Herman Rulison his order for a proper headstone. It would take a week to finish and when it was placed at the gravesite, only the Gallagher family was in attendance. The twelve foot tall, white granite obelisk, topped with a cross, had MARIA C. carved in bas-relief on one side. Chiseled below her name was, WIFE OF R. GALLAGHER & DAUGHTER OF DR. J. SHERWOOD along with her age and date of death.

It was the time of the year when yellow, blue, and purple wildflowers had burst forth in profusion in nearby fields. The children picked several bouquets and placed them on their mother's grave. When strewn in front of the marker, they completely covered the ground.

The family wept anew.

CHAPTER 24

After seven days of intense mourning, Richard's thoughts slowly returned to his business and the latest reports he'd been hearing about the St. James pastor. The priest had intensified his demonization of the Carthage parishioners to any and all agreeable ears in his far-flung mission. The majority of Clarke's parishioners in the far reaches of his mission were workers of the earth who had become sensitized to the emerging stratification of class in America. These rural residents had been given good reason to believe the St. James people felt themselves superior to them, both educationally and socially. News of the intensifying war with their Pastor in Carthage only exacerbated these bad feelings.

Less than three weeks after Maria's funeral, Carthaginians went to the polls for the annual election of the village board of trustees. Richard, the Democratic candidate for president, feeling it would be unseemly for a man in mourning, did not campaign. No one seemed to mind being spared the usual handshakes and political promises from the lips of an aspiring politician. The nominally Republican Carthaginians did indeed vote for the man, as Dr. West had predicted, and Richard was elected in a landslide. He soon was sworn in to begin serving a one-year term as village president.

Bent on enlisting additional support for his dispute with Albany, Gallagher continued leaning on George O'Leary to become more active. The jovial and erudite Squire was a born politician but, unlike his good friend Gallagher, had aligned himself with the Republicans. The cherubic Celt came to America just two months after he had finished his shoemaker apprenticeship in Ireland. Arriving in Canada as a penniless, friendless youth, he succeeded in reaching Prescott, Ontario where for the first time he saw the stars and stripes wafting in the breeze across the St. Lawrence River. Like thousands of other Irish before him, he immediately crossed into the US.

He later commemorated the event by composing a poem, which was published in *The Carthage Republican Tribune*:

> When first I saw that flag of freedom,
> I hailed it with childish glee.
> Though the St Lawrence was 'tween it and me.
> Then I was an exile from the land of green,
> Where a flag of freedom ne'er can be seen,
> Then I crossed the flowing river,
> And prayed on bended knee
> That God would preserve Freedom's flag
> For all eternity.

O'Leary came to Carthage in 1838 where he set up a small shop producing quality shoes and boots. A jovial *bon vivant,* he subsequently was elected or appointed to several public offices. At various times he was a peace justice, deputy sheriff, or a school board trustee. As the census taker noted, the Squire was also a "speculator," a label used to identify those persons wealthy enough to dabble in real estate.

Virtually no one in Carthage, except his wife Alice, called O'Leary by his given name George. He still proudly spoke Gaelic, a rapidly dying facility among his fellow émigrés. The broad shouldered, freckle-faced man not only wrote poetry but would also belt out an Irish tune at the drop of a Tammy. These songs, learned in his youth in County Cork, were always delivered in an enthusiastic and melodic tenor voice.

Among the impressive credits O'Leary garnered over the years was the tribute paid him by the internationally famous contralto Antoinette Sterling. Writing from England, she fondly recalled O'Leary from the time she lived in her eponymous village of Sterlingville, New York. "I received my first inclinations towards literature and voice from Mr. O'Leary," she wrote. The accolade, published in all the area newspapers, was highly treasured by the Squire.

O'Leary was a cautious man for he believed, and often said, that *The end of a feast is better than the beginning of a fight*. His most recent appointment as deputy sheriff was bestowed by Jefferson County Sheriff Cross in the February past. Because of his reputation as a peacemaker, certainly a useful quality for a judge and deputy sheriff, Gallagher often thought the Squire's abilities could be employed to mediate the current St. James dispute. Thus far they had not.

After four years of observing the church scuffle, the Squire finally took up his pen to add his voice to the litany of complaints against Pastor Clarke. In his letter he conspicuously omitted the trailing e from Clarke's name. The Census taker Almont Barnes, a writer, reporter, and newspaper editor, always took care to spell names correctly. Yet, he also recorded both priest and brother as Clark. O'Leary knew it was an affectation, one that was meant to separate his lineage from the other half-dozen or so plebian Clark families in the village. The practice was popular among those who sought to be assigned to the upper class. It was widely rumored that Mary Todd's family, Abraham Lincoln's in-laws, had added a second d to their name for the same reason.

In May of 1860, O'Leary wrote the following lines to Bishop McCloskey.

> I am aware of the responsibility that I take upon myself when I address the Bishop of this Diocese, but why should I hesitate, although for writing to you I should be held up to ridicule and branded as an infidel by the Reverend Mr. Clark, but matters have at present gone and carried to such an extent that I consider it a sin before God if I did not at least inform your Lordship of the total disregard of all Religious precepts. Why should I hesitate when I see, in this Congregation all respect for the doctrines and precepts of that Church of which I claim to be an unworthy member trampled under foot and disregarded.

I write to you not to find fault with the pastor or people. There is a great responsibility somewhere which this pastor or people has to answer for. There is at present over half of this Congregation which do not attend Divine worship and those charging the pastor with being guilty of acts and Language which I think is not fit to mention and near all the congregation do not partake of the Sacraments. About 200 children who has no religious training whatever.

The greatest portion talk aplenty charging the pastor with turning the confessional into a place of Speculation in proposing to Peter Kelly that he should sell his land and that in a few days after that his Brother called on Kelly to Sell it to him. Kelly says that he made him promise on his knees to sell it and that if he did not Sell it he was living in a State of Mortal Sin and that he has turned females of tender age away from the confessional because they went to the fathers to Watertown to confession. Refusing to attend to the Sick and dying. One of those cases is a Woman about 3 miles from here. He was called on did not go the woman died. She was a practical Catholic. These are only a few isolated Cases.

There is nothing here only dissention and strife in this congregation. There are about 250 Children. No first Communion not for years. No confirmation.

There is Great Excitement at present. Mr. Clark has commenced suits against the following persons, that is, they are sued to Redwood he has transferred what he calls his accounts to be Sued in the name of a man that resides in Redwood 26 miles from here.

Enclosed I send you one of his Claims which he has sued for. The following are the names that are Sued William Reily, Lawrence Cunningham, Farel Neary, John Gormanly, James Moran, Philip Sullivan, Patrick Reily who resides in Harrisburgh and a number of others. Reily's suit is to come off on next Tuesday in Lewis Co.

This was the first time anyone had accused Clarke of using language "not fit to mention." The priest was losing his temper more frequently, and using graphic language to give voice to his anger, much to the dismay of peace-loving people like O'Leary. Gallagher, a man given to some temper himself, had not mentioned this behavior in his complaints

One of the more serious charges to be leveled against the pastor-using the sacrament of confession to profit his own family-was intended to draw the bishop's attention to the charge of simony* previously leveled by Arnold Galleciez.

O'Leary took pains to relate, in spite of Clarke's revulsion at being dragged into court by others, that he himself was not hesitant to seek judicial redress. Given this bent, it was not surprising he had a number of suits going on at the same time. When the pastor previously wrote McCloskey about Gallagher suing Joseph Savage in the pew dispute he said: "[Gallagher was] intending to draw odium and disgrace upon... the Catholic Church in a crowded Court Room..." a consequence that did not seem to apply to his own actions.

O'Leary ended with:

> I tell you Bishop that if you were to know the Deplorable State of Religion in this Section you would at least investigate the matter.

Bishop McCloskey privately lamented these letters but remained steadfast in supporting his priest. His reply to O'Leary reminded him he had an obligation "to listen to the dictates of his Church and not bear witness against the clergy." The Squire shook his head as he read the letter aloud. "This will all come to no good end," he prophesized.

The Rev. Mr. Clarke was behaving like a man seemingly possessed. Contrary to the admonitions he had received from Albany, and a few of his friends among local parishioners, to tone down his rhetoric, he continued his rants from the pulpit whenever he was in Carthage. Haberer, for one, had mentioned to Clarke that Gallagher was considering a lawsuit for slander. The news only emboldened the preacher and he continued his crusade against the miscreant furniture dealer even more vigorously.

Gallagher had reached the end of his patience and retained lawyer George Gilbert to file suit against Clarke for slander. The small courtroom was yet again packed with spectators as Judge Bickford convened the trial.

"We're here to determine if plaintiff Richard Gallagher was slandered by one Rev. Mr. Michael Clarke," he intoned in a voice matching the gravity of the charge. "The plaintiff may call his first witness."

The spectators, shuffling in their seats, muttering to each other, rubbed their hands in anticipation. Another recitation of the juicy details from inside St. James Church would be great entertainment indeed. Gallagher's lawyer called a series of parishioners who attested Clarke had slandered Gallagher from the pulpit. "Aye, he said the man was dishonest and couldn't be trusted," testified Anthony Walsh.

"Did he mention him by name?" asked the judge.

"Nay, but everybody knew who he was talkin' about." A roar of laughter from the gallery followed.

Aunt Nancy wanted to testify but Gallagher's attorney thought it unseemly for a woman to appear in such proceedings. "She's too forward," his counsel advised. "She behaves more like a man than a woman. It could work against us."

Patrick and James Walsh also appeared on Gallagher's behalf. They testified Clarke had used "unseemly language" in describing the plaintiff during his sermons.

"Did he mention the man by name?" Judge Bickford asked yet again.

"No sir, but everybody knew who it was he meant." Another outburst of laughter followed.

"Well, you can't sue for innuendo," said Bickford and he proceeded to ask each and every witness the same question, and each and every one had to answer in the negative.

When the parade of witnesses was exhausted, the judge pounded his gavel and gave his decision. He didn't require the accused to call any witnesses as he said, "I find for the Rev. Mr. Clarke. The plaintiff has not proved the allegation."

The surprised Clarke couldn't hide the self-satisfied elation that overran his normally dour visage. He had bested his sworn enemy and would tell the bishop of Gallagher's latest sacrilege of dragging the Church into court. This was exactly what he'd been warning McCloskey about.

The fuming Gallagher was upset at what he felt was a travesty of justice."He knows what he's doing," he muttered. "And he'll overstep himself one of these times."

The same Protestant judge, whom Clarke had accused of bias in the pew trial, now ruled in his favor. But this would have no remedial effect on the emboldened priest's attitude.

Bishop McCloskey was not pleased when news of this latest incident reached his eyes. Although he had problems with other priests around his diocese, Clarke's actions were keeping him at the top of a list the bishop would rather did not exist. Another thorn pierced McCloskey's miter when he received a letter from Father James Mackey of Ogdensburg. The priest complained Clarke was poaching on his territory. The bishop wrote Clarke demanding an answer to Mackey's complaint. But as had increasingly become *de rigueur* for the embattled priest, he was unapologetic and offended at the suggestion of misfeasance. Clarke sought out the high road in defending his actions.

> So, a good clergyman who loves his flock cannot leave his own mission according to Rev. Mr. Mackey's principle, in search of that which is necessary for their comfort.

Ever the misunderstood missionary, Pastor Clarke blamed the alleged infringement on his missionary zeal for serving anyone in need-a notion that would certainly had been disputed in Carthage. He explained he was on a trip to buy equipment for his church at Rossie and was awaiting a stagecoach when approached by a man asking him to baptize his child. Clarke saw no need to heed territorial strictures, especially since the man had a ready stipend. Father Mackey, who heard of the priest's alleged refusal of the sacraments to those in Carthage who couldn't pay, was not amused.

The diligence with which priests guarded their turf, and the income yielded there from, was because such monies often were their main source of income. One could reasonably question what was paramount in both priests' minds-serving the spiritual needs of the faithful, or the accrual of moneys from such services? If it was truly the former, Clarke could have remitted the stipend to Father Mackey and that would have ended the affair. Perhaps the charges of simony were worthy of examination-if the bishop was so disposed.

Although McCloskey continued to feel his choices were limited, an observant chess master might say his unyielding position had backed him into a tight corner. His continued insistence that his parishioners simply obey the Church was buttressed by his fear of being seen to accede to trustee rule. If Gallagher was privy to what McCloskey had written from Rome about the Nyack seminary, "But for my part I would rather see the whole establishment at the bottom of the Tappan Zee than see it under the control of lay trustees," he would have been able to predict his bishop's actions.

Would McClosky just as soon see the church in Carthage lay at the bottom of the Black River before he would see it under the control of its trustees? If the dispute continued on its current course, he just might get his wish.

Chapter 25

"The people of Carthage have no respect for the Church or its missionaries. They don't appreciate all that I do for them." Statements such as these became a staple of Father Clarke's well-developed mantra, and were often repeated in sermons out on the mission trail. He also mentioned the scandalous lawsuits brought against him by the disrespectful Gallagher.

"Whatever is wrong with those St. James people?" his parishioners in Antwerp asked.

"They don't have your faith," Clarke replied. And those farmers thrust out their chests and tugged on their suspenders as they condemned those Carthage apostates.

Gallagher was identified as the ring leader of the revolt, not only by Clarke and the bishop, but by many of his fellow parishioners as well. His spiritually starved rebel band continued to carp about the infrequency of services. Several paraded into Gallagher's place of business to personally voice their complaints. They would brush by the furniture pieces laid out on the floor and proceed directly to the rear of the store. The salesmen, practiced at spotting potential customers, would roll their eyes and mutter, "Ain't makin' no sale here."

The businessman in Richard wasn't happy about the procession of non-customers, but felt his church and community leadership roles obligated him to listen. It soon became evident the emotional squabble generated complaints that became exaggerated in direct proportion to the number of ears they passed through. Surely many gripes were real, but Richard recognized some had to be taken with a proverbial grain of salt. The priest had been avoiding St. James for the last two months so some of the reported indiscretions couldn't have happened since he wasn't there.

As the seasons came and went, rumors continued to surface. "He's going to take the money and build in Montague," reported Patrick Flynn on one of his Saturday sojourns from Lowville. "There's a lot of grist in the gossip mill," he said. "Those people are thinkin' they have a say in your affairs and how your money's to be spent. The priest told 'em so, and now they want to be in on yer decision." Flynn had several acrimonious things to say about the priest and wasn't selective about whom he told.

"I don't know if we can trust what Flynn says," O'Leary ventured. "I've heard he's left the Church entirely."

"Haven't you?" asked Gallagher.

"You know what I mean," said the Squire. "I don't need to listen to the priest rant. But if it's true Flynn is on a vendetta, we have to be careful about believing what he says. He may be grinding his axe a bit too fine."

"Well you couldn't blame him, 'cause he's not the only one thinking about leaving the Church," Gallagher said to the raised bushy eyebrows of his friend.

"You're not serious, are you?"

Gallagher didn't respond and scrutiny of his features would not betray a firm position one way or the other.

It also became known, as O'Leary had noted in his letter to McCloskey, that Clarke was bringing suit against parishioners in other venues. The pew rebellion had spread to other churches and the contentiousness did not go unreported in the press. On June 21, 1860, *The Republican Tribune*, the reincarnated weekly newspaper now published by Marcus Bickford, seized upon these insurrections to file this report.

> Church quarrels are always unpleasant. We are sorry to learn that the difficulties existing in the Roman Catholic Church in this place are growing worse. We hear that several suits for pew-rents have been instituted in the Town of Alexandria, some 25 miles distant against prominent Catholics in this vicinity, the suits being brought in the name of a certain Alexandria constable. The parties sued, we understand, contest the suits, denying that they owe the pew-rents. We are sorry for this state of things, and desire that the members of this church as well as all others may live

> in peace among themselves. 'Behold how sweet and how pleasant it is for brethren to dwell together in unity.'

Judge Bickford, unlike former publisher Almont Barnes, had no qualms about publicizing church controversies. His Reformationist views spurred a willingness to criticize any centralized church authority. He also made no pretense about his obvious political preferences as the paper's masthead revealed his Republicanism. He molded his paper into an organ of support for his party's presidential nominee, Abraham Lincoln. He unabashedly declared Abe to be the man best suited to run the country and his pages regularly contained articles supporting that view.

Two months later another article about St. James appeared in *The Tribune,* copied in its entirety from the *Lowville Journal.*

> We clip the following from the LOWVILLE JOURNAL of last week, as a matter of current news. It would seem from its perusal that the unhappy difficulties which have for some time disturbed the members the Roman Catholic Church worshipping in Carthage are extending into parts of the parish where Mr. Clarke officiates. Why cannot these difficulties be adjusted, and peace prevail among these people? We do not undertake to decide who is in the wrong; it seems to us that the Bishop of the Diocese ought to investigate the matter thoroughly, and whoever causes the strife ought to be reproved. The Bishop, from what we have seen of him seems to be a fair man and his appearance is like that of a lover of peace. We think if his attention was properly called to the unhappy state of affairs among his flock in this vicinity he would initiate such measures as would effectually restore the accustomed harmony and peace among them.

The paper's public call for the bishop to "reprove" the offending parties was heard all the way to Albany and duly criticized by the bishop as yet another example of Protestant interference. For the paper to intimate the bishop's attention had not been "called" to the unhappy state of affairs was tantamount to an accusation of dereliction of duty. Although he struggled not to show it, McCloskey's patience was over-taxed by the paper's chiding him about his duties. He unconsciously grasped the crucifix hanging from his neck as he said to his aide, "I'm told this reporter is not Catholic and has not been privy to the negotiations that have taken place. Who is giving this newspaper these false reports? Is it Gallagher?" Conroy said he didn't know but he would try to find out.

Although a weekly advertiser in both the Carthage and Lowville papers, Gallagher was naturally suspected as the instigator of the reportage. In fact neither of the papers' editors had asked his opinion before the stories ran. Had they done so, he would have no doubt given his blessing. "They can give him hell for all I care. The man deserves it," he said. In fact, he didn't think the papers went far enough.

The *Lowville Journal* was published in Lewis County where five of Clarke's missions were situated. When asked about it, the editor said his territorial interests trumped any concerns about the impropriety of reporting church squabbles. He continued his reportage with the following article.

> For some time past a portion of the citizens of the Town of Harrisburg have been somewhat agitated in relation to a difficulty which has arisen among the members of the Catholic Church of that place.
>
> The circumstances, as we gather them, are these: Sometime in 1855, Rev. Michael Clarke - desirous of paying the debt which existed against this church, and also for the payment of his salary, as officiating Priest-appointed Mr. Wheeler his agent for the purpose of soliciting subscriptions to defray such expenses.
>
> A Mr. Vaughn subscribed three dollars, and shortly afterwards paid it. Mr. Vaughn thought nothing more of the matter until some six weeks ago, when Thomas Phillips, of

> Jefferson County, presented an assigned claim from Mr. Clarke, against Mr. Vaughn, for eleven dollars.
>
> Payment was refused, whereupon Vaughn was sued before Justice Newton, of Montague, by Phillips, and the case was tried last Friday, Mr. Ballard of Watertown, and A. H. Kellogg of Copenhagen, for plaintiff, and George L. Brown, Esq., of Lowville, for defendant.
>
> The defense was that the $3 was only to be paid for one year and not to continue from year to year - and that, it having been paid, the plaintiff could not recover. The jury, composed of the most intelligent and substantial men from Montague, returned a verdict for the defendant.

The increased publicity prompted McCloskey to take a more decisive step. He reluctantly decided to send his aide to Carthage to see if he might somehow ameliorate the situation. "Fix this problem," he commanded Conroy.

"I'll do my best, Your Eminence," he replied as he left the chancery. Conroy knew Clarke and was, of course, privy to all of the priest's correspondence. The disturbing reports accumulating about this man, not only from the laity but also from other priests in the diocese, troubled him. "He's eccentric," Conroy once volunteered to McCloskey. "They say he hears voices and has visions."

The bishop took little note of this and said he was inclined to attribute these characteristics to the man's piety. "He has a difficult circuit." McCloskey said, recalling the reason for Father Roche's resignation. "It has exhausted lesser men."

The imposing Conroy presented an unusual sight for Carthaginians when he alighted from the stagecoach. His six foot frame, draped in a long black cassock, was capped off with a round brimmed saturno (a hat so called because it evoked a popular sketch of the planet Saturn).

"He could blot out the sun," said Anthony Walsh when he first laid eyes on Conroy.

"I didn't know you'd taken up O'Leary's humor," Gallagher laughed.

Conroy was huffing and puffing after the short walk up State Street to Gallagher's store. "We need to have a meeting," he said sternly. Gallagher felt he was in no position to refuse.

"I'll gather everyone at my home for this evening, if that's alright."

When the meeting convened, the bishop's delegate listened patiently, and painfully, as Gallagher recited the litany of parish grievances. "Is there any way we can conclude this peacefully?" Conroy interjected. He would dearly love to be seen as one who resolved thorny problems. And he knew if this situation persisted he would inherit it whenever he became bishop of Albany. Although the rite of succession was not chiseled in stone, everyone accepted that the vicar general would be elevated if and when the post became vacant. Thus, Conroy didn't want the Carthage dispute remaining on his plate when he ascended to the bishop's chair. And, to be seen as a peacemaker would be an important feather in Conroy's saturno.

Gallagher pondered the vicar general's question for some time before answering. "I don't see how we can fix this without the removal of that priest," he said monotonically. Conroy sensed a hint of regret in the man's tone. The litany of trustee complaints added nothing new to what he had heard and read before. He dearly needed to rest his weary frame and therefore rose to bid adieu to the trustees. He accepted Haberer's offer of a ride to his hotel. On the morrow, he said, he would go down to the Irish Settlement to see the pastor.

As soon as he entered the Clarke farmhouse, Conroy came under attack. "How could you reach out to those apostates?" the pastor bellowed. He had already heard a report of the previous night's meeting and was extremely displeased. Although the bishop's aide did not expect a joyous welcome, the force of Clarke's vituperation caught him by surprise. With spittle foaming at the corners of his mouth, the priest shouted, "They've heaped abuse on the Church and its clergy! By meeting with them, you've dignified these calumnies against me!" His anger seemed hot enough to burn. Conroy waited until Clarke's vituperation was spent and watched as the priest turned cold and abrupt. "Go home and mind your own business!" he said bitterly. "I don't need some drunk coming here to tell me how to run my parish!"

Conroy was stunned, and with his huge body shaking, he struggled to suppress the urge to take Clarke by the throat and throttle him. He took a step forward, paused for a deep breath, while laboring to regain his normally calm demeanor. But his anger too did not easily abate. When finally he regained his composure, it would be his turn to vent the long-felt frustration he had towards this impertinent brother of the cloth. He shouted, "You are a stupid little man!" and turned abruptly to rid himself of the place. "Stupid, stupid," he said again and again as he stormed out the front door.

Clarke's brother William emerged from his listening post in the hallway and said to Michael, "Di' ya think that was wise?" The priest scoffed, turned, and went to his room.

The vicar general's unpleasant ride back to Albany seemed interminable. As his thoughts about his visit alternated between anger and frustration, he frequently and involuntarily shook his head. When finally he arrived home to report to his superior, his first words were dripping with anger. "He's an arrogant man. Told me to mind my business and go home! Can you imagine!?"

McCloskey's furrowed brow showed displeasure at the disrespect but, upon reflection, drew a deep breath and calmly asked, "Do you think he had a legitimate point? You did dignify the trustee's position by meeting with them."

Although he felt completely justified in his peacemaker's approach, Conroy's face flushed. *Isn't that what an emissary is supposed to do, meet with all parties?* he wondered as he swallowed hard and hesitated before replying. "How can we make peace if we don't meet with both sides?"

Every gesture, every utterance, betrayed the bishop's displeasure at the way things were regressing. Yet, he was more determined than ever to reinforce his position that steadfast obedience to the Church was not only required, but demanded. A brief look of worry trotted across his face as he searched for the words that would allow him to continue this conviction. "We cannot give in to the laity on this matter, can we?" he finally asked. Conroy shrugged reluctant agreement for he knew that pressing the issue further would not carry the day.

Meanwhile, Pastor Clarke became strangely energized by his encounter with the bishop's emissary. His perilous ploy had worked, at least to his satisfaction. *Who do they think they are?* he smugly wondered. *They have no idea what I put up with here. Let them walk in my shoes before telling me how to run my parish!*

Yet, only he knew how far he was willing to go in this dangerous game, both with his diocese and the trustees. Was he willing to sacrifice his bishop? The chess pieces lined up for the end game but it remained to be seen if the priest really had gained an advantage or not.

CHAPTER 26

"**A** great day for a parade," George O'Leary announced to the gathering crowd on Independence Day of 1860. The celebration had become a ritual revered across all population centers in the North. And no man loved the patriotic observance more than the Squire. The village's parade, held annually since 1820, today featured two brass bands leading the marchers up and down the main thoroughfare.

The festivities began at 11 am with the Lowville Saxe Orchestra and the Carthage Military Band promenading eastward up a pennant festooned State Street. Their destination was Gallagher's Grove where a red, white and blue bannered stage awaited them. Spectators took their seats on benches in rapt anticipation of the cast of orators who were ready and eager to regale them with their patriotic speechifying.

Besides the stirring music provided by the bands, the program included prayers and a reading of the Declaration of Independence, to which all gave shouts of "hooray" and loud applause. Once the orations were finished, the procession re-formed and marched back down State Street with a black arm-banded Gallagher and high-stepping O'Leary leading the way. The column halted at the Harris House where the dignitaries entered to partake of a sumptuous repast served up by the hotel staff. After the meal, a series of thirteen toasts, one for each of the original colonies, were given in honor of the Republic, George Washington, the signers of the Declaration of Independence, soldiers of the revolution, and anyone else they could think of.

Designated "President of the Day," George O'Leary was called upon to assume the role of toastmaster and he offered the first salute titled *My Adopted Country.* The Squire recounted his youthful memories of Ireland reading about the American Revolution. "Little did I then think that in the year 1860, I should preside at your festive board, to pay tribute to the memory of those men whose swords flashed at Yorktown and Bunker Hill." He concluded with his sense the annual commemoration was, "A thing much needed in this place. May this celebration be the means of uniting our citizens in all matters of interest to our village. And may we place ourselves in a position to realize the sacred promise that 'If two shall agree as touching anything that they shall wish, it shall be done for them."

After dinner, many in the gathering repaired to the Water Street docks to board the *L.R. Lyon* and *Richard Gallagher* for excursions up the Black River. The steamboats noisily pulled away from shore with smokestacks belching and the captains serenading passengers with merry tunes on their steam whistles.

Those who remained ashore made ready for a mock battle between the Carthage Union Guard and the German Battalion, a local group of ethnic German veterans of the Mexican war. The Union Guard would represent the American Army invading a Mexican town, while the German Battalion, with uniforms made especially for the event, played the role of Mexicans defending their territory.

The Black River Bridge was the scene of the first battle where the "Mexicans" would endeavor to defend their town of Carthage. With loud discharging of muskets on both sides, creating huge smoke clouds obscuring everyone's view, the Mexicans retreated east up State Street to the corner at Mechanic Street. The spectators followed along, spitting the taste of gunpowder residue from their mouths, while lustily cheering the "Americans" on.

The retreating forces stiffened at the crest of the hill where they tried to make a stand amid the usual battlefield confusion. After skirmishing for a while, the "enemy" forces were routed anew and took flight all the way to upper State Street, where they finally surrendered. An "honorable treaty signing" was executed to conclude the reenactment.

The crowd drifted back downtown towards the river and took seats along the bank where, after dusk descended, they enjoyed an extensive fireworks display. Loud explosions reverberated through the valley to the accompaniment of more cheering and copious clouds of smoke. The celebration went on until 11 pm when it finally concluded with a rapid volley of pyrotechnics, and the large gathering dispersed and went home.

"'Twas a beautiful day," O'Leary said to Gallagher the next morning.

"Aye, 'twas." And abruptly changing the subject asked, "Who do you think will be our next president?"

The national election of 1860 had moved to center stage, trumping the St. James parishioners' parochial concerns. The partisan *Tribune* gave a large number of column inches to Abraham Lincoln and his party, while only causally mentioning the opposition, and then always in critical terms.

"Abe's our man," said O'Leary.

Gallagher, the Democratic president of the village, had supported Col. John Freemont in the 1856 election, especially because of the anti-Catholic campaign run by the despised Know-Nothings. But he was now faced with the unpalatable prospect of choosing from three pro-slavery candidates his fragmented party had nominated. The political lines were not as sharply drawn in the village as they normally would be because both the Catholic Democrats and the Protestant Republican were mostly abolitionists.

The noted newspaper publisher Horace Greeley came to Watertown on July 14 to promote Lincoln's candidacy, and was greeted by a huge crowd of Republican supporters. "There were lots of stirring speeches," O'Leary reported to *The Tribune*. "Even those who disagree with Greeley's politics felt he made a sensible and fair address."

"Do you think the Know-Nothings will be felt in the election?" Gallagher asked the Squire.

O'Leary' words had the ring of an insider's understanding of the tactics Lincoln's opponents would employ. "They've come up with a cockamamie scheme to deny the state's plurality to Abe. They are trying to get everyone to vote for Douglas so Lincoln won't get a majority, even though they aren't for Douglas. They want the election thrown to the House of Representatives so their candidate John Bell can be appointed. But I don't think that has a chance in hell of happening."

Southerners, hostile to the prospect of a Lincoln presidency, actually offered up two candidates, Stephen Douglas and John Breckenridge, in addition to the Constitutional Union (Know Nothing) Party's John Bell.

Bickford's paper didn't let this division of ideologies go unnoticed. He went so far as to lecture southerners about the doctrinal differences held by each of the candidates. "If you are undecided as to what principles you approve, it is very likely that on examination you may like the principles represented by 'Honest Abe' Lincoln." It's not likely the pages of *The Tribune* reached any further south than the Lewis County line, some five miles away, so is uncertain to whom Bickford's rhetoric was directed.

The Irish weren't left out of the political equation by the Lincolnites, despite their Democratic leanings. A meeting was held at the schoolhouse in the Settlement where O'Leary gave an impassioned speech reminding his confreres the Catholic Church "had always opposed slavery, up to the time of the present pontiff." He also mentioned one of the previous popes, St. Leo, had condemned slavery in the strongest terms. He claimed even Protestant historians declared the Roman Catholic religion was the chief instrument in effecting the abolition of slavery in Europe.

When O'Leary waltzed across the street from his shoe factory to the furniture store the following day, Gallagher proceeded to quiz him about his speech. "As far as the Church is concerned, it depends on your definition of slavery, doesn't it? Isn't McCloskey's position, and the Church's, actually a form of slavery?" He repeated what his lawyer had said in the pew trial. "If you don't have a say in what goes on, can't express your opinion, and are always told to obey their dictates with no respect to the laws of the land, then you're a slave, aren't you? And if you don't obey they tell you calamities will befall you. How is this anything but slavery?"

O'Leary mulled over the words and hesitatingly said, "You make a good point." As an ardent student of the law, the choice between church and state had always posed a dilemma for him. "There has to be a middle ground somewhere," he said as he retreated out the door.

The national election was held on the first Tuesday of November, and two days later when all the votes were counted, *The Tribune* headlined:

FUSION COLLAPSED ! !
THE UNION SAFE ! !
Lincoln Elected by the People

Gallagher, although he didn't campaign for him, voted for Honest Abe. He was a dedicated and outspoken abolitionist so he had to cross his party's lines and vote his conscience.

Happy the national election was now relegated to the pages of history he turned his attention back to his struggles with his Church. He wondered what the rascal priest had been up to. He would not have to wait long to find out.

Chapter 27

Pastor Clarke had made a big decision. Just as he had used his authority to relieve Maria Gallagher of her position in the Altar & Rosary Society, he was now ready to use the same tactic to get rid of her pesky husband as the parish house committee chairman. He posted a notice dismissing Gallagher and appointing himself in his place. Surprisingly, there was no great uproar, no letters to the bishop, and most importantly, no transfer of the disputed funds, which remained in Gallagher's hands.

"What took him so long?" was Richard's sarcastic response when he read the notice. "'Tis illegal and won't stand because he's ignoring State law. Hell, he can say he's running it for all I care, but his mitts won't caress one pence of the fund he covets so much."

Clarke then put part two of his plan into action. He submitted an item to be printed in *The Tribune* announcing a meeting, ostensibly to finalize plans for the long delayed parish house. On Thursday, December 27, 1860, *The Tribune* printed the following:

> A notice is posted about town for a meeting of the subscribers to the fund for building a Parochial House on the Roman Catholic Church lot in Carthage; to be held at the church on the 1st of January next, at 1 o'clock PM. The meeting is called by the Building Committee, and the object is stated to be to determine whether they shall go on and build, or whether the money shall be refunded to those who subscribed and paid it.

"We'll see about that," an agitated Gallagher said at an impromptu meeting with the trustees still in his camp. "What else do you think he has up his sleeve?" Rumors circulated Clarke had invited a large contingent of outliers for his last Mass of the year.

"Why would they be coming here?" James Walsh asked.

"I don't know," said the equally puzzled Gallagher. "But for sure he's got something up his sleeve. Make sure the word gets out for our people to attend, especially all those who've quit coming."

"That's about half of the parish," said James.

As daylight broke on the final Sabbath of the year 1860, Carthage awoke to a bitterly cold winter's day. The temperature had dipped to five below zero during the night and everyone hoped the rising sun would warm the air sufficiently to make the trek to church tolerable. Most parishioners suspected a momentous meeting would be taking place. The frigid air seemed to crackle with electricity as the local contingent began filing into St. James Church.

Few of the parishioners brought children with them for word had spread it might be imprudent to have the young 'uns present. The church would not only be crowded, but words not meant for juvenile ears might be passed.

Mass was scheduled for one p.m. but with the clock now at 1:15, the priest had yet to appear. He could be seen peeking through a slit in the vestry door from time to time, surveying the attendance. "He's waiting for all his supporters to come in from the sticks," ventured Gallagher to the nodding assents of the Walsh brothers, whom he had invited to share his pew. His family, at his insistence, had remained at home.

Visitors' carriages had been pulling up outside the church since 12:30. They braved the cold roads to arrive from Belfort, Copenhagen, Harrisburg and Pinckney. The last to appear were from the furthest points of Antwerp and Montague. And by 1:45 pm, there was standing room only in the church.

A low murmur had begun to arise from the impatient crowd, and many began asking about the delay. Gallagher's contingent seated on the bride's side, was soon exchanging stares and glares across the aisle with the priest's allies and the visitors

When the church could hold no more, the priest made his entrance and began with the usual opening prayers. At the service's midpoint, the celebrant took to the pulpit to read the gospel. When finished, he looked around at his audience, nodded to the visitor's gallery, and began his sermon.

His oration wasn't exactly what the Carthage faithful wanted to hear, as it contained some fresh invectives directed against the dissidents, and Gallagher in particular. "I see before me a group of sinners," Clarke began as he waved his arms and pointed directly at Gallagher's pew. A murmur arose but the preacher continued in a louder voice. "Yes, many sinners are seated before me. There are those who would dictate to the Church how it should conduct its ministry. And you know who you are!" he thundered.

The murmuring grew louder with each charge hurled by the priest. "We have guests here today who respect their Church and its clergy. They are as much a part of this mission as anyone here and have the right to express their opinion on parish affairs. Therefore we will conduct a trustee election today, and I insist everyone have an equal vote."

The Carthage contingent recoiled with anger as Clarke's plan became clear. He intended to have the parochial house meeting, scheduled for two days hence, to be run by a new board of trustees. It took but a few seconds for the dissidents to absorb the priest's plan, and their reaction was swift.

"No, no, no," a woman's voice was heard to shout. Aunt Nancy, seated in a front pew, stood up and cried in a shrill voice while shaking her fist, "Put him out. Put him out!"

A roar of approval rose from the rebels that drowned out the priest's red-faced objections. The rebel faction soon coalesced into a mob, a single force that stood in unison ready to act on the rallying cry. Two young Settlement farmhands began a menacing stride towards the altar, intending to obey Aunt Nancy's directive to drive the priest from the church.

A look of terror crossed Father Clarke's face. Sensing personal danger he made a dash to flee the sanctuary. Two

Montague allies seated close to the altar jumped up to block the two boys who had quickened their pace once they saw the priest's move to retreat. Others, impelled by the heat of the moment, began hurrying up the center aisle, jumping the chancel and making for the vestry door. But Clarke's allies body-checked and knocked them down. The beleaguered priest, along with two supporters, made it into the vestry and locked the door behind them.

The shouting, which had quickly grown to a passionate pitch, prompted the adversaries seated across from each other to begin trading menacing barbs, accompanied by shaking fists. A fight broke out between two hot-blooded youths, soon followed by more of the same until a general melee was underway. The few women present cowered against the walls on both sides of the church while the men engaged in hand-to-hand combat in the center aisle. A pair of belligerents wrestled their way up towards the sanctuary, landing on the altar table, which crashed to the floor. The men seized legs from the broken framework and began using them as clubs to attack each other. The fisticuffs continued with the more experienced Settlement brawlers steadily gaining the upper hand. After nearly ten minutes of spirited engagement, with bloodied heads and bruised fists decorating the participants, the tide turned decidedly in favor of the locals. The visitors and their allies, realizing their position was untenable, embraced retreat rather than continued fisticuffs, and ran from the church.

The anti-Clarke forces pursued the interlopers out the double-doors onto the boardwalk in front of the church. Once he saw the battle was won, Gallagher shouted, "Let 'em go, let 'em go!" As his forces reluctantly gave up the fight, the alien brigade quickly jumped on their double parked buggies and, amid shouts of giddyap and the whinnying of horses, fled in the directions from whence they had come.

Meanwhile inside the church, a few of the hot-bloods had continued beating on the vestry door, which was being fortified on the opposite side by the two Clarke supporters. The attackers finally broke through, but the priest had already made his escape. He had hastily mounted his buggy, parked at the rear of the church, and was soon galloping down the South Mechanic Street hill to the Irish Settlement.

The triumphant faction, despite the biting cold weather, milled about the front of the church patting each other on the back and basking in the glow of victory. With gasps and snorts of steam still coming from mouths and nostrils, congratulations were passed from man to man. Gallagher was nursing his right fist, which had connected with a hardheaded farmer from Copenhagen. Others had blood on their coats and some on their faces. Yet all sported smiles that, to them at least, vindicated their spontaneous, if unseemly, defense of their principles. No matter the pain of their wounds, or the criticism that was surely forthcoming for desecrating the church, they had made their point to the priest, and for them that would carry the day.

Aunt Nancy was hailed as a latter day Joan of Arc because of her spontaneous rallying cry. "I guess we showed Pockey a thing or two," she proudly said while taking a victory lap in front of the church.

Clarke arrived at his brother's farm in record time with his horse on the verge of collapse, exhaling plumes of steam from its nostrils. He rushed into the house and exclaimed to his brother, "They're mad! All of them, mad!"

"What's happened?" asked William, who was a bit under the weather and had decided against attending church on this day. "I knew you was askin' for trouble."

"They've driven me from the altar!" Michael shouted. "Why weren't you there to help me?"

His brother continued laconically puffing his pipe. "Well, I'm not surprised," was his answer.

Back at St. James, the summoned lawmen, in the persons of Deputy Sheriff O'Leary and Constable Lingenfelter, had arrived. The Squire, who had stopped attending church since

McCloskey's summary dismissal of his letter, was surprised when he received the call to duty. He soon observed that the vanquished party had fled and a calm of sorts had returned. There was nothing for him to do except take notes. "What's happened here, Richard?" he asked and listened carefully to the excited recitation for he felt someone would surely be bringing a lawsuit over this incident.

The trustees gathered, and adhering to their understanding of the letter of the law, took charge of the church. They summoned blacksmith Will McGraw to put new locks on the doors. The building was tightly secured and Gallagher took charge of one of the new keys. “It'll be a cold day in hell before that shoemaker sets foot in this place again,” he said. "No offense to shoemakers, Squire," he added.

The rumblings from this affair would be trumpeted near and far, causing many to wonder how long it would be before the echoes from Albany would be heard.

CHAPTER 28

"Scandalous, just scandalous!" A mortified Thomas Brady [no relation to the man of the same name who ran the Latin School in New York City] was sitting in the parlor of the Clarke farmhouse the Monday morning after the melee in the church. He had come to offer his support and Father Clarke could see at a glance Brady was genuinely offended by the incident. The man owned a rope factory on the west side of the river and was beyond appalled at what he heard had taken place. After the requisite number of headshakes that set his jowls atwitter, with several tongue clucks escaping from his clenched jaw, he assured his pastor he would write the bishop directly to inform him of the affair. He also suggested Clarke get supporting letters from prominent people in the village. "Perhaps the lawyer Stewart is one who will oblige you," he offered.

The emotional wounds from the incident had cut the priest deeply. His usual display of confidence had disappeared and evidence of worry was stitched across his face. Whenever the previous day's events bubbled up from memory, Clarke visibly recoiled. His mind was a jumble of random thoughts, uncharacteristically unable to concoct a cogent plan. Brady's suggestion, however, shook him from his depression and made his eyes regain some semblance of sensibility. He began speculating who else of prominence in the village might send a testimonial to the bishop.

As his cunning normalcy returned, he pounded his fist into his palm when he suddenly remembered the ushers never got to take up the collection. There was no time to think of that now for he must prepare to go to Albany and present this latest sacrilege to the bishop in person. He could not risk Gallagher, or any others, sending a preemptive and biased rendition ahead of him. He spent the rest of the morning writing his version of the event and poring over what other evidence he should take with him. Given his past interactions with both the bishop and his vicar general, he realized it would be imprudent to expect them to rely on his word alone.

That afternoon, Clarke paid a visit to the Le Ray Land Office on West Street and as politely as he could, asked the respected lawyer Stewart if he would not mind writing a letter to Bishop McCloskey on his behalf. Stewart, muttering about the disrespect shown towards church and clergy, immediately sat down and took out a sheaf of paper. "I don't understand what is wrong with these people," he said to himself. He had recoiled at the latest news of the St. James dispute making the rounds and, as expected, reflexively leaned to the side of the clergy. He had known Clarke for a long time and remembered him from his days as one of the village's many shoemakers. Their paths had intersected many times in the Church's land transactions and, of course, in the courthouse. The litigious Clarke's frequent lawsuits made it inevitable they would cross paths there.

The priest eagerly watched as the attorney's elegant script was made to flow onto the paper in long, decidedly firm strokes.

> To Rev. Mr. Michael Clarke,
>
> I have known you for many years, but more particularly since you have had charge of this Parish. I have and still do consider you as a very laborious, indefatigable priest. I have never heard anything against you except in this place. I know the Catholics at Redwood and Sterlingville & some at Copenhagen, and those who I have heard speak of you has been in your praise. The difficulties that have existed here I know but very little about, except what all know, but the merits the right or wrong, I have not inquired into or investigated.
>
> You have been ill treated as a Priest by those who should have respected you, not only in a recent lawsuit, but yesterday after Mass a very uproarious time was had outside the Church. I heard loud hurrahs when I was several hundred feet from the Church. The idea I have of the duties

> of Catholics towards the Church and their priests has been violated by men who know or should know better.
>
> I heard that the persons who I refer to did last Sunday shut up the Church by nails & locks, and they had a meeting in the Church yesterday. I heard that these men had applied to the Military to aid them if you and your friends interfered. I say I heard so - and I think it is so.
>
> Great disrespect has fallen on the Catholic Religion in this place, and I say for one taking into account all I have seen & heard, that the authority of the Roman Catholic Church and her Priests have been set at nought & indeed trampled under foot.

When Stewart finished the letter, he took a few pinches of sand and sprinkled them on the paper to blot the ink. Clarke was surprised to see it was addressed to him and not the bishop. *Why not write directly to McCloskey?* he wondered, but didn't dare question the endorsement. He thanked Stewart for his show of support, put the letter in his large pouch, slung it over his shoulder, and left.

When Clarke had time to examine Stewart's letter in detail, he found the consummate lawyer had taken care not to attest to things he hadn't seen or didn't know for sure. He concentrated his disdain on those raucous Irish, without any judgment as to who might be right or wrong. One sentence that raised the priest's curiosity was the mention someone had appealed to the military for help. No doubt this claim was the result of the many wild rumors making the rounds as news of the affair blanketed the village. When it became known, the notion that government troops might take sides in the church squabble caused a great deal of humorous commentary among the St. James dissidents.

Clarke started on his journey to Albany early the next morning. When finally he arrived at the bishop's residence, he was greeted by a dour Father Conroy. "I must see the bishop," he announced.

"Oh, and what would be the nature of this unscheduled visit?" Conroy asked rather dryly. The residual animosity he harbored over their last meeting was painfully obvious. The vicar general's body blocked the entrance to the residence and his figure now assumed an even more imposing silhouette.

"The bishop will want to hear what I've got to report," said Clarke in a voice trembling with anxiety. "There was no time to schedule an appointment."

Conroy, with arms akimbo, looked down on Clarke as if ready to fall on him, much to the smaller man's discomfort. *He's on my turf now, so I'll decide what's important. Maybe I should tell him to mind his own business and go home.* Clarke panicked as he considered he may have come all this distance only to be refused an audience with his bishop.

"So, what's this all about?" Conroy asked in a voice only one irritated note above a growl.

"I'll be telling the bishop about the grievous sacrilege committed by Gallagher and his gang in Carthage. They've driven me from the altar and seized the church!"

Driven from the altar? This could be a serious matter indeed. "Wait here, I'll see if the bishop's free," instructed Conroy.

"Your Eminence, Father Clarke is here from Carthage. He says there's been a grievous sacrilege committed against him and the Church." McClosky's ears twitched involuntarily as he clasped his crucifix and embraced a look of concerned. No matter how much this affair vexed him he could not refuse to listen to such a serious charge.

"Do you know more?"

"He would not divulge anything other than to say he was driven from the altar."

"Show him in."

Clarke bowed, genuflected, and with quivering lips kissed the bishop's ring. He could barely control his excited utterances when he began relating the events of the past Sunday. When finished, a self-satisfied look crossed his countenance, in reaction to the bishop's apparent horror. *He will now see I've been right all along and he'll have to take action,* Clarke thought.

McClosky was indeed disturbed by the report and took his time reading Stewart's letter. This was worse than even he could imagine. Indeed it was a sacrilege to desecrate a consecrated church.

"You'll be getting letters from other respected parishioners attesting to what I've reported here," added Clarke.

"I've heard enough," the bishop said as he rose brusquely in signal to Clarke he should take his leave. Clarke obsequiously kissed the ring again, and Conroy rose to usher him out.

"I'm not surprised, given all that has transpired," the bishop's aide remarked as he led Clarke to the door. "Not surprised at all."

Clarke wasn't happy at Conroy's comments but decided not to respond. He was gripped by a mix of emotions as he walked down the steps of the bishop's residence, unsure he had been accorded the appropriate respect by the chancery. He was, after all, the injured party, was he not? His head was shaking as he mounted an omnibus to the railroad station.

True to his word, Thomas Brady sat down in his office at the rope factory to write the promised letter. Although not a party to the goings on at St. James, he privately harbored ill feelings towards the renegade faction, especially "that ring-leader Gallagher." He would vent his pent up recriminations in his angry report to his bishop.

My Lord Bishop of Albany,

A sense of duty induces me to embrace the present opportunity of conveying to you an expression of my indignation at the Ruffinly Conduct of a Lawless faction of nominal Catholics. This Rascally mob led by Patrick Walsh and the Renegade Gallagher has committed acts of violence in the Catholic Church on last Sunday which has outraged the feelings of all the respectable inhabitants of this place.

You are aware that for some time past the prospect of building a house for the Priest on St. James Church lot in Carthage was in contemplation but owing to the opposition of Gallagher and his faction the work has been retarded but thanks be to the praiseworthy exertions of our worthy Pastor, the Rev. Mr. Clark who is determined that the building of a parochial house shall not be abandoned.

I know that for the earnestness in which he has devoted himself in the faithful Discharge of his duty he seeks no human praise but Looks up to him for his reward who will render unto every one according to his work.

However it may be interesting to you as it is highly gratifying to me to be able to state that since he came to this Mission he has diligently exerted himself with his money and his services in promoting the harmony and advancing the interest of all the Catholics who happened to come under his care.

But principles such as I have just stated and a character that proves the sincerity of them was not sufficient to secure him from the abuse of some of his own Rebellious flock. On last Sunday, a number of Catholics from all parts of the Mission, who felt interested in the Erection of a priest's house met at Carthage and cheerfully subscribed for that purpose but instead of receiving thanks from the Rebel faction of Carthage Congregation, they received the most unsufferable abuse. They were taken from their seats and dragged like fellons into the street. Next they abused the priest, Broke in the door to the vestry, took the Books and papers they found there and carried them off. Then they walked up on the alter with their hats on and shouted three cheers for Garibaldi.

All these indignities our worthy pastor and the virtuous members of the congregation patiently endured, recollecting that our saviour suffered far more without making any resistance.

Now, Rev. sir, I feel a sort of anticipated consolation in reflecting that the religion which gave us comfort in our early days and enabled us to endure the stroke of affliction

> and endeared us to each other and when we see our friends sinking into the earth fills us with the expectation that we rise again that we but sleep for a while to wake for ever.
>
> But what kind of communion can we hold, what interchange expect, what confidence place in that renegade Gallagher who is labouring under an incurable disease and fond of his own blotches when the belief of Eternal justice is gone from the soul of man, horror and execration take up their abode. I have the honour to be Reverend Sir with profound respect your Faithful humble Servant,
>
> Thomas Brady

Brady singled out Gallagher and Patrick Walsh but curiously did not mention his brother James. Their spinster sister Aunt Nancy had become the talk of the town, and Brady had heard enough about this woman whom he felt didn't know her proper place. As far as he was concerned, she was no better than that Dickensian character Madame Defarge in *The Tale of Two Cities*.

Brady had bragged he'd fix those renegades by telling the bishop the truth and leaked the contents of his letter to anyone who cared to know. Patrick Walsh said he expected as much from that "bastard" Brady. "We should take some of his rope and tie it around his neck!"

Brady's understanding of the building project seemed incomplete at best. He didn't mention the issue of where and what kind of parish house would be built. Gallagher would certainly tell him it was Clarke who didn't like Father Roche's house; Clarke who wanted a barn and farm animals on the church property; Clarke who threatened to not build the in Carthage-independent of the fact Gallagher led the drive and raised most of the funds. Why would he go to the trouble of soliciting subscriptions if he didn't intend to see the parish house built. Those words would rain down on his antagonist should he desire to defend himself. But he said he couldn't be bothered with the likes of Brady.

The claim Clarke was using his own money to promote harmony was amusing to several parishioners. They were the ones who alleged Clarke refused them sacraments because of their inability to pay. Many also said Brady never came to their discussions, otherwise he'd have known the true story.

Thomas Brady, as did the clerics in Albany, thought the Garibaldi cheer was an egregious display of disloyalty to the Church. And they felt the St. James dissidents who applauded and admired the Italian's opposition to the papacy were in violation of their required obedience to their faith.

"Aye, there's no love lost between the two," said James Walsh about Brady's animosity toward Gallagher. "He's jealous of Richard's success." It seemed plausible that while he had struggled to succeed with the rope factory, his opponent had become successful in both the public and private sectors. Others mentioned a falling out over some business deal struck years ago when Gallagher was setting up his water-powered cabinet shop on the Black River. It was likely that, if the rumors had any merit at all, only the two men knew the true story.

Gallagher sighed and said there wasn't anything anyone could do, so it was best to ignore it. “It'll all come out in the wash,” he said rather stoically. Indeed the laundry had gotten very dirty and would need a good washing. But who would be the one to do it?

CHAPTER 29

On the day following the regrettable church incident, State Street was all abuzz, with gossipers stopping by Gallagher's store, not to buy furniture of course, but to hear his side of what happened and what might be done next. "Well, the priest wanted to elect a new building committee so we'll do just that. We'll have the meeting in the church at one o'clock tomorrow, just as it said in *The Tribune*."

The rowdy but unfortunate confrontation had not only become the talk of the village, but also in all the towns throughout the mission territory. Most of the participants, when their temperatures got back to normal, agreed it was an embarrassing bit of publicity for their religion, one that was ostensibly dedicated to peace and harmony. Small towns don't require large events to set them abuzz and this was, even by Carthage standards, a large event. The gossip the brawl generated, when looked at by people with more sober dispositions, did not reflect well on either side. The incident caused the town to discuss, and become even more divided over the merits of either party. "'Tis the Devil's work," some said, a statement difficult to dispute. Both sides nominally embraced the Christian precept of brotherly love that, they had to admit, was woefully absent on that fateful Sunday.

At the appointed hour on Tuesday, the church was unlocked and members of the congregation who wished to vote filed in. None of Clarke's supporters showed up, fearing a repeat of the previous Sunday's fisticuffs, and knowing they would be outnumbered. When the meeting came to order, a motion was made and seconded that Patrick Walsh be appointed treasurer in lieu of Clarke, and Ed Galvin would replace Michael Kenna as a committee member. Gallagher was retained as chairman and suitable motions were made and passed by acclamation. Another action put forth by Gallagher called for the removal of Clarke as their pastor. It was passed with loud cheering and a few whistles. There ensued a spirited discussion of what they should do next, but it was finally agreed they should wait to see what moves were forthcoming from Albany. The meeting was then adjourned.

A *Tribune* reporter was on hand hoping to observe some fireworks but left disappointed. Two days later the paper filed the following story.

AN EXCITED CONGREGATION

> On Sunday last, an exciting affair occurred in the Roman Catholic Church in this village, which we venture to say was unprecedented in this community, which is usually so quiet and peaceful. We confine ourselves to a statement of the most prominent facts, as we have not room for all the details.
>
> It is well known here that there has been for some time a feeling of dissatisfaction existing in this congregation: Owing to a variety of causes, a large part of the church profess to have lost confidence in the priest in charge. They have frequently petitioned the Bishop of the Diocese to send another priest in his place, or at least, to investigate the causes of their complaints. Though four or five years have elapsed since these complaints were made, the Bishop, as we are informed, has disregarded them; and we have long feared that the end would be disastrous to the peace and good order of this community.
>
> Several years ago, money was subscribed and paid to the priest to build a parochial house on the church lot. Many difficulties arose out of this, and several lawsuits. Finally, Mr. Gallagher sued the priest for fifty dollars, which he claimed to have paid on this subscription, and which he sought to recover back, on the ground that as the house had not been built as contemplated, the priest ought in conscience to refund the money. The suit was decided in favor of the defendant, after a long trial. Thereupon the building committee called a meeting of the subscribers to be

> held at the church on the 1st of January (Tuesday) to determine what should be done with the funds. The priest thereupon, as we learn, gave notice to the churches at Antwerp, Redwood, Rossie and other places, to have the people come from these places, last Sunday, to the church at Carthage, to help elect a new building committee. As last Sunday was not the regular day for a meeting here, and as no notice of a meeting was given to this congregation, the party opposed to the Priest, on hearing of it, supposed a trap was laid for them. But as they got news of it, they resolved that they would not submit to what they called foreign dictation without some resistance. So, many of them attended, some to look on, and some to make opposition. The house was filled at an early hour, and about 150 attended from other congregations. After service, the Priest brought forward his project, and thereupon a scene of discord ensued which beggars description. Both parties became highly excited; there was loud and angry talking, and apprehensions of a fight. The priest fled to the vestry, with a few of his home and foreign friends. It soon began to be surmised, by those in the body of the church, that a business meeting was being held in the vestry, and thereupon the door of the vestry was forced open, and the priest and his friends went away. Those who remained passed a resolution to close the church, and to deliver the keys to the police constable of the village, which was done.

After claiming that a scene of discord occurred "which beggars description," such scene was not further described. The reporter contradicted himself in the next paragraph when he claimed that a "row" had already commenced before the authorities were summoned. Yet it "probably prevented a fight."

> After the row had commenced, police constable Lingenfelter and Deputy Sheriff O'Leary were sent for, to preserve the peace, and their arrival and prompt action, probably prevented a fight, and perhaps bloodshed. It was an affair

> much to be regretted. Our laws properly guarantee to every religious denomination the right to worship according to the dictates of their own consciences. But the laws contemplate peaceful assemblages, and not riotous ones. It is the opinion of many, that until this Church quarrel is appeased, there will be little use in trying to keep up the Roman Catholic worship in this place. And we do not see how the present pastor can appease this quarrel, even if he were so disposed; of which disposition we confess we see no evidence. Every community has a right to insist on quiet and order, and the means necessary to that end. And those who have the matters of this church or any other in charge, should not disregard the cause of public morality.

The report only added to the confusion as to who controlled the church, and continued with a tamer account about the building committee meeting that took place two days later.

> LATER - "Order reigns in Warsaw."* The meeting on Tuesday called by the Building Committee, as mentioned in the preceding article, was peaceable and orderly. The meeting appointed James Walsh, an old and much respected resident, to be Treasurer, in place of Rev. M. E. Clarke, the pastor; and Edward Galvin, a member of the Building Committee, in place of Michael Kenna. They also resolved to commence building the parsonage on the church lot, as soon as the new Treasurer received the funds, and also passed a resolution expressing want of confidence in the pastor, and a desire for his removal. They also appointed a committee to take charge of the church, and resolved to open a Sunday school to attend to the religious education of the children, which they allege has been almost entirely neglected during Mr. Clarke's pastorate.

The following week, *The Tribune* reported that "Worship at the R. C. Church was held on Sunday although the Priest was not in attendance. We understand, also, that there is regular appointment for worship there every Sunday." Reports of the church being "shut up tight" were obviously wrong. Given the number of street corner discussions taking place, this would not be surprising. Such chatter focused more on entertainment value than truth. If the details were juicy enough, few saw the need for confirmation.

Other members of the anti-Clarke faction decided to join the letter-writing campaign. The Lowvillian Patrick Flynn, who had regularly reported happenings in the Lewis County missions, decided to send McCloskey his perspective on the affair. His letter, which was dated two weeks after the infamous brawl, fairly dripped with venom for the Church and all its emissaries. The only personage he neglected to criticize was the pontiff himself. The long and rambling letter introduced a few issues not previously mentioned. He also stripped the concluding e from Clarke's name, perhaps in an attempt to take the man down a peg or two, and return him to the peasant class.

> Sir:
>
> I write to you for the purpose of informing you what my own sentiments are and to inform you what are the sentiments of three quarters of the Roman Catholics of the Carthage mission on the subject of your endorsement of the damnable villiannies committed by Michael E. Clark among those to whom he was sent in the capacity of a Catholic priest.
>
> It is scarcely necessary to inform you of the many crimes and iniquities that this clerical imposter has committed during the time that he had officiated as priest in this mission; for I am well aware that you have been informed of all these things repeatedly, and that is by the most reliable and trustworthy Catholics in father Clark's mission, that you are well aware of the injustice practiced against the members of the catholic church, and of the scandal given to all Catholics thereby, and that this villianny and scandal is still farther aggravated by the fact that father Clark's conduct

receives your official sanction and endorsement, in your utter refusal to remove him from this' mission.

The causes stated above are the only inducements I had in addressing these lines to you. For I am not foolish enough to suppose that anything that can be said or written to you will have the effect of causing Father Clark's removal from this place but merely for the purpose of informing you that Clark during his ministry here, has been a disgrace to that religion which it is our interest to respect and honour , and which has honoured you by elevating you to the high and holy office of one of its Bishops, in return for which, in connection with father Clark, you are a disgrace to the high office you hold - to the religion you profess - and the country that gave you birth.

For it is a notorious fact well known to both Catholics and Protestants that you have been informed, that father Clark has attempted in numerous instances to pervert the sacrament of confession to objects of his own personal interests such as speculating in bonds and notes upon real estate, for purposes of personal revenge, for manufacturing witnesses to give in testimony in his favour in the numerous lawsuits in which he is steadily engaged in the business of horse-trading, the confessional box also furnishes him with all the information he wants with regard to the good points and comparative value of his parishioners horses.

Among the rest of his astounding feats as a Catholic Priest, has been the Plaintiff in not [less] than thirty lawsuits during the last eight months, and he also been the Defendant in as many as two or three suits in each of which he has committed perjury as many times, and as often as he thought it was necessary for his own interests to do so.

He has sold out the Catholic vote of his mission as often as he could find a purchase for it; and made his boast that before he came to this place he received one thousand dollars from O.B. Mattison* of corruption money for his influence among the Catholic voters of Oneida County.

But of what use is it to multiply facts of this nature, and of which the above is but a mere outline, and the truth of which you are as well aware as is father Clark himself for Clark has never dared to challenge an investigation of those charges that are in every mans mouth in this part of the state.

You have been informed of those both when you were in Carthage and in Watertown, but you pretended that you did not believe them because they were not proved by witnesses under oath and yet you refused to give the individuals who made those statements time to produce the witnesses which they offered to do thus showing your anxiety to support father Clark in all his villianies whatever they may be.

The last specimen of his piety that I have heard of occurred one week ago last Sunday in the village of Carthage where he assembled all the offscourings of Catholicity that he could find in Lewis, Jefferson and St. Lawrence Counties to take possession of the church in Carthage and elect trustees of a suitable degree of villiany who would be his pliant tools in any emergency that might arise, the result was what might have been expected, a fight took place in the church, during which pews were broken, a table was torn to pieces that the legs of it might be used as offensive weapons, the priest made his escape into the vestry, the door of which was smashed in, and the priest was obliged to make his escape bare-headed through the streets of Carthage followed by the contemptible rabble that he had brought there for the purpose of taking possession of the church.

In conclusion I will now say that you are wholly responsible for all the scandal and disgrace that has fallen upon the church in this place for you are well aware, and this fact is as well known by Protestants as by Catholics. Your conduct in supporting the Priest in the manner has driven many from the church forever men ... who have spent their youth and middle age as Catholics are now going down to the grave, with nothing but hatred in their bosoms for the faith in which their ancestors from time immemorial lived and died and for your comfort. I will tell you that all the writings and publications of the whole Protestant world

> combined would never be able to do this even father Clark himself could not do it; but when they seen the bishop supporting the Priest in his criminal designes they then bid farewell to the catholic church.
>
> There are many who still remain in the church firmly as they ever did who declare firmly and emphatically that if Bishop McCloskey ever reaches heaven they do not want to go there. The truth of the matter is your reputation in this place is worse than that of any states Prison convict in the United States for it is the general remark in this place that a man who will support a murderer, a thief, and perjurer as you have done is none too good to commit the same crimes himself.
>
> In conclusion I have only to say that I consider you to be a damnable and sacrilegious villian who willingly sacrifices the whole catholic church rather than desert the Priests interests in anything he may undertake.
>
> There is one conclusion that everyone has arrived in this place with regard to you; that is the money has been plundered from the poor Catholics of this place by this clerical despot your agent, has been divided with you, that your decisions on this subject have been dictated by bribery and corruption instead of being the offspring of that disinterested regard that a Bishop should feel for the church of which he is a member.
>
> Patrick Flynn.

Mr. Flynn obviously had several irritating burrs under his saddle. One of his most salient points-that the bishop was by his inaction culpable for the deeds of Clarke-was an opinion shared by quite a few in Carthage. As his letter rambled on, he seemed unable to exhaust his vituperation. He was at pains to remind the bishop that Albany was at the root of, and responsible for, this mess. He is bent on driving a proverbial stake into the bishop's heart as if trying to slay a vampire.

Some of Flynn's charges against Clarke had never before been aired. The complainant reaffirmed O'Leary's contention that the pastor's litigious nature had involved him in a large number of unjust lawsuits. The charge that he was caught up in political shenanigans would cause Gallagher to speculate this could have been why the priest was available from Utica in the first place.

Upon reading his letter, one could easily get the impression Mr. Flynn was no longer a communicant of the Catholic Church. The complainant accused McCloskey of being in financial cahoots with Clarke, a charge even the most dedicated members of the dissident faction had not thought to make, nor in the final analysis even believed.

McCloskey resisted his first impulse to destroy Flynn's letter. He summoned Conroy and instructed him to file it in the proper cabinet. He would present it at subsequent meetings with his brother bishops, thinking it might serve as a case in point of the ever-present threat of the Protestant Reformation.

Conroy could see McCloskey's ears were burning when the bishop handed him the offending letter. "It is time to act," the bishop said. All the reports about the Carthage affair had been reviewed, his archbishop in New York had been consulted, and he must now publish his decision. "You will be my witness," he said and thereupon began dictating a letter of censure that must be delivered post haste to each of three St. James trustees.

"It is with solemn regret that I inform you..." the letter began.

Chapter 30

"That bastard priest!" Richard Gallagher said once more. He cradled his head in his hands, elbows resting on his desk, looking down in disgust at the letter that had caused his outburst. He read it yet again.

> Dear Mr. Gallagher,
>
> It is with solemn regret that I inform you of the Holy Roman Catholic Church's decision that you hereby be excommunicated from its membership rolls and henceforth denied the sacraments of salvation.
>
> This action is being taken in accordance with your being found guilty of serious and continued infractions regarding your longstanding disobedience of our Church's instructions, desecration of a consecrated church, including the expulsion of Father Michael Clarke as your pastor. Your continued obstinacy in this matter has caused grievous harm to our sacred Church and to the faithful of the parish of St. James.
>
> I trust in God that you will see that persistence in the error of your ways will bring untold misery down upon your head as well as the others in your community. You will be required to publicly repent your sins and swear allegiance to the Holy Church before you can return to God's good grace.
>
> Sincerely in Xto,
> Rt. Rev. Bishop John McCloskey

Gallagher looked down at the bishop's letter after he had loosed the sacrilegious epithet for a third time. His face was on fire as his eyes burned holes into the offensive parchment. He then became lost in time as his mind tried to release the pent up tension. He thought of Maria, and had she been there for him, he would have bolted the store, gone home and vented to her. Her counsel and restraint in times such as these was greatly missed. He needed someone close to confide in, but there was no one. It was just as well she was not here to witness this, he finally conceded.

The Walsh brothers, James and Patrick, had also received letters and together they mounted a farm wagon and galloped up from the Settlement to see Gallagher. Aunt Nancy insisted on coming along. "What're we gonna' do now?" asked an extremely agitated Patrick.

"There's nothing to do," Gallagher replied, having had time to regain his composure. "We have to remain united, that's the important thing."

Both Patrick and James betrayed their misgivings with furrowed brows, darting eyes, and halting speech. Their small frames seemed to shrink inward, giving Nancy cause for alarm. "Get hold of yourselves," she scolded.

Gallagher wondered if his cohorts could hold up to the pressures that lay ahead. "Come on," he said, "you both were leading the parade in church. Don't change your minds now."

"Well, I... I got caught up," Patrick said defensively, as he remorsefully remembered being one of the ones who beat upon the vestry door.

"Surely I di'not think it'd be grounds for excommunication," said a wincing James, while cringing at the memory of shouting anti-clerical epithets while throwing punches. He wondered who had snitched on him with the bishop.

"Let's all take a deep breath and sleep on this," Richard said, clearly signaling he wasn't happy with the course the discussion had taken. With that, everyone retreated to solitary ruing of their deeds. Aunt Nancy carped all the way home, telling her brothers to buck up.

By the time February rolled around, more members of St. James parish were expressing concerns about the path the events had taken. Under the interdict, no services could be held in the church even if they had a priest to perform them. And the absence of religious services and administration of the sacraments, no matter how infrequent, would be greatly missed. Among many, especially Patrick Walsh, the bravado of dissent was replaced with a whispered and heartfelt remorse. The rebels had never anticipated or actually thought through all the possible consequences of their actions. Their misery was compounded by increased rancor from the pro Clarke segment of the congregation. As time wore on, divisiveness deepened with the warring factions being driven further and further apart.

Gallagher heard that Patrick Walsh had taken to his room at the farmhouse and was neglecting his chores. Among the dissidents, he rued his excommunication *in extremis* and repeatedly admonished himself with, *I should'na got caught up in it, 'specially on that Sunday in church. What was I thinkin'? I wasn't doin' nothin' nobody else wasn't doin'.*

His sister Nancy, and Gallagher, along with a diminishing core of rebels, remained resolute and focused their anger on the priest. They did worry aloud that Patrick had lost his grip on reality, and James wasn't far behind. Aunt Nancy, never one to mince her words, called them both cowards.

"You will see," Father Clarke sermonized to an audience of loyalists who had gathered for Sunday Mass at the farm. "Retribution will be delivered to those who disobey the Church." Prior to the interdict, the priest was absent from the village much more than he was there. He now appeared for services at least twice a month, either at the family farm or a large private home in the area. It was speculated that this was his way of "putting salt in the heretics' wounds," a notion he would not deny, had he been asked. The Clarke farm, which had been made the *de facto* parish manse, had now become the parish's *sub-rosa* church. The previously unavailable sacraments were dispensed in greater abundance, sometimes two weeks in a row, but only to the Clarke loyalists.

The pastor kept control of the parish record book, in which he recorded several baptisms and marriages after the church was closed, rites that seemed to have now taken on more immediacy than before. "'Tis just another way this Shylock has to make us pay," Gallagher said, quoting one of his favorite Shakespearian plays for effect. "He's out to get his pound of flesh one way or another."

As the weeks slipped by, Gallagher became distracted by something else he had on his mind. Coping with the loss of his wife in isolation, he knew he was not spending enough time with his children. Mrs. McManus had been filling in, helped out by the servant Mary, but it was too large a burden for them. "If I di'not have my two girls to look after, I could manage," said Mrs. M.

Adelaide Masury, the music teacher, had gone on a singing tour with her sister Elise shortly after Maria's death. Richard missed not seeing the bright-eyed girl, who had continued her steady march into attractive womanhood. He admitted he had developed a fondness for her and enjoyed those mildly flirtatious encounters that made her blush. It was in those moments he began wondering if Addie would ever consider stepping in to replace his departed wife. Oh, he didn't mean replacement exactly, and he reproached himself at the thought. But loneliness was taking its toll during the few months since his wife had passed away. *'Tis not natural for a man to be alone,* he ruefully noted.

Adelaide and Elise returned to Carthage in June to give a recital at Walsh's Hall. Richard made sure several friends attended with him, including Squire O'Leary. He was so moved by the performance he suggested to his party they send a card to the ladies the next day, asking them to consider extending their engagement. The card was delivered by messenger and the girls responded immediately, promising an encore musicale on that very same evening. *The Tribune* published both notes in its next issue, which caused a few raised eyebrows when Gallagher's name appeared at the top of the card. It had, after all, been only three months since he had been made a widower.

Raising his brood without a wife and mother dominated Richard's thoughts, even pushing his excommunication to the background. As a practical man, he was lately giving the idea of remarrying a lot of thought. Friends began dropping hints that this or that widow might make a good match, but those ladies held little attraction for him, certainly not in comparison to a girl like Adelaide Masury. The lass had gained a prominent place in his mind, and soon he could think of little else.

Whenever young Miss Masury was in town, she found time to drop in at the Gallagher household to see the children. At least that's what she said was the reason for her visits. This gave Richard some added time with her, which he not only welcomed but began to anticipate. When his thoughts turned to romance, he began debating himself about the propriety of such a relationship. The age difference wasn't unheard of but try as he would he couldn't ignore that the lady was twenty-three years his junior. He rationalized that her maturity belied her years and soon convinced himself that this disparity didn't matter. Yet, he had to wonder if the lady would think him too old. When he looked into the mirror and ran a comb through his thick crop of salt and pepper hair, he allowed that at forty-two he felt pretty damn good.

Whenever Richard saw Addie, he thought she perked up and even flirted back with him. Her ready smile and fragrant perfume made him conjure up flowers dancing in the fields. *She gets prettier by the day,* he thought.

Addie seemed to delight in making conversation with Richard and mentioned how much the children had improved in their music. "You must let Helen and John play a duet for you," she enthused. "They are really getting good."

Even after the children went off to bed, Addie would linger to continue conversing with Richard. Mrs. M had long noticed the attraction and would politely retire to give them privacy. Richard, ever the studious salesman, put his best assets on display. "What do you think of Carthage's future?" he asked in an attempt to broaden their conversations. Despite a look of wonder in Addie's eyes, he sensed she not only understood what he was talking about, but might actually become a sounding board for his ideas, just as Maria had been. He could see the lass really enjoyed these tête-à-têtes, and there was no mistaking what started as a spark had become a flickering flame of interest... for both of them.

"The future certainly looks bright," she answered, "what with the canal being completed and all." Richard smiled.

The infatuated widower was not a man who took rejection easily so he studied Addie ever more intently to be sure she was interested before he took the next step. Finally, he screwed up his courage and suggested a courtship. "What do you think, my dear?" he said a bit sheepishly one evening. "Do you think we could make a go of it, you and me?"

"Well, I'm flattered," Addie blushed. "This is quite a surprise, so I'll need some time to think this over."

Richard had done his homework and knew Addie had other admirers. In fact, she was being pursued by the baker's apprentice from her brother-in-law's shop. He was a handsome boy, the same age as she, but woefully lacked his maturity and prominence, or so he reckoned.

"I'll have to discuss this with my sister," Addie said.

"Do that," responded Richard, trying to sound as casual as he could under the circumstances.

When she got back to the Chase residence, Addie broached the subject with sisters Elise and Hattie while her brother-in-law Justus listened. He couldn't help but weigh in with his opinion. "You'd be lucky to make such a catch. Jeez, the president of the village and one of the wealthiest businessmen in town? How could ya turn that down?"

Sister Hattie was not as enthusiastic. "He's quite a bit older than you," she demurred. "Are you sure this would be right for you?" Elise was non-committal, although she didn't look forward to losing her touring concert partner, she was only concerned her sister would make the right choice.

"But he doesn't look his age," Addie said a bit defensively. In truth, Richard didn't look forty-two, despite the streaks of white in his hair. By all outward appearances, he was a strong and virile man. Addie recalled the stories about the account he gave of himself in the church brawl. "Look at the way he walks... straight and tall with strong strides. I don't think his age is a problem. I just wonder if I'm up to his need to have someone to talk over his business deals with. I remember his wife Maria was good like that."

Hattie advised her sister should "Take your time. You're still young."

"Well you were only seventeen when you married,"

Her sister blushed as she replied, "Yes, and my husband is still only two years older than me."

"Everyone in the village knows he's looking for a wife and there are a lot of eligible ladies hanging around his store," Addie said. "That Nancy Walsh woman is always stopping in with some widow or old maid."

Richard was mildly surprised when the twenty-year-old girl said yes to his overtures. In moments of more sober reflection he was pessimistic about his chances. When he thought about it, which was most of the time, he unconsciously walked more erect, with an exaggerated spring in his step. He began thinking of moving their relationship past the encounters at his home, perhaps to a concert date at Walsh's hall.

Richard eyes couldn't stop sizing up the young lady's enviable figure, especially her well developed bosom jutting out over her slim, cinched waist. She was taller than the petite Maria, and Richard began imagining what this lady looked like underneath all those layers of clothing. The dresses, except for their size, weren't much different than those worn by Mrs. McManus. But no matter how hard he tried, he couldn't stop comparing Addie to Maria. *She's a bit fuller in the hips, and probably won't have problems birthing children,* he mused. Addie blushed for her suitor couldn't hide his thoughts very well. Richard would then shake his head and force himself to return to more proper thoughts. With every ensuing encounter, however, he became visibly more and more distracted by the young lady's physical beauty.

"He's good-lookin' and a fyne catch," said Mrs. M, dragging out the word 'fyne.' Young Addie had sought her advice so she gladly gave it. "You could do a lot worse. And just look at this house."

Addie's brow appeared to wizen and her eyes narrowed as she pondered the older woman's words. *Mrs. M knows what she's talking about.*

When Richard and she were next alone, Mary McManus asked, "So what're your plans with this lassie?" The opportunity arose because Addie was away on an engagement in Watertown.

"I been thinking I have to find a mother for these children," he said, "and the lady seems up to the task. I know she's young, but she's old enough, don't you think?"

"Oh, she's old enough alright. But what about her Da? Do ya think you'll have any problems with him?" Mrs. McManus had a habit of ending each sentence with a rising inflection that gave her words a ring of authority.

"Why, do you think he'll be a problem?"

"You know 'ee's a bloomin' snake-oil salesman, don't ya?"

"He's a doctor, that's all I know."

"'Ee's worn out his welcome in every town 'ee's been in, or so I've 'eard. I asked Addie 'bout 'im but she won't say much. Doctor my foot! You'd best be careful or he'll be feedin' you extract of sarsaparilla or somethin' else he's cooked up called Wau-Au-Moo. And I di'na think it comes from a cow either."

Given the practice of medicine, opportunities abounded for so-called "snake-oil salesmen" who roamed the countryside peddling their "cures." *The Tribune* ran a full page of advertisements in every issue for one treatment or another, to remedy one affliction or another. Why, for an investment of only fifty cents, a person could heal their "nervous liver" or alleviate catarrh.* The multitude of concoctions they hawked was "guaranteed" to provide unparalleled efficacy in the prevention and treatment of a litany of diseases that looked as if they were taken from the index of a medical text. There were preparations called Peruvian Syrup, Balsam of Wild Cherry, Iodine Water, and Grace's Celebrated Salve. The list of products was mind boggling.

"'Ee's like one of them "Doctors" or "Perfessers" who use'ta roar into town in one of them covered wagons. They'd have a flunky beatin' a drum and slogans painted on their canvas sayin' they could cure anythin'."

How Mrs. M knew all this, Richard could only wonder. The inquisitive woman prattled on about the bogus patent medicines they dispensed saying many were concocted by the "doctor" himself. "They're naught but drummers," she said, "They can't stay in one place too long 'cause the fools find out these cures di'not work. 'Tis a wonder ole Doc Masury hasn't been tarred and feathered."

Dr. Masury, however, didn't ride into town in a covered wagon like some ordinary drummer. He would put up a "medicine stand" from which to dispense his potions. His shills were not rubes placed in the audience, but letter writers to local newspapers lauding the efficacy of his wares. He stayed in a town from one to two years before selling out. In 1854 he was at Boonville when he found his "stand" had run its course, just as it previously had in Boston and Rochester. He advertised his "medicine stand" for sale and relocated to Ogdensburg where the family was currently situated.

"'Tis no wonder the poor lassie has moved around so much," Mrs. M continued. Her melodic voice trilled ever more true as she rocked in her chair, arms folded beneath her matronly bosom. "She's lived in six different places in just fourteen years. Why, the girl was only five when they first come down from Canada to Watertown. He'd sell the business each time to some poor unsuspectin' bumpkin, promisin' they'd make a bloomin' fortune. No tellin' where he'll be off to next."

"You're too hard, Mary," Richard said. Although he respected her wisdom, he knew she indulged in gossip, along with a bit of exaggeration now and then. Yet, he also knew the woman had an uncanny ability to ferret out information from unsuspecting folk. Nonetheless, he felt compelled to defend Addie's father, even though he'd never met the man. "You're too hard," he repeated.

"Smitten men di'na think straight," said Mrs. M. The matron had a point; Richard was indeed smitten and desperately seeking a way to rationalize his courtship. He noticed the children didn't listen to him as they did when Maria was about. He was increasingly impatient, delivering spankings, something he never did when their mother was alive. His civic duties required lots of time, causing him to neglect his family, and the disciplining of his children.

"I don't care," he finally said, "I've already put a proposal to the lass." Just as Addie realized other women had designs on Richard, he too worried some "stage door Johnnie" might attract her attention while she was on the road performing.

Richard wasn't worried about the bakery apprentice for he figured the only asset the boy had he didn't was youth. Orrin Jones might be the same age as Addie but failed every other important test.

Addie had weighed all her options carefully. *I can't be tied to a bakery shop. I've seen what that has done to Hattie.* All in all, she was too practical, too ambitious, to see herself following in her sister's footsteps. Observing those struggles first hand was enough to convince her Richard Gallagher presented a better life for the taking. *Why not enjoy the finer things?* She asked herself as she surveyed the fine appointments decorating the Gallagher mansion. A steady diet of this would be alright with her.

"Trust me sweetie," Mrs. M. counseled, "'tis far better to have a bulging bank account than a breathless suitor."

CHAPTER 31

"HOSTILITIES COMMENCED!" the newspaper's headline screamed. "FORT SUMTER BOMBARDED!"

The residents of Carthage, along with the rest of the nation, were jarred out of their provincial concerns by news of an attack on Ft. Sumter in South Carolina. The thunderclouds of war that had continually flashed their warning signs finally exploded with a surprise attack on the Union installation. The stage for this eruption had actually been set four days before the melee at St. James Church took place, when South Carolina passed its articles of secession. The bill said the state had ownership rights to all property within its borders regardless of Federal claims.

"Our problems with the bishop and his priest are certainly looking mighty small this morning," Gallagher said to the group gathered on State Street. Everyone admitted the St. James insurrection was miniscule when compared to the potential dissolution of the Union. Placed in the proper context, this made Carthage's religious turmoil look like a tiny pustule on the broad face of national concerns.

"Aye, 'tis a bad omen," O'Leary said, and a discussion ensued as to how they might support the war effort.

As the river of patriotism swelled in the North, spilling its banks and flowing into Carthage, it drowned out all other concerns. "The Union must be preserved!" exclaimed O'Leary, a sentiment felt by all.

The conversation went on into early evening with people aimlessly milling about on State Street like lost sheep waiting for a shepherd to appear.

The grocer John T. Walsh noted, "We don't even have a flag flying anywhere in the village."

Squire O'Leary suddenly shouted, "By God almighty, before the sun rises tomorrow, Old Glory will be waving from the spire of St. James Church!"

Overcome with the passion of the moment, the Squire abruptly left the gathering, bent on procuring a flag to make good his oath. He went from store to store but nary a flag could be found in the whole of the village. Undeterred, he went to Horace Hooker's dry goods store and purchased a bolt each of red, white, and blue cloth. He took the bundle home and told Alice what he had promised. Mrs. O'Leary gathered up the material and rushed over to her dressmaker, the widow Ann Coyle. The seamstress in turn enlisted the three ladies of the needle she employed, and who coincidently boarded with her. Margaret and Katherine Kinney, along with Margaret McNulty, were anxious to help fabricate a proper Stars and Stripes and soon the bevy of Betsy Rosses was hard at work. They sewed on through the early hours until a large flag was completed. The next morning as the village rose to meet the dawn, O'Leary's flag was seen waving from the cross atop the St. James Church spire.

"Now there's a sight for sore eyes," said Gallagher as he passed the church on his way to open his store. The vision of Old Glory fluttering in the morning breeze energized the crowd that soon gathered on State Street. When word was passed that Squire O'Leary had placed it there, the villagers sought him out to lead an impromptu parade. The Carthage military band was assembled and soon a procession headed by O'Leary was parading up and down State Street, to the cheers of a swelling throng of bystanders. The crowd began shouting slogans such as, "Preserve the Union!" and "On and on forever!" The onlookers gathered at the church, which had been opened by Gallagher. Not that he cared, but this would not be a violation of the interdict since it was not a religious service. The throng that filed in had as many Protestants in their number as Catholics, an ecumenical first for St. James.

"Speech, speech!" they chanted and O'Leary rose to address his fellow citizens.

He began his oration with outstretched hands pointing towards the vaulted ceiling, above which the cross and waving flag was stationed. "Make no mistake," he said in stentorian tones, "'tis no coincidence that two great emblems are joined today. The cross of man's salvation and the flag of our nation's freedom have come together so God may bless our struggle." His words of passionate association between the two symbols were met with frequent and loud applause.

Upon conclusion of the impromptu celebration, the Squire went home and penned yet another of his stirring poems to commemorate the occasion. Judge Bickford gladly published the text in the next issue of *The Carthage Republican Tribune.*

RAISE HIGH THE BANNER

Ye sons of old Ireland, honest and true,
Your country adopted appeals now to you.
Her banner unfurled to the breeze let flow;
'Tis the flag of Columbia, down ne'er let it go.
Behold it dishonored, and trailed in the dust,
By tyrants and helots whose names are accursed.
Grasp, grasp the loved banner, and raise it on high,
For 'neath its proud fold we all fain would die -
Yes, raise it on high, and march right along
With the drum, and the music, and the patriot song;
Grasp, grasp the loved banner, and ne'er let it go,
For freedom is crushed the moment you do.
Lift up the loved banner, and high let it be,
For I see by its stars it was made for the free.
True sons of old Erin helped to raise it on high,
And 'neath its proud folds did Montgomery die.
How oft we have struggled, how often in vain,
In hopes for dear Erin a flag we might gain!
But here we are now, in the home of the free,
The Star-Spangled Banner insulted to see.
Then raise it on high, I implore yon once more;
'Tis the banner which Washington honored of yore

> Your countrymen helped him to raise it on high,
> And prayed that the chieftain's work never would die.

O'Leary, of course, didn't realize what he had started for soon the town's merchants began competing with one another to hang flags on their buildings. Old Glory was soon raised on the Liberty Pole* by the Union Guards. Not to be outdone by the Catholics, the Presbyterians placed a flag atop the tower of their church, and to mark the occasion rang their bell with a "merry peal."

Never far behind a trend, and unwilling to be overshadowed, Gallagher commissioned the fabrication of the largest flag of them all, to be placed atop his business block. Soon Old Glory was waving from Wm. A. Peck's store, Gilbert, Atwood & Stiles law office, and the printing office of *The Carthage Republican Tribune.* And not long after that nearly every child in the village was waving a miniature flag of the Republic. Patriotic fervor was never more in fashion as the nation's revered symbol burst forth in profusion around the village like mushrooms in the woods after a spring rain.

As the Civil War heated up, a dash by Carthage men to join the conflict was soon underway. The cheerleading *Tribune* published calls by President Lincoln for volunteers to help put down the insurrection. Most men and boys who rushed to join had no reason to doubt the pundits' prediction of a short war. "You'll be home by Christmas," was a slogan uttered with such confidence everyone believed it to be true. The soldiers recruited in the South were being told the same. Talk of joining the war soon reached fever pitch on both sides as the respective armies rushed to fill their ranks.

When the war began, the federal government had but a small standing army, led in both North and South by the cream of the crop from West Point. Many of the Southern officers had to now make an agonizing choice between a state's right to secede and preservation of the Union, as both sides hurried to assemble their militias into larger armies.

Lincoln's secretary of war scoured the landscape in search of military veterans who could be chartered to raise a regiment or company in their respective locales. Men with any military experience, such as the Mexican-American or Indian Wars, obtained commissions along with a writ allowing them to enlist men in their outfits. The officers proceeded from town to town to raise cavalry, artillery, and infantry regiments. Some towns formed companies of volunteers who elected their own officers by popular vote.

News of volunteer units being formed around New York State filled the columns of *The Tribune*, as recruiters began making their way into Carthage and Champion. A platform would be set up and stirring speeches flowed from uniformed men, complimented by martial music from the local military band. A revival meeting-like atmosphere descended on the gatherings, one that glassy-eyed, patriotic boys found hard to resist as they ran up to the stage to be "saved." The audience cheered each time a volunteer came forward and a few would shout, "Good boy, Ezra!" or "Good lad, Levi!"

Within two weeks of the Ft. Sumter attack, local shoemaker Abel Nutting was commissioned a Captain and proceeded to raise a company of 25 volunteers. The initial rush to join was intense and the ranks of the military soon swelled.

The Tribune reported on May 2 twenty-eight more volunteers had departed Carthage to join Capt. Angle's company at Copenhagen, some ten miles south of Carthage.

> Their departure was the occasion of great enthusiasm and excitement. They are a fine set of men, and all good fellows, who we doubt not, will give a good account of themselves. At their departure our cannon was fired, and the villagers crowded around to shake hands and bid good bye. Some tears were shed at parting, but it was a call of the country... Col. O. Holcomb gave each of these recruits a dollar.

Although most enlisted in a particular regiment, some men would be transferred to a different one a few months later. One Carthage boy ended up in an Ohio regiment. But, given the casualties piling up, with numbers equally divided between bullets and blight, the rolls began to attrit. Generals began complaining they didn't have enough men to fight their battles, and asked that recruitment be speeded up.

As the patriotic Carthage boys soon realized, the reality of war was quite different when seen up close. When rivers of blood began flowing freely on the battlefields, the initial rush of patriotism abated along with an alarming rise in desertions. Even some of the sturdy men of Carthage found war to be inglorious when actually having to fight in it. *The Tribune* neglected to mention desertions in their reportage, especially for any boys from Carthage.

CHAPTER 32

"I can't be worried about the war," Richard said to Mrs. M. "I've got to conclude this liaison with Addie." Despite Gallagher's genuine concern about preserving the Union, and the nagging problms with his Church, both issues would have to be put aside for the sake of his family.

Addie, as any twenty-year-old might, had agonized over what she should do. After weighing the pros and cons, with age disparity doing battle with her desire for security, the young lady decided to accept Gallagher's proposal. Following her concurrence, an ecstatic Richard set the wedding date for the second week of May. The scheduling, Richard said, was because of the pressing need for a mother for his children. Of course, the widower's human appetites played no small role in his haste. He hungered for the warmth of a woman at his bedside, although to openly admit this would be unseemly.

The bride to be threw herself into preparations for her wedding. There was a dress to be made, bridesmaids to be chosen, and a reception to be planned. She knew this wouldn't be like the romances she'd read about in those English novels, but she had to do what she had to do.

The bride to be was crestfallen when Richard told her she would have to scale back her grandiose wedding plans. The elaborate preparations she had in mind wouldn't do because, "There's a war on. We've not the time to spend ferrying people to Ogdensburg. Just one couple to attend us will have to be sufficient." In any event, if the truth be known, he wasn't even happy about having the wedding in Ogdensburg.

Censure by his Church prevented Gallagher from having a Catholic sacramental ceremony. All Roman priests were forbidden to preside over his marriage, even if he could find one who was sympathetic to his cause. And it was rumored there were a few, but they could not risk a breach with their bishop. As an option, Richard could avail himself of a peace justice. Why, even O'Leary might oblige him, as he did for several others from St. James when no priest was available. But Gallagher feared making his marriage a spectacle for the local gossip mill. He had enough problems without inviting more talk. A civil ceremony would no doubt damage his standing within the Irish community, and even create a challenge to his leadership. He suspected a few stood ready behind the scenes to take his place.

The prospective bride knew all too well the ecclesiastical problems in which her intended was embroiled. Nearly everyone within the circumference of the Carthage mission, Catholic or Protestant, knew, or thought they knew, the whole scandalous St. James story. The newspapers had done their best to entertain their readers with the juicy details. But all this mattered little to Miss Masury for she was an Episcopalian, just as was her predecessor Maria Sherwood. Her English given name was the same as King William IV's consort queen.

But any thoughts Richard had about avoiding an Episcopal service were moot. Addie had her heart set on getting married in her family's church in her adopted town of Ogdensburg.

On May 12th, the entourage ventured north on the afternoon stage. The first leg took them to Antwerp and from there on to Ogdensburg. Hattie and Justus Chase would attend the couple as matron of honor and best man. Although disappointed that her wedding plans had been scaled back, Addie did not betray her chagrin to Richard.

When they arrived at Ogdensburg, a broadly smiling Dr. John Masury met Gallagher for the first time. He beamed as if he was about to conclude an important business deal. He was cordial and smooth and comported the look and dress of a prosperous personage. He had assessed his daughter's union from a completely practical point of view, and in light of the economics involved, deemed it a quite desirable coupling. He casually wondered if there might be an opportunity for a medicine stand in Carthage. Richard sized up his prospective father-in-law and could see the man had sold a thing or two in his time. It took one to know one, he conceded.

Dr. Masury made arrangements for the wedding ceremony with Pastor Harold Peters of St. John's Episcopal Church. The cleric knew his church was not Gallagher's first choice because tradition in most religions called for the woman to embrace her husband's faith. He didn't get many Irish Catholics coming to him for weddings, especially given their long history of resistance to conversion to the Church of England. He knew about the St. James troubles because Ogdensburg was not that far from the Carthage mission in Gouverneur, and people talked a lot.

The marriage took place on the next day, the third Monday of May, at eleven in the morning. The day and time was not the most popular choice for weddings, which underlined the notion of convenience. It was a small affair attended only by Addie's parents and siblings, along with Chase and Gallagher. Except for his immediate family, no one else from Carthage was even privy to his plans. Bickford's *Tribune* carried no mention of the impending nuptials and the only public notice appeared four days later in the weekly *Ogdensburg Advance.*

> MARRIAGE ANNOUNCEMENT - In this village on Monday morning, May 13, 1861, by Rev. H. R. Peters, St. John's Episcopal Church. Mr. RICHARD GALLAGHER, of Carthage, Jeff. Co., to Miss ADELAIDE MASURY, of this place.

A modest reception was held for the wedding party at a nearby hotel. Dr. Masury, his face aglow with the assurance his daughter had married well, rose to render a toast. "Here's to Richard and Addie, may they prosper and be happy."

After a few more toasts, followed by a light lunch, the wedding party boarded the 3:30 stage for the trip back to

Carthage. The new Mrs. Gallagher was now ready to take up permanent residence at Gallagher's State Street home.

A few days after the nuptials, when the story of the coupling had made the rounds in Carthage, George O'Leary ran into Gallagher and offered his congratulations. "What's with all this secrecy? Why no announcement in Bickford's paper?" he asked.

"'Tis of no concern," said Gallagher. "He only worries about Republican news anyway."

The staunch Republican O'Leary chortled at the jibe. He was surprised at the normally humorless Gallagher's attempt at whimsy. In fact, *The Carthage Tribune* would never mention the prominent village leader's wedding at all.

"Alice and I are going to throw a reception for you and the missus. Will that be okay?"

"I'll speak to Addie about it and let you know."

"Let me tell you what news is important here," O'Leary said, his visage turning serious. Due to a spate of burglaries in Carthage, his deputy sheriff duties were keeping him quite busy. His recent experiences put the lie to the notion anyone had about small towns and low crime rates.

"It's hard to believe," the Squire said, "but some rascal robbed Eli Horr's residence last night." Horr was one of Carthage's most wealthy and prominent businessmen. "He forced a window and grabbed some money, clothing, and nine timepieces. The loss is over $400."

"What the hell was he doing with nine watches?" Gallagher wondered. "I'm thinking you only need one to tell the time."

O'Leary couldn't help but chuckle yet again at his friend's attempt at humor. "Now, that's the kind of news that's important hereabouts!"

"What's the world coming to?" said Gallagher with a few more tsks.

"Lord only knows," Squire said. "Lord only knows."

CHAPTER 33

"Oh, this is quite lovely," Addie remarked at Alice O'Leary's reception for the Gallagher newlyweds. The bride was appreciative as the gala took a bit of the sting out of the paucity of publicity and the sparse wedding ceremony she endured in her adopted Ogdensburg.

"Did ya hear the bishop's comin'?" Jimmie Walsh said to Gallagher as they sipped punch off in a corner. Although the war consumed the headlines and was the leading village concern, St. James' dissidents were caught off guard when they heard Bishop McCloskey would be paying a visit to the area. "'Ee'll be here for Mass on the 30th, or so they say." The rumor further alleged he would be saying Mass at none other than the interdicted St. James Church. This intelligence caused quite a stir and many eagerly awaited the service. "Aye, maybe this'll be the end of the mess," he added.

"I don't know," said a pensive Gallagher. "I don't expect the bishop to be quite that easy."

When the appointed day arrived, parishioners of St. James found their church open but neither bishop nor priest was in residence. "McCloskey's saying Mass down at the farm I betcha," O'Leary speculated. This idea soon spread among the crowd and the Squire suggested, "We ought to form a troupe and go down there and meet with him."

The idea energized Patrick and James Walsh and they suggested the Squire lead the delegation. Both brothers had secretly pined for the opportunity to offer their personal contrition to the bishop and be absolved of their sins.

"It's worth a try," O'Leary said, "long as he's in the area, what would be the hurt?"

The council would not include Richard Gallagher, who declined to participate. "You're wasting your time. I'll not be a part of it."

By the time the group arrived at the Irish Settlement, the bishop's open-air Mass had ended. Over a hundred Clarke loyalists were in attendance. "You're not welcome here," the priest's allies shouted, but O'Leary stood his ground and insisted on an audience with McCloskey.

A discomfited Father Conroy told him, "The bishop's time is reserved today for people who have been loyal to him." And when the Squire persisted, he finally said, "Come back tomorrow."

Clarke, who was lurking in the background, smiled at the rebuff, pleased that his stance was finally being vindicated. The dissidents reluctantly agreed to return on Monday.

When the delegation sat down in the Clarke parlor the next day, they were greeted by an irritated and unsympathetic McCloskey. He fidgeted in his chair as he repeatedly fingered his crucifix. He listened impatiently as the group unapologetically broached the subject of getting another priest. "Father Clarke will not attend us," said O'Leary, "or when he does, he always comes late."

McCloskey, recoiling as though someone had stuck a pin in his cheek tartly replied, "You could have asked the Watertown priest to visit St. James."

O'Leary said the parish couldn't afford a priest from another mission because the cost of ten or fifteen dollars per visit was way too high.

McCloskey scoffed at this. "Isn't a priest worth at least that much to you?"

If the group had any hope the bishop would alter his position, such expectations soon evaporated. "I will not replace the priest you have driven from the sanctuary," he said bruskly. "You must listen to the teachings of our holy faith and submit to the laws of the Church." And then repeated his threat: "If you persist, you people will surely bring calamities down around your heads."

No amount of oratory from the glib O'Leary could sway the prelate. Those delegates who didn't live at the Settlement picked up their traces and headed back to town, dragging their dashed hopes behind them.

"I knew it was useless," Gallagher said after listening to the meeting report. But he generously refused to gloat.

On Independence Day, 1861, Judge Bickford's *Republican Tribune* felt compelled to report on the bishop's visit, without attribution. Gallagher speculated O'Leary had fed Bickford the details.

> The Rt. Rev. John McCloskey, R.C., Bishop of Albany, was in the vicinity on Saturday and Sunday last. A report was circulated that he would be at the Church in Carthage and preach, and the Church was opened for the purpose, and many of the people assembled.
>
> But after waiting some time it was reported that the Bishop would not visit the Church, but was to officiate at the house of William Clarke, brother to the priest. Some of those who came to church, expecting the Bishop to come, went to Mr. Clarke's house, and others who were before aware of the arrangement were also there.
>
> Mass was said and the Bishop made some remark, applicable to the difficulties which have for some time existed in the Church formerly worshipping in this village. The point of the Bishop's remarks, we are informed, was that the congregation must submit to the Priest, and acknowledge that they had done wrong in opposing him, should have no other Priest while he lived.
>
> We had hoped that whenever the Bishop came, these unfortunate difficulties, which have so long in this Church, to their own great injury, and that of the public, would be settled, and that peace would be restored among them.
>
> Those dissatisfied with the Priest, we understand, have asked for an investigation and have professed themselves ready to submit to whatever determination should be arrived at, on such investigation. But as the thing now stands, we judge the prospect of peace is more distant than ever. This we much regret, and without assuming to decide who is wrong, or who is right, we still think that community has a right to insist that whoever is in the wrong should cease the wrong, and do what should be done.

> If the bishop ought to investigate the complaints made, he is blamable for not doing so; and if the congregation ought to submit to what the Priest enjoins, without any appeal, they are blamable for their conduct.
>
> Meanwhile this large, wealthy, and respectable congregation are without the regular public worship of the Church in which they believe, and the community suffers much detriment in consequence.

Bickford showed no hesitancy in lecturing McCloskey with his "understanding" of the situation, and Gallagher had no quarrel with the prelate being taken to task in the press.

Of all the repentant parishioners, Patrick Walsh felt the rebuff most profoundly. His genuine contrition prompted him to make another attempt at repatriating himself with McCloskey. He wrote a letter to him expressing his sorrow and asking for forgiveness. Gallagher scoffed at the news of Patrick's intentions, an undertaking he felt would do no good. "The man's got a heart of stone," he said to Patrick's brother James. "Don't let him be making more of a fool of himself than he already has." But the repentant sinner was undeterred, and brother James privately applauded his effort.

> Dear Reverend Bishop McCloskey,
>
> After leaving your Lordship on last Monday I saw Mr. John Collins and made arrangements with him to call a meeting in the Church on next Sunday which is today and he was to send word round in his part of the town and I was to give them notice in the Irish Settlement. I did so and it was well understood that there was to be a meeting this morning at ten o'clock. I went there at that hour and there was but few there and the Church was closed. I called on Mr. Haberer and requested him to open the Church and he refused saying he did not recognize my authority to have the Church opened. I told him he heard the Bishops direction and wish and if he did not open the Church he must expect

> to assume the responsibility. He said he would be no worse than he was. I went to the Church prepared with the written resignation of myself and my Brother James of all offices in the Church which I herewith enclose to Your Lordship. My Lord you see the position in which I have placed myself for I blame no one and I hope you will see fit to remove the Censure pronounced against me and I solemnly promise never to interfear in Church matters again. My Lord please accept my thanks for your kind treatment to me last Monday and believe me to be your effectually Humbled Servent.
>
> Patrick Walsh

Patrick's written contrition was rebuffed as firmly as was the delegation's personal appeal, even though he had formally withdrawn from Gallagher's dissident camp. "There's a traitor in every group of apostles," Richard said with a voice betraying rising anger. "I wonder why I bother with these people." Filled with contrition, Patrick Walsh began actively campaigning for a counter-revolution.

Pastor Clarke, unable to expel the bitter taste of anarchy from his mouth, deemed Walsh's supplication inadequate. He effected the look of a wounded lamb as he reminded his flock, "Just as they did to Christ on the cross, they have heaped indignities on me, and believe me when I say the Church will require much more than a letter for forgiveness. They must suffer as I have." He also reminded them they should not patronize any of the businesses of the dissidents-especially Gallagher's furniture emporium. Even imperfect contrition, the usual requirement for Christian absolution, was not good enough, neither for Clarke nor the bishop, which some observers thought a bit unchristian.

The crestfallen and penitent Patrick Walsh knew not what it would take to move the bishop. His only option now was to ask God in his daily prayers to let His mercy flow down on him and his brother. And this he fervently did.

CHAPTER 34

"Oh, you think he's laid a curse on us, has he," Gallagher said with a smirk whenever people brought the subject up. More than a few suspicious Carthage folk began taking the prelate's latest threat of "further calamities" seriously.

The Walsh brothers had taken the warning to heart. "We shu'na dismiss this," they said.

Aunt Nancy remained resolute, saying it was "a lot of malarkey."

Just two weeks later, in the early morning hours of Sunday, the 15th of July, Carthage again heard the clanging of fire bells. Gallagher hurriedly dressed and went outside to look towards downtown. He saw a faint glow emanating from the direction of lower State Street. "Jesus," he exclaimed in a low voice, "not another fire!" He was soon urging his steed downtown to investigate.

Firefighting in Carthage had remained as primitive as before, causing Gallagher to be gripped with anticipation whenever the alarm bells rang. And once a fire started, more often than not, it burned until there was nothing left but ashes. During the winter months, weekends proved to be most perilous since businesses were shuttered from closing Saturday evening until reopening Monday morning. Because it was now the middle of summer, everyone wondered what could possibly have started a fire.

Carthage's business section, like most small towns, had buildings that were primarily constructed of wood, the most abundant and economically available raw material. The nearby forests provided seemingly endless supplies of pine and spruce so there was no compelling reason to use the more expensive brick or stone. As a result, whenever a fire started, its flames had a banquet of timber upon which to feast.

In the wee hours of that fateful Sabbath day, a fire had started in Walsh's grocery store directly across the street from Gallagher's furniture business. Walsh's block, which housed the popular music hall, was sandwiched between the Baptist Church and Brown's Hotel.

When finally discovered, the fire had spread to Walsh's neighbors, setting both of those buildings ablaze. The flames consumed the structures as if they were kindling. Its appetite was not satisfied with just those three buildings and tongues of flame licked at other storefronts on the same side of the street. They too were soon ablaze.

The inferno belched thick acrid smoke that made it next to impossible to see across the street. Horr & Hooker's store was next to ignite. It was followed by Guyot's building, which also housed the post office and a large meeting room for the Disciples religious denomination. The blaze soon reached enormous proportions and began sending incandescent plumes across the smoke-filled street to threaten the Gallagher block and his neighbors. The furniture store, undertaker's parlor, law offices, and *The Republican Tribune's* printing facilities were all now in jeopardy.

The blaze illuminated the nighttime sky and could be seen twelve miles away, causing many observers to rush to the scene to see if they could help. Soon, bucket brigades stretched all the way down State Street to the river as an engaged citizenry pitched in to help.

Gallagher arrived in time to hear the Baptist Church's bell toll for the last time as it fell to its death into the ashes of its former home. It was a depressing death rattle for the instrument, which had been installed only five months prior.

As the coughing Richard joined the bucket brigade, he had good reason to worry his block would be next to go. But two factors joined forces to help save his building. The first was the weather with its shifting winds and intermittent rain showers. Just when it appeared the capricious flames had crossed the street to envelop his structure, the wind changed or a sheet of water came down to dampen the flames' enthusiasm.

The second factor was Gallagher's insistence that the lower floor of his new block use brick facing, one of the few so constructed in Carthage. With the exception of the wood trim and cornices, it provided an excellent barrier against the fire.

Across the street, everything from O'Leary's building to the corner at Mechanic Street was ablaze. The fire, as Gallagher had forecast, overwhelmed the underequipped fire department's ability to contain it. The inferior equipment did not deter the men, however. The horses had quickly dragged their 20 year-old pumper to the site from the Church Street station only a block away. The blaze, already out of control, prevented the firemen from driving their team down State Street to the Black River. Instead they had to run their hoses eastward to the cistern at the corner of School Street. With connections finally in place, six husky volunteers took up positions on either side of the pumper and with great effort alternately pushed the bars up and down, forcing water through the antiquated tubing and on to the fire. But, as predicted, they proved no match for the blaze. The small diameter hoses leaked at every joint and, in addition, the 400 barrel cistern was soon exhausted. The fatigued firemen, with their hands calloused and bleeding, gave up the futile exercise and joined the bucket brigade.

"Poor bastards don't have a chance," Richard muttered. "I hope nobody's died because of this." He could only shake his head as he surveyed the charred scene.

When the fire finally consumed itself five hours later, Gallagher's block was intact even though the heat cracked every window and the drapery inside had caught fire. The wood-sided upper floors, although blackened by smoke, survived relatively unscathed. The furniture store suffered only $500 in damages, which was covered by insurance.

Squire O'Leary was another of the lucky ones, and he thanked the Lord for his good fortune as he surveyed the collapsed hulks of neighboring buildings. Why he was spared, he did not know.

When the damage was totaled, twenty-four buildings had been consumed-two stores, nine dwellings, and three sheds and out buildings. Total losses were estimated at $60,000, with only 50% covered by insurance. The business casualties, besides the grocery store and hotel, included two places of worship, a drug store, hardware store, two clothing stores, a blacksmith shop, and a carriage manufactory.

Grocer Walsh, in whose building the fire originated, was also a resident of the demised Brown's Hotel. He, along with twenty-two other merchants and craftsmen were permanent guests there and would now have to find new living quarters. Carthage's sparse housing market had in effect converted the hotel into a large boarding house. Thus, including the six lost residences, over forty Carthaginians would have to find new lodgings.

Some of the more superstitious St. James parishioners began whispering aloud that this calamity was caused by Bishop McClosky's Curse. "Poppycock!" Gallagher protested whenever someone mentioned this.

Just two days after the fire, at 9 o'clock in the evening, as if to reinforce notions about the supernatural at work, Carthage was treated to the rare occurrence of an earthquake. The area was not known for such phenomena but the rumbling noise, along with a good dose of window and crockery rattling, caused many to wonder anew if McCloskey's Curse was indeed behind it all. News reports later said the temblor was felt as far away as Canada to the north and in Utica some 70 miles to the southeast.

Patrick Walsh, who had taken up nervously fingering his omni-present rosary beads, said yet again, "'Tis the bishop's curse. I know that it is."

Gallagher said he hoped the temblor was felt in Albany. "Perhaps it might wake them up."

Father Clarke couldn't help but smile when news of the fire was given to him upon his return from the Sterlingville mission. "And what happened to those apostates Gallagher and O'Leary?" he inquired. When told they had escaped the wrath of God, he had difficulty hiding his disappointment.

"But one of the Walsh brothers lost his shoemaker's shop," the informer said.

"God punishes those who flaunt the Church's authority," the priest said to the faithful who gathered at his brother's farm the following Sunday. "The hand of divine retribution has visited the village."His sermon seized the opportunity to reinforce that obedience to the Church was required to stave off further disasters. He immediately sat down to write to his bishop with the news.

> Just as you warned, the miscreants of this parish suffered a huge calamity as a fire punished many, although the rebellious Gallagher and his allie O'Leary escaped this time. Many properties were destroyed and a great punishment has been levied upon their heads.

The bishop nodded in agreement after reading the priest's note that Conroy laid on his desk. "Disobedience will not go unpunished," he solemnly said. This latest news vindicated his position and served to harden his resolve to continue the course he had chosen-pressing his advantage and accepting naught but full capitulation to the Church.

Chapter 35

"We'll survive this," Gallagher said somberly to all who came by to survey the damage. "It's got nothing to do with any goddamned curse. That's the kind of shite they'd like us to believe."

As Carthage nursed its wounds, craftsmen came from as far away as Rome, New York and beyond to help rebuild the business section. Clearing away the debris commenced as soon as the embers had cooled, and less than two months later, R. R. Brown laid the cornerstone for a bigger and better hotel. A ceremony was held for the insertion of artifacts in the front brickwork of the new hostelry. At the dedication the pastor of the demised Baptist Church said, "This will allow future generations to remember what took place here." The villagers had contributed coins and other small articles to be interred along with an issue of *The Republican* that described the great fire. They hoped the time capsule would be uncovered by some future generation of Carthaginians to resurrect a forgotten chapter in the town's history.

"In its own way, the fire is but a blessing in disguise," said Gallagher as he watched the construction of larger and more elegant buildings rise across the street from his store. The new construction was mainly using bricks, as the lesson from the survival of Gallagher's block was taken to heart.

The disaster would also effect an emotional change in the minds of many. The noticeable renewal of civic vigor reaffirmed in Gallagher's mind that the village of Carthage had nowhere to go but up-the very idea he had prophesied to Bishop McCloskey many times before.

The village fathers, now imbued with renewed resolve to make the village safer, pushed through the required tax assessment to purchase more modern firefighting equipment. "It's about damn time," Gallagher said.

Construction proceeded apace and only three buildings did not rise from the ashes by year end. O'Leary said

Longfellow aptly put it when he wrote, "Noble souls, through dust and heat, rise from disaster and defeat the stronger."

The news of the Civil War continued to march into Carthage, unrestrained either by fire or church quarrel. Now several months old, the battlefields exhibited an enormous appetite for the blood of its countrymen, on both sides of the divide. Among the war reports reaching the village was news about a recent battle that took place near a town called Carthage in Missouri. *The Carthage Republican*, seizing on local interest due to the identical names, labeled this outcome a "glorious victory" for the Union. The combat had begun in another town in close proximity called Boonville (also a nearby New York State town), and the Union forces under the command of German immigrant Col. Franz Sigel,* were driven into retreat. But bulletins about who was gaining the upper hand, as always, depended largely on which side was doing the reporting. Various newspapers used opposing battle dispatches that were often in disagreement.

The reason for the battle centered on a division among the people of Missouri between the pro- and anti-slavery forces, similar to the division in New York's Carthage between the pro- and anti-Clarke factions. As was shown in the battle for the hearts and minds of Missourians, which faction was seen as winning, influenced the opinions of the undecided, all of whom would prefer to be on the victorious side.

As the Church battle in Carthage reached for a climax, several Protestant villagers began taking sides and criticizing the Catholic Church. Father Clarke saw this as an opportunity for his sermons. "Those who cast their lot with the renegades are aligning themselves with those Reformationist devils. It's all part of the Protestant plot to interfere in the Church's affairs." The priest, well-schooled in antipathy for Protestant precepts, was perhaps too eager to frame the dispute in those terms. The specter of a Protestant threat was never far from the Church's collective mind, and Clarke knew any such interference would harden Bishop McCloskey's position.

As summer turned to fall, Catholics adroitly tried to balance their concerns about war, rebuilding the village, and the church problem. "We really need a priest," was the parishioners' continued lament, one Gallagher had heard so many times he'd lost count.

"I know, I know," he replied with exasperation because the subject never failed to both frustrate and renew his concern. He knew everyone who tried to intercede with the bishop on their behalf had failed. "Hell, even the Squire couldn't talk our way out of this, so who can?" he observed.

Despair crept into the renegade ranks and disputes arose among them. This made it more difficult to agree on whether further entreaties should even be made to the bishop, or if they should just give up. Some said they should form their own Church, an idea Gallagher dismissed as pure folly.

One fall day, as Richard was supervising the refurbishing of his store, a man in a priest's or monk's garb approached him. "Are you Mr. Gallagher, the head trustee of St. James?" the robed man asked. Richard, cocked his head, squinted, and looked with wary eye at the tall, muscular man. He noticed the stranger's speech tumbled out in a heavy brogue complete with rolled arrs, an accent the stranger didn't try to disguise. Gallagher couldn't place the native tongue exactly, which seemed to encompass more than one dialect.

The bearded man brushed back the cowl on his cloak to reveal a growth of long reddish-brown hair that didn't quite match his variegated beard. "I'm Father O'Connor, Father Sean O'Connor," he said with a wide grin while extending his hand, which Gallagher hesitantly shook. "I'm passin' through from out west, and I hear youse be need'n a priest."

"Oh, and where might you have heard that?" Gallagher asked.

"'Tis fairly well talked about what's 'appened 'ere. I've even 'eard the bishop is now regrettin' what's gone on in this parish. But, ya know how 'tis. Sometimes those from the city di'not know about life here in the wilderness."

"Aye, that's for sure. And you have experience in the wilderness?"

"Aye, do. I know you people be needin' a priest, and I di'not have an assignment at the moment so I 'ave come to see if I can help."

Gallagher gave a second, more thorough look at this rough-hewn specimen who certainly looked like one used to life on the outer edges of civilization. "So, you'd be available to minister here?"

"I'm 'ere ta help any way I can. I know the souls of this parish ahrr in sore need of the sacraments so I coulda make myself available. 'Tis bandied about many 'ere are in danger of fallin' away if Catholic services aren't performed soon."

"That's the truth," Richard replied. "And many have left already."After asking several more questions, he said, "Let me discuss this with the other trustees."

Gallagher knew all too well several St. James parishioners had begun attending Protestant services. Most went to the Episcopal Church where his new wife Adelaide worshipped. On occasion he also went there, just to please her. He briefly reflected on how he had to be married by an Episcopal priest, and it wasn't a happy memory for him. He wouldn't forgive Clarke or McCloskey for that. Yes indeed, something has to be done, he agreed.

Gallagher gathered the trustees in the church to have them listen to what the stranger-priest had to offer. After Father O'Connor finished, he was asked to wait outside while the church elders caucused. Gallagher began, "I just met this priest yesterday. You heard what he had to say. He wants $500 a year to run the parish." Richard also mentioned that Father O'Connor had reported that the hierarchy in Albany was worried "we'd all become Protestants."

The trustees grappled with hiring of this priest in their usual manner, with the discussion focusing on the demanded salary of $500. They saw that this clergyman presented an opportunity to put one over on Clarke and their bishop. Of course, itinerant priests with no diocesan affiliation were not unknown in the outback, but the timing of this appearance was seen as a gift from heaven. Could their luck, which had definitely been running south, be about to change?

“Why don’t we give him a try,” said Patrick and James Walsh eagerly. They were the most desperate to get back in God's good graces.

“Do you think he’d take any less?” Ed Galvin asked. "Remember we told the bishop we couldn't afford $10 visits by a priest. How can we afford it now?"

“He says he'll do with naught less than $500,” Gallagher replied.

"But he'd be here all the time for catechism, weddings and funerals," said Patrick.

Desperation trumped business judgment as the men reluctantly agrèed to the fee. Under normal circumstances the cost might have been negotiated down to $350 or at most $400. A smiling Father O’Connor was waiting outside and readily agreed when Gallagher offered him the job. A hearty handshake sealed the agreement. There would be Mass on the following Sunday and every Sunday thereafter. "We've no parish house for you," Gallagher said.

"Not'ta worry. I've a room at the Essex House till I find a permanent place," said Father Sean.

Happiness descended upon St. James parish. There would be no sharing this priest. Father Sean O'Connor would be "their very own!"

CHAPTER 36

"We've got a new priest!" was the news soon being passed around to the St. James faithful. It sounded too good to be true. "'Tis excitin' news indeed," everyone agreed. When Sunday rolled around, the interdicted church was opened well in advance to let the spiritually starved Catholics in to attend Mass. This was what they wanted and needed, and the diocese be damned.

The church was soon more than half filled with smiling parishioners. Gallagher arrived trailing four of his children, clad in their Sunday best. Baby Richard Sherwood Gallagher, and his four-year-old sister Isabella, remained at home with their step-mother. "Reminds me of the first Sunday that rascal Clarke arrived," he offhandedly mentioned to Aunt Nancy.

"Nay, 'tis much better than that," she airily answered, marching up to her usual front row pew.

Pastor Clarke's allies, dismayed at this turn of events, sent him the news via messenger to Copenhagen, where he was ministering. The pastor reportedly released a vituperative monologue that included some "hard language." He hurried back to Carthage, worried that some of his faithful might be tempted to attend the interdicted church. Supporters were told to spread the word that Pastor Clarke would be saying Mass on Sunday at the mansion on Tannery Island. Having two Masses on the same day with two different celebrants in Carthage would indeed be historic. It was a far cry from the usual month or two, a situation to which the Catholics of Carthage had reluctantly become accustomed.

Nine months had passed since services were held at St. James and the apprehensive attendees sat quietly to await the new priest's entrance. The ebullient Father O'Connor briskly entered through the since repaired vestry door and approached the altar to begin the service. The vestments were too small for the large framed man and the tight-fitting alb caused him to shimmy as he walked. The celebrant seemed tentative at first, stumbling over the opening prayers, and more than a few parishioners looked at each other in puzzlement. Gallagher thought the priest slurred over the Confiteor but passed it off as nervousness.

As the Mass wore on, Father O'Connor became acclimated to his new surroundings and found a pace in harmony with the ritual. When he genuflected, he struggled to rise because his knee was restricted by the snug vestments. His sermon rambled a bit as he repeated the statements he made to the trustees only a few days before. "All will be well in the confines of this 'ere parish soon," he said, and the attendees breathed a collective sigh of relief.

The altar boys glanced at each other as Father O'Connor bade them to empty the cruet of altar wine into the chalice at the consecration. The priest gulped the spirits, which he seemed to overly enjoy. "Father likes drinkin' Christ's blood," one boy whispered to the other with a chuckle.

"Just call me Father Sean," he said after Mass while shaking hands with those who insisted on more formal address. Many Settlement residents invited the new pastor to their homes to share a meal, and made sure to invite him to their next Saturday night soiree. The priest seemed delighted and said he'd be sure to make it.

As he walked down the boards to the street, Richard said to the Squire, "He's a bit rough around the edges, don't ya think?"

"Perhaps, but knockin' around in the wilderness will do that to a man," O'Leary replied. "Just look at us!" And both men laughed.

The dissident Catholics of Carthage were generally upbeat throughout the week. No one was more delighted than Patrick Walsh, who was positively giddy he could again receive the cherished sacraments. Also, marriages and baptisms could be planned, along with the consecration of burial sites. The long absent cloud of happiness reappeared and hovered over the parish.

When Saturday came, the Irish Settlement rose early to prepare for its final week-ending bash of the season. The area was experiencing Indian Summer, a welcome period after the first killing frost when the weather turns unseasonably warm in a last ditch effort to stave off the long winter ahead. The growing season had been over for a month, with potatoes and cabbages long since clutched from the fields. The women busily prepared traditional Irish stew for the feast along with soda bread and potato scones. The town butcher, Reed Crook, and his apprentice Simeon Ingraham, had delivered sides of beef and pork that were soon turning on spits. Tables were set up, kegs of beer put in place and at five o'clock people started gathering to begin the festivities in earnest.

"Aye, here comes the priest," a young lad hollered. Sure enough, one of the earliest arrivals was none other than the robed Father Sean. The crowd was swelled by several non-Settlement residents who, upon hearing the priest would be there, decided to join the soiree. Squire O'Leary brought along his boarder, the apprentice shoemaker Charles Doherty. He tried to persuade Gallagher to attend, to no avail.

After looking over the vittles laid out on the tables before him, the Squire felt impelled to recite a couplet from an old Irish poem. As he filled his plate he sang out loudly,

Then hurrah for an Irish Stew
That will stick to your belly like glue.

A roar of laughter greeted the Squire's jocularity, serving to cap the cheerful mood that was greatly enhanced by the new priest's appearance. And Father Sean fit right in as he downed his first draught of beer and piled copious amounts of beef and potatoes onto his plate. He accompanied his victuals each time with another large mug of beer. "He's got a healthy appetite," said Patrick Walsh, and everyone agreed this man was far different from Father Clarke, whose stern and pious demeanor always seemed to get in the way of having a good time. Observers also noticed Father Sean's actions were unrestrained by any need for an appearance of solemnity. Why, he didn't even insist on saying grace before diving into the sumptuous spread set before him. "All in all, a very likeable chap," said Patrick. He offered the priest a nip or two from the pint he kept in his coat pocket, which the priest gladly accepted. "Yessir, a likeable chap," he said again.

After the eating round of the feast was over, two men took up fiddle and pipe and launched into a series of familiar Irish ditties. This prompted couples to rise and begin dancing around the Settlement green. Their gyrations were accompanied by lots of shouting, clapping and stomping of feet.

As the evening wore on, the beer flowed unabated, and more than a few of the imbibers became tipsy. The older generation began drifting back to their homes or heading back to town. They were anxious for a good night's sleep in order to be rested and ready for Mass in the morning.

Tradition at the Settlement held that as long as there was beer, the young bucks would remain drinking until it was all gone. There would be dares and double-dares as to who could drink the most, or who could balance a mug on his head the longest, and other such juvenile tomfoolery.

Father Sean chose to remain with the younger lads, while chugging on his tankard. The liquid often dribbled down his chin and onto his tunic, leaving a trail of foam that turned his beard white, which he promptly wiped off with the sleeve of his robe. The burly priest seemed unusually at ease and was eager to join in when the wrestling started. The husky farm lads, unused to physical familiarity with a man of the cloth, were hesitant. But Father Sean insisted, and at his first lunge slipped and fell, ending up splayed on the ground. A few boys couldn't help but snicker while most admirably restrained themselves. When one of the lads tried to help the priest up, he brushed him aside while muttering a curse. The startled young man recoiled because he'd never heard a priest cuss before-nor seen one drunk for that matter. The boys were stunned into silence.

"Wat'cha lookin' at?" Father Sean bellowed. "I can 'andle any one of 'ya! I di'not spend all those years in the bloody British army for nothin'. They could'na best me there and neither can youse. I'll take on every bloody one of 'ya!"

After a stunned but short silence, one boy shouted, "In the army? What's a priest doing in the army? But ain't youse a priest?"

"Nah, I ain't no bloody priest," he slurred with a sneer, followed by an uproarious laugh. "Come on now, who wants to be next?"

"He ain't no priest," one of the boys said in astonishment. And after the statement sank in, he shouted, "Let's get 'im!"

The crowd, which had dwindled to fewer than a dozen, surged and fell on the would-be wrestler, pummeling and kicking him before an older lad intervened. "Let 'im be! We di'not wanna' kill 'im!"

The beaten and bloodied ex-Father Sean was then lifted up and taken to his horse. Once mounted, one of the boys gave the animal a slap on a hindquarter, and the steed galloped off into the night. "We'd best not see youse roun' 'ere again," they shouted as the priest, clinging to his animal's neck, disappeared into the darkness.

"This'll be worth wakin' up the old folks fer," shouted one lad as he hurried home. The incident had a sobering effect on the remaining boys, and many of them ran off to wake their elders and tell them what had transpired.

This Sunday, so anxiously anticipated by the St. James parish, would not be a Sabbath with a glorious celebration of Mass, but one that would set tongues wagging like never before. The melee in church the previous December might pale by comparison.

CHAPTER 37

Who can that be knocking on my door at this hour? Richard Gallagher was halfway up the stairs, on his way to bed, when he heard the loud rap, rap, rap on his front door. He tugged on his watch fob and pulled his timepiece from his vest pocket to see it was five past eleven, which only made him wonder all the more who could be calling. He ambled back down the steps and opened the door to find Ed Galvin standing before him. His face had splotches of worry splayed across it as he pushed his way inside without waiting for an invitation. "You've been duped, you've been duped!" he announced.

"I've been duped? What the hell are you talking about?"

While still standing in the hallway, Galvin struggled to right his spectacles which had come askew in his haste to dismount his carriage and climb the steps to Gallagher's door. He breathlessly proceeded to relate the Settlement's goings on, just as he had heard them from one of the boys.

As Richard listened to the lurid details, his face contorted in anger and he repeatedly pounded his fist into his palm. "Damn, damn," he muttered, chagrinned and embarrassed beyond description. He finally seethed, "They shoulda' killed the bastard. I knew there was something funny about that chap! I just knew it! Father O'Connor indeed. I should have listened to meself."

The shame of being duped, when it finally struck him, was compounded by the fact they had all participated in a bogus "black Mass"* on Sunday last. Why they even received communion from the blackguard. "Sacrilege! Lordy, lordy, they'll have fun with this in Albany," he said as he tried to think of what to do next. "Let me ponder this," Richard said as he ushered his visitor out with a curt goodnight. While ascending the steps anew he realized he'd have no choice but to go down to the church on the morrow and face the people.

A way would have to be found to mitigate the damage this scandal would have on their cause. And he wasn't hopeful.

When he reached his bedroom, Addie, awakened by the noisy voices from below, was sitting upright. Seeing Richard's worried expression, she pressed him to tell what had happened. "'Tis a mess," was all he could say over and over. He related the story as he knew it and said they both should try to get some sleep, an effort that would prove to be only sporadically successful for the agitated Gallagher.

The dawn broke rather forebodingly over the village that September Sunday morning. The sky was filled with gray-black cloud slivers that menacingly crept from horizon to horizon. Most of St. James parishioners would arrive at church unaware of the previous night's doings at the Irish Settlement. When the story about the pseudo-priest who had smoothly bamboozled them circulated among the faithful, their brimming smiles 'neath their bonnets and hats soon transformed to drooping frowns. They buzzed about outside the church as the lurid details passed from ear to ear.

"The fella wot called 'imself Father O'Connor got drunk. Imagine that!" said Aunt Nancy. "The byes beat 'im good when they discovered he weren't no priest but an army deserter! And British at that!"

"Will there be no end to this affair?" her brother Patrick moaned. And it wasn't long before the whole town was again gossiping about the Catholics and their troubles.

J. T. Walsh reported the impostor priest had vacated the Essex Hotel, where he himself had lodged since the great fire. "He was gone at the crack of dawn. Skipped out, they say."

Father Clarke's loyalists crowed uncontrollably when they got wind of this latest *cause célèbre*. The priest's brother William would be among the first to give him the news of the symbolic defrocking when he next arrived back at the farm. He relished relating his version of the story, emphasizing the beating the impostor was given. The priest's normally dour countenance was soon grinning in appreciation of this turn of events. He went to his room, opened his hutch and immediately wrote a report of the affair to his bishop. He began with the rather optimistic assessment that his faction was gaining the upper hand in the ongoing conflict. His supporters were demanding the dissidents turn over the key to the church, a subject he'd sought legal advice about from a Watertown lawyer.

> I intend to see you before long and I am sure with regard to Carthage, I think there is a better appearance at present than there has been for some time. The people are very uneasy and unhappy about their Church & I think that it will be given over to them before long. I hear many rumors about the Key asking me what right has such a man [Gallagher] with our Key. I tell them I have nothing to say on the matter. I can see evidently great trouble. [Patrick] Walsh called on Mr. Wynn [a Watertown attorney] lately for advice about opening the church, and it appeared then that if it were necessary that the door would be forced in and take possession and keep it for the people and then give it over to you. Mr. Wynn told me this only yesterday on my way from the North. We conferred together and I told him to write to you for advice. Those few bad men had a suspended Priest amongst them for a while offering him five hundred dollars per year. He was very witty he said you were very sorry for what you had done at Carthage & would soon revoke the sentence. That you sent him to examine the whole matter and he found them innocent, etc. He received a few dollars and decamped. His name H. H. McDonough here & Father O'Connor in other places, to be certain who he was, I cannot tell. He got drunk on their hands and told that he was a British deserter. They are now very still. Any directions that you may have to give me regarding the opening the Church I will wait for it. Still I think it well to let them work for a while amongst themselves...

For the contrite Patrick Walsh, this embarrassing affair was the last straw. He was fifty-seven and feeling a bit unwell and was again ready to openly defy Gallagher and the other trustees. Life on the farm was hard and, and not knowing how much time he had left, was fearful of dying outside the Church's good graces. He made no secret of his wish to get right with his God. And the only way he knew to do this was through the Church.

His brother James's mindset was not far behind and he re-committed to the same objective. Given the entrenched defiance of Gallagher, the penitent Patrick now saw himself cast in the role of a savior, the one who would "keep the people of Carthage from going to Hell." Deftly disregarding his past performance as a rebel instigator, and ignoring the recent rebuff he received at the hands of his bishop, Patrick consulted a lawyer as to the legality of forcing the church open. He reckoned leading the charge to reclaim the church in the name of the diocese would be an act of penance McCloskey would have to acknowledge. He would have no further discussions with Gallagher because they had now become enemies.

Family bonds and lifelong friendships were now being tested as never before. Aunt Nancy refused to speak to Patrick and his red-faced brother, James, even cussing them out and saying they should act like men. "I di'not know we had Judases in the family," she sputtered in disgust.

The wounds from this battle were cutting deeper and deeper, causing many to believe they could never heal. The St. James landscape now resembled a war zone, not unlike the battlefields further south where the shooting war was being hotly waged. The bloodshed in Carthage, although symbolic, was hemorrhaging from the souls of the combatants.

CHAPTER 38

"I'll settle for nothing less," boomed Gallagher in answer to those who sought to find out what it would take to make peace with the Church. The only way to right this dispute in his mind, and on his tongue, was for Pastor Clarke to slink off into the night, just as the fake Father O'Connor had. The years of dispute had colored his character in ways some friends found alien. He was one of those people with whom you invariably knew where you stood. But he now was showing a stubbornness even Squire O'Leary said was a bit over the top. He wasn't ready to back down, even in the face of lost business. "I don't give a damn if they don't shop here!" he said to his worried salesmen.

Gallagher, as a businessman-politician, necessarily went out of his way to have cordial relations with prospective customers and potential voters. He couldn't help but notice foot traffic at his store was declining. Other cabinetmakers and furniture stores in the village also took notice and lurked in the background ready to fill any void.

"I haven't seen the required penance," Father Clarke remarked to those who questioned the wisdom of continuing the war. "That blackguard Gallagher will pay, and pay publicly, for his sins." To the priest, the slights he endured left marks no less injurious than if he'd been flogged on the path to Calvary. "The man deserves to be whipped, or at least put in the stocks, on the corner of State and Mechanic," he said during one of his tirades. He was not inclined to turn the other cheek, and more than willing to let his detractors stew in their own juices for as long as it took to pay for the indignities he had suffered.

But problems elsewhere in the pastor's mission began cropping up. People in Redwood also filed letters of recrimination with the bishop, and the priest was forced to respond to each allegation. Of course, as the injured party in the dispute, Clarke was unwilling to accept any blame for the alleged misdeeds, no matter from where they came. It was obvious to him the responsibility for any discontent lay at the door of his nemesis Gallagher. He saw his nefarious hand behind everything that had gone wrong, even in the outlying missions. The complainant from Redwood had to be a rabble-rouser in the employ of the conniving furniture dealer.

> In reply to your favour which came to hand today, asking the truth of a statement made in a letter from a Redwood correspondent, I beg to say that I have taken one Sunday from all the old Churches, that I might thereby be enabled to pay the indebtedness of the New, which I have accomplished sometime ago. Furthermore, I refused to attend funerals unless they occurred whilst I was in the place. Perhaps this might be the great sin with Mr. Gallagher's influence who has a Dept Chair Seller in that place. I remember that Mr. Tass came for me to attend the funeral of a near relative of his, whilst I was engaged in duty at Montague, and I refused him and he left indignant. ...

Bishop McCloskey shook his head as he read Clarke's latest letter. Conroy took the opportunity to quote aloud the pastor's admission that he refused people the rite of Christian burial. "He's gone a bit far, don't you think, Your Eminence? For sure his priorities are confused."

The bishop ignored the needling, but did notice such jabs had lately been increasing in frequency. McCloskey's, greatest priority was destroying the trustee system, and defending his priests in their relentless pursuit of this goal. "We must do all we can to achieve the end result."

***

"What's happened, my dear?" Richard asked with alarm when arriving home to find Addie in tears.

"I've just received word that Willie and Georgie have enlisted in the Army along with Johnny," she said tearfully.

“The youngest want to be drummer boys.” Even though the brothers she spoke of were but thirteen, fifteen and eighteen years of age respectively, they had decided to join the war effort. Patriotic fervor was as high in Ogdensburg as it was in Carthage, perhaps even higher. “But they’re so young!” she sobbed. "This is all because of my father." Dr. John Masury often proudly spoke of his service as a bandmaster for the British during the War of 1812. "They want to prove to Father they can follow in his footsteps. They think this will be a glamorous adventure,” Addie sobbed.

Richard went over to the divan and sat next to his bride, placing his arm about her shoulders and drawing her close. “They may be right. Drummer boys aren’t really in any danger, or so I’ve heard.” But his attempts at assuaging his wife's concerns went for naught.

Richard wasn't being completely frank with Addie because he wanted to spare her feelings. Anyone who followed the war, as he most avidly did, knew how it was being fought and would have reason to worry, even about drummer boys. The bulletins and dispatches gave a fairly unvarnished perspective of the dangers faced by men and boys alike.

“They’re like mascots for the older troops,” Richard dissembled as he continued trying to comfort his wife. This statement contained a kernel of truth, of course, for they were treated like mascots, but that wasn't the whole story. All too often drummer boys found themselves in the line of fire, and when more guns were needed on the line, the youngsters were pressed into service and shouldered rifles just like regular troops. It wasn't something that Addie needed to know.

As the days and weeks passed, and the calendar crept into the Northern New York winter, the grim realities of the Civil War dominated center stage. Young men were forced to contemplate the prospect of dying for one’s country in its more sanguinary and less heroic light. Carthage's inclination to parade and shout slogans was being dampened by the flow of battlefield blood on both sides.

Recruitment in Jefferson County continued unabated, but after the initial rush to "save the Union" subsided, a number of eager recruits found military service not to their liking and deserted. Faced with providing more fodder for the hungry cannons, Lincoln talked of imposing national conscription, an idea greeted with universal derision. Many believed it an infringement on free will-considered a democratic as well as theological principle. It was commonly believed volunteer soldiers were better fighting men than the conscripted variety. Drafting fighters would "undercut morale" many said, and comrades in arms would despise them.

The desertion rate soon climbed to 10% and showed little sign of abatement. Some men fled after less than 24 hours-mustered in one day, gone the next. Madison Barracks, the closest military base to Carthage was at Sackets Harbor, New York, where the Black River emptied into Lake Ontario. Canada lay just one mile across the bay, close enough to tempt those with thoughts of desertion. Three brothers of a Carthage family had enlisted, but within a month two had deserted and were never heard from again. It was assumed they made it to Canada or perished in the attempt. *The Carthage Tribune* failed to mention any of these infamous acts.

Although Lincoln's supporters claimed the North was uniformly supportive of the war, the reportage seemed to indicate otherwise. The "seceshers," as Bickford's *Tribune* called them, prowled about the landscape trying to generate opposition to Lincoln's plans. Questioning of these policies in print caused some newspapers to be banned from the mails as "traitorous" and "disloyal." Lincoln's Postmaster singled out *The Freeman's Journal*, the *Day Book, The New York Daily News,* and *The Journal of Commerce* for censure.

As Bickford gleefully reported in his paper:

> Those seceshers in Carthage will no longer be able to receive these treasonous papers. Uncle Sam has concluded he should no longer carry these papers that try to ruin him."

That a newspaper publisher would applaud this action puzzled Gallagher. "The free press has its limits," Bickford answered when the question was posed to him.

"Seems this is more than a limit," Gallagher replied. "I thought the Constitution supported free speech." He especially took issue with the ban when he found he could no longer receive his *Freeman's Journal.*

Bickford's editorial positions, although he would strongly deny it, had come under the influence of his ministerial background. Moralist themes leaked into his reportage, as evidenced by his explicit approval of the mob of women who stormed a house of ill repute in West Carthage, giving both men and women found there a merciless beating. He ignored the opportunity to condemn such vigilante justice.

On the other hand, as Gallagher noted, the editor wasn't above taking a "bribe" now and then. Merchants dropped off samples of their wares to his offices for which they expected, and received, a plug in Bickford's columns. He recently reported "J. T. Walsh has received a shipment of fine cigars, $1 for a hundred," after the merchant wisely delivered a box of same to *The Tribune* offices.

Because of the war, and despite an occasional item in the local paper, the problems at St. James receded to the background. The Church dispute would not totally disappear, however, and it would rear its ugly head again when the imposed interdict entered its second year.

CHAPTER 39

"There's enough animosity to go around," Father Conroy said, "without our adding to it." The vicar general had made it his mission to persuade Bishop McCloskey the dispute had gone on far too long. "Some are saying we at the chancery lack the Christian charity to forgive as Christ would have directed."

McCloskey was visibly stung by the sharpness of this jab and looked malignantly at his aide, as if ready to reprove him. Insubordination aroused feelings he could not suppress and caused a reflection on his reputation as a humble, devout and exemplary Christian. He was at pains to understand Conroy's assault. *Am I being openly challenged?* he wondered. *Do not I pray at every opportunity? Do not I say Mass and administer the sacraments as often as my duties allow?* He suspected Conroy's ambition was behind these comments, yet was forced to consider whether his contempt for the trustee system had actually colored his judgment. After a short contemplation, he concluded it had not.

Even though he knew his bishop as well as anyone, Conroy was navigating in dangerous waters. *His Eminence is just as stubborn as that man Gallagher, and that fool priest in Carthage is worse than either of them,* he mused. He sincerely believed that after eighteen months it was time to call a truce, get this problem out of the papers, and most importantly, the people back in Church at Carthage. Other clerics in the diocese also subscribed to this sentiment, one they felt had taken far too long to reach.

Father Clarke mulishly continued trying to prove it was he who was truly the injured party in the dispute. He was one crying in the wilderness, just as he now shouted to the trees while traveling between missions. *Nobody seems to understand what I have had to put up with. Haven't I done everything possible to demonstrate it is the bishop who needs to take decisive action?* Indeed, every time he wrote Albany he proved, to his satisfaction at least, it was the renegade Gallagher who was at the root of all his problems. He asked the trees why the bishop hadn't taken more drastic action. If the trees could have answered his pleas, their objections to this version of events would surely have echoed throughout the forest. The excommunication and interdict were not enough in the priest's eyes. If he had his way, the bishop would send an army to quell the rebellion, just as Pope Pius IX had done at Castelfidardo. He was only discharging his duties on that last Sunday of 1860, and would do the same again if given the chance.

When arriving back to home base, Clarke decided to again seek counsel from the same Watertown lawyer that Patrick Walsh had retained. The attorney advised him he would be within his rights to yet again hold an *ex oficio* election of trustees. Emboldened by this opinion, the priest promptly scheduled another election, this time to be held on the 29th of May, at his brother's farm where he could control the attendance. Notice was posted in *The Tribune,* and Gallagher's renegade forces, exhausted by the conflict's duration, weakly cried foul to no avail.

On the day after this latest meeting date was announced, Carthage was visited by another priest, a stranger who sought out Squire O'Leary. "I want to meet with the principals in this dispute," he said. "Can you arrange it?"

After quizzing the prelate as to his credentials and determining he was genuine, O'Leary said he would speak to Gallagher. "He's the one you've got to talk to if there's anything to be done."

"Once bit, twice shy," said Gallagher after being asked to meet with the new emissary. "I'll not make the acquaintance of another bogus priest. I'm still smartin' over the last son of a bitch who called himself a priest."

O'Leary shook his head but decided to introduce Father Francis to the Walshes, Galvin, and Neary. The priest said he'd like to convene a meeting to explain the bishop's position, which he said had been misinterpreted. Most of the principals, worn out by the dispute, said they would welcome talking to this emissary. Aunt Nancy thought otherwise, saying, "Some of you would listen to the Devil himself if you thought it would open the church!"

The mysterious Father Francis had his meeting on the 27th, and Pastor Clarke had his four days later at the family farm.

Bickford's *Tribune* of June 10, 1862, reported this new wrinkle in the continuing saga. Showing an uncommon bit of sensitivity for the embarrassment many of his readers felt, his paper never mentioned the previous year's fiasco with the impostor priest O'Connor. However, Bickford couldn't resist reporting both Clarke's and Father Francis' moves. This was the perfect opportunity for the self-appointed conscience of the village to scold all the participants, suggesting it was time they put an end to the affair.

WAS FATHER FRANCIS AN IMPOSTER?

> The difficulties in the Roman Catholic Church in this village have lately assumed some new phases.
>
> The priest, Mr. Clarke has been holding meetings, and saying Mass in a private house on the [Tannery] Island, and of course those who were opposed to the priest did not attend. Some time since, the priest gave notice that an election of trustees would be held at the house of William Clarke, his brother. The opposite party had intended to attend the election and vote.
>
> But in the meantime a priest named Francis came here, who claimed to have authority from the Bishop to settle the difficulty. He held a meeting at Walsh's Hall on Tuesday the 27th of May. This meeting was largely attended, though Mr. Clarke was not there, and Francis told those dissatisfied with the priest what the Bishop required of them, and they concluded to submit to what was demanded.
>
> The election of trustees, Father Francis announced, was contrary to the wishes of the Bishop, as he did not wish to

control the people, nor did he want to appeal to the law of the land for that purpose. Under the advice he gave, the opposers of Mr. Clarke concluded to keep aloof from the election.

The election, however, was held on the 29th. Only a small number, and those entirely of the priest's adherents attended. There were, however, some present from Lewisburg, Montague, Watertown and other places.

As soon as the trustees were elected, they came to the church, and under the advice of a Watertown lawyer, with the assistance of a blacksmith, forced the doors open and put on a new lock, and took formal possession. The priest announced, so we learn, that the election was according to the wishes of the Bishop. It is a question for somebody to decide when the two priests disagree as to the wishes of the Bishop.

The opposers of the priest claim that the election was void, because it was not held at the proper place. But it rather seems to us, that the present aspect of the case is with the priest, unless the Bishop shall decide against his late proceeding, as it is claimed he will.

What is stated above is by hearsay, entirely, and the name of our informant will be given if required. We have no other interest in the matter than what is common to the whole community, who ardently desire that this most irritating controversy, now of some three or four years' standing, should come to an end, and that peace may be restored in some way.

Father Francis disappeared as quietly as he arrived, never to be heard from again. His appearance had mysteriously opened the door to new discussions for both sides. Armed with a legal opinion, Clarke boldly marched down the board to capture the queen-his church.

Would this move lead to checkmate or a draw?

CHAPTER 40

"Yes, you may go to Carthage," said Bishop McClosky. Father Conroy's insistence prompted his superior to sanction yet another trip in pursuit of resolution of the St. James dispute. "'Tis against my better judgment, but you may have your way one more time. Remember but this," he instructed, "we must break the back of trustee power. There can be no compromise on that."

Conroy always dreaded getting off the train at Utica to board the Boonville stage. He was not alone in wondering why the railroad hadn't yet run to Carthage. His commodious frame afforded little comfort to the unlucky passengers seated next to him, and this made him even more uncomfortable. To relieve the tension he tried his best to be jovial, cracking an occasional joke about his bulk and the cramped quarters,.

Traveling was not kind to the priest's constitution and each time the stage stopped to change horses or let the passengers stretch, he headed for the nearest outhouse. He tried to maintain a good humor because, as a representative of his Church, he was conscious of setting a good example. It was bad enough that hostility to men of the Roman cloth was often painfully overt. He did his best to offset such behavior with humor. His thoughts, however, continually returned to plotting how he could put an end to the St. James affair. The begrudging endorsement of McCloskey only served to stiffen his resolve to find a solution.

When the last leg of the journey finally deposited him at the stage depot near the boat docks of Carthage, he collected his bag and started the short walk up State Street to take a room at Brown's new hotel. He would need a good night's rest to recover from the trip. The next morning the refreshed priest stomped into Gallagher's furniture store, and spying his quarry in the rear of the building, wove his way around the furniture display to confront him. Richard looked at the big man in surprise and wondered what in hell the man could possibly want now?

When Conroy reached the rear of the store, he drew up his large frame and said in a loud voice, "I want to have a meeting with the St. James trustees."

"Do you mean the new ones or the old ones?" Gallagher cynically asked. "You'll need to talk to O'Leary. He's our intermediary for negotiations. His place is across the street."

Conroy harrumphed, turned and left. He drew many stares as he made his way across the street. His unique garb and large size was not often seen on the streets of Carthage.

O'Leary didn't blame Conroy for the problems St. James had with Albany and was much more cordial than Gallagher. After a short conversation, he agreed to meet with him over lunch at his hotel just two doors up the street. "We can discuss how you want to go about this," said the Squire. "Lord knows 'tis time it was settled."

After a couple of drinks and a large t-bone steak, Conroy took charge of the discussion. "I'm here to make the peace," he said as firmly as he could. "And believe me when I say it was a great struggle to get this far."

The Squire could see from the set of the priest's jaw he meant business. "Who do you want to meet with?" he asked.

"The legitimate board of trustees, including Gallagher."

"I don't know if he'll come," said O'Leary. "He's mightily aggrieved. This ruckus has cost him plenty."

"Please beseech him on my behalf. If we have an agreement without him, others may not go along. It is my mission to bring everyone back to our Mother Church."

The Squire said he would try, even though he sorely regretted having gotten into the middle of this mess. He had declined trusteeship in St. James several times because he thought it would conflict with his civic duties. He did write a letter of complaint to the bishop, but only at Gallagher's behest. Upon reflection, however, he admitted as a peace justice he was the logical candidate to mediate the dispute.

O'Leary met with Gallagher that afternoon and was not surprised to still see a face full of bitterness. The store was empty even though it was a Saturday, the busiest shopping day of the week.

After hearing O'Leary's proposition, Gallagher burst out with a litany of pent up grievances."I've poured my heart and soul into this struggle and what has it cost me? I've been slandered, lost friends, lost business, and had indignities heaped on my family. I've been denied the sacraments and had to have a Protestant wedding. These are things I don't think I'll ever be able to forgive."

"Look, Richard," said O'Leary, "You're a friend of mine. Can I give you a little advice?" He didn't wait for a response as Richard stiffened like a schoolboy about to be lectured. "Here's what I'd do if I were you. Meet with the man. He dearly wants a deal that will make everyone as happy as possible under the circumstances. This is the best chance since the whole mess started. Hasn't everybody had enough?"

Gallagher became pensive and after a long pause said, "I won't stand in the way. If the others go along, so will I."

A meeting with the seven trustees, Conroy, and the arbitrator O'Leary, was scheduled for Gallagher's store that evening. It was felt this was the only way to be sure he'd attend. Tension hovered in the air as everyone took seats on the comfortable furniture. The Squire tried to warm up the group with a few old Irish jokes everyone had heard before, and they listened politely and laughed appropriately. The meeting began in earnest with Conroy repeating his mission.

Gallagher interrupted and said, "I can't be part of any deal the keeps that priest here, and that's final."

The visiting priest was a bit discomfited by the dictatorial tone in Gallagher's voice but recovered to say, "We're here to make a settlement, not demands. Please Mr. Gallagher, consider that all parties believe they are aggrieved and any agreement will require everyone to give a little."

Justice O'Leary agreed and tried to defuse the tension. "Let's reserve our judgment until we hear what Father Conroy has to say. What do you suggest, Father?"

"I have given this dispute much thought and what the diocese has in mind is the following: First, we will rescind the interdict from the St. James Church." There was a collective sigh of relief at this, especially from the Walsh brothers.

"Second, upon proper confession, the bishop will lift the excommunication from the three individual trustees." A murmur arose at the suggested admission of wrongdoing, and echoed throughout the empty store. "Wait, wait, hear me out," Conroy admonished, and the voices grew quiet. "Third, we will reinstate Father Clarke as pastor." The groans grew much louder, with Gallagher rising from his chair.

"Please sit down, Mr. Gallagher, and hear me out," the priest demanded again. After Gallagher reluctantly retook his seat, the priest continued. "He will say one last Mass at St. James and be immediately transferred to another parish." The groans subsided and everyone smiled, all except Gallagher, that is. "Fourth, you will agree to turn over the church deed to the bishop." A few more groans erupted but soon died out.

"I can see that this is grounds for a settlement," O'Leary said, seizing the opportunity to fill the void of stunned silence. "It looks to me as if everyone can save their faces here." Gallagher's expression turned very serious as he pondered the proffered peace treaty, and finally he said, "I think we should discuss this among ourselves before putting it to a vote.

Conroy, his satisfaction broadcast by his determined smile, rose and walked to the front of the store. He felt he need say no more because he saw they were coming around to his point of view.

Haberer, Kenna, and Patrick and James Walsh each took turns telling of their frustrations and worries about the church remaining closed. They were ready and eager to accept the terms as offered. They knew their majority would not need Gallagher's acquiescence to pass the final resolution.

There was some grumbling about the priest being allowed to say a last Mass but they decided to take a vote on the offer. "Well gentlemen, what do each of you say on the diocese's proposal?" Gallagher asked. It passed six to one. Gallagher, to everyone's surprise said, in a gesture of magnanimity, "Let's make it unanimous."

The group called Conroy back to the meeting and told him he had a deal. The long battle had come to an abrupt and undramatic end.

Patrick made sure to remind the vicar general, "Ee's gotta lift the curse, ya know." All except the puzzled Conroy laughed. The priest decided to ignore the remark.

Addie was awaiting Richard when he arrived home. She had always maintained the whole Church business was an overblown tempest in the proverbial teapot but wanted to support her husband in his time of need. "What happened, dear?" she asked. Her young face puckered to a point as she tried to interpret her spouse's expression. The toll it had taken on him evoked her pity. *He looks so much older tonight,* she thought. "Can you tell me about it or must it wait?"

"Let's have dinner and we can talk about it then."

A relatively quiet meal was had as Gallagher was lost in thought about the day's events. After the couple finished eating they repaired to the parlor. "I think I'll have a drink," Richard said. This no longer surprised Addie as taking a drink or two after supper had become a ritual for her husband. He went over to the liquor cabinet, took down a bottle of Irish whiskey, and poured a healthy portion into a tumbler. They sat together on the divan as Richard began sipping his drink. With each swallow bits of worry drained from his face. As the spirits took their desired effect, he wondered why he so avoided this pleasure in his youth.

When his first glass was finished, Richard had completed relating what transpired at the meeting. He couldn't help project the feeling he had lost the war, one he had fought so valiantly with heart and soul. "I've been maligned maliciously and without so much as an offer of redress," he said bitterly. "I've lost business, lost friends, and just about lost my religion. What could be next?"

Addie knew she had to be supportive, this despite never completely submerging her misgivings about the Catholic Church and the way it behaved. *Isn't that what Maria would do?* "Well dear, you've done your best, I know that."

Richard took Addie's face into his hands and gently kissed her. "Well, I haven't lost you," he said softly as passion rose in his husky voice. "Let's get on to bed. There will be plenty of time to talk of this on the morrow."

Richard arose the next morning in a much better frame of mind. He felt a great weight had lifted from his shoulders, and was only mildly puzzled as to why. When he kissed Addie goodbye, they both smiled contentedly. "Have a good day," she said cheerily.

The first Sunday of September in 1862 was the day Father Clarke said his last Mass in Carthage. Father Conroy, representing the Diocese of Albany, sat in the sanctuary throughout the service. Some thought it was to make sure the outgoing pastor didn't take the opportunity to vent his spleen one last time. The celebrant periodically glanced over at the imposing vicar general and decided, under the circumstances, to be as charitable as possible. He thanked all his "friends" for their support, concluded the Mass, got into his buggy, and drove off never to be seen publicly in Carthage again.

Richard Gallagher did not attend Clarke's farewell Mass. His wounds were still raw and he felt the time, effort, and price he had paid had not been worth it. His bitterness towards the departing priest and his enabling bishop would take a lot more time to heal.

Epilog

The rebellion in Carthage affected many lives. Let us examine how some of the principals involved fared after the Bishop's Curse was assumed to have been lifted.

Arnold Galleciez

The French millwright, and builder of Gallagher's house, had written one of the more scathing letters to Bishop McCloskey about the malfeasance of Father Clarke. He would have had reason to wonder if the "bishop's curse" had paid him a visit because of this.

Two and a half years after sending his letter, while the church was still under the interdict, he and his family were poisoned with arsenic and nearly died. Arnold's sister, who was visiting the family, had volunteered to prepare breakfast, complete with some pieces of fried pork. She went to the pantry to get some flour with which to roll the meat. There she spied a plate on which some flour had already been placed. In the spirit of frugality, she decided to utilize the dish, which unbeknownst to her contained a mixture of arsenic for the purpose of ridding the house of rats. The whole family was thereupon poisoned, with Arnold, who ate the largest portion, getting the major dose. Dr. West was immediately called to administer first-aid and a week later, all had thankfully recovered. The family forever credited Dr. West with saving their lives.

Galleciez would be the builder for the new St. James Church, the construction of which was begun just two years after Father Clarke left. The new building was completed in late 1865 and was heralded by Bickford's paper as the "most costly and magnificent building in our village." It measured 60' by 100' with a bell tower, including its spire, which reached 92' into the air. The church is still in use today.

Galleciez lived to age seventy-five, passing away in 1902.

Judge Marcus Bickford

Bickford had come to Carthage from Lowville in 1838 to practice law. In 1849, he was bitten by the "gold bug" and embarked on a journey to California with two Hammond brothers to make his fortune. The Hammonds were a prominent and prosperous Carthage family. After an arduous and perilous journey across the plains, the group arrived at Donner Pass where they panned for gold, with "ordinary" success. Bickford remained in California for two years before returning to Carthage, no better off financially than when he left. Soon after returning home, he married Jane Van Horn Hammond, the sister of his gold seeking companions.

Bickford, you will remember, was the "Protestant judge" who questioned Father Clarke mercilessly during the pew trial. As was told in our story, he was not only a lawyer, justice of the peace, elder and pastor of the Disciples Church, but also founder, owner, publisher, and editor of *The Carthage Republican Tribune.* In his first issue, Editor Bickford unabashedly laid out his paper's philosophy in an editorial:

> We deem it proper on this occasion to inform our readers what our program is. We intend to make our paper what its name imports, Republican in politics, firm and decided yet dignified; and courteous towards those whose political views differ from ours... While giving the paper a high moral tone, and not entirely ignoring the subject of religion, we shall, nevertheless, abstain from intruding religious views which may be regarded as peculiar or sectarian.

Bickford wasn't always true to his stated mission, as was seen during the 1860 presidential election. He felt completely at liberty to often, and discourteously, lecture the opponents of "Honest Abe," and did so with relish. He often moralized in the pages of his paper, as in the summer of 1862 when he castigated the "evil" intrusion of two billiard tables into the village. It was to "the detriment of the morals of the place," he said, while implicitly calling for some vigilantes to correct this social evil by editorializing, "It is in the hands of the virtuous of the community."

Of course Bishop McCloskey and Father Clarke took a jaundiced view of Bickford's reportage. They thought the newsman was biased by his religious beliefs, and saw his columns as "Protestant interference" in Church affairs.

After the fire of 1861 consumed his place of worship, the Judge could have rightfully claimed to be a victim of the McCloskey "curse." Three years after said "curse" was supposedly lifted, he became painfully ill with rheumatism and had to sell *The Tribune.* He recovered just enough to remain a contributing editor on the paper until 1876, a few months before his death. His wife Jane, said to be quite well educated, and a devotee of local history, spoke fluent French. She was then the oldest living resident born in Carthage, and outlived her husband by eighteen years, passing away in1894 at age seventy-two.

Bickford was sixty-one when he died of what the doctors said was "inflammatory rheumatism." *The Tribune's* obituary concluded with the following verse that endeavored to sum up the man's life and pay tribute to his crusading values.

> The pitying heart that felt for human woe
> The dauntless heart that feared no human pride;
> The friend of man, to vice alone a foe;
> For even his fallings leaned to virtue's side.

Patrick Somerville Stewart

The stalwart Protestant lawyer Stewart was born in Edinburgh Scotland on the 4th of August in 1796. At age fourteen he shipped as a sailor and came to America finally arriving at Carthage in 1815. Stewart adhered to a strict moral code and maintained a reputation for honesty and sagacity throughout his life. His respect for men of the cloth of all denominations impelled him to, albeit reluctantly, involve himself in the Catholic Church struggle on Pastor Clarke's behalf.

Stewart's reputation along with his hard work was rewarded when the Le Ray family entrusted him with virtual control over all their vast land holdings and the conduct of their financial affairs.

The senior members of the Stewart clan seemed blessed with longevity. Patrick and his wife Mary Jane lived long and productive lives although they did suffer the loss of two children—seventeen-year-old James died in 1836 and two-year-old Julia who died three years later in 1839. Stewart's brother John L. lived to age eighty, while his spinster sister Helen reached the superannuated age of one hundred years, passing away in 1904.

Patrick Somerville Stewart died at age seventy-eight, and wife Mary Jane who was five years his senior, died fifteen months later in 1876 at age eighty-six.

The Walsh Family

The three Walsh brothers, James, Anthony, and Patrick, along with their sister Aunt Nancy (nee Ann), were all born in a place called Course, County Monaghan, Ireland. They came to America via Canada in the early 1820s as part of the horde escaping their country's pestilence and persecution. Finally settling in Carthage, they all resided at the Irish Settlement, where the brothers James and Patrick were farmers while Anthony plied the shoemaker's trade on State Street. Three other siblings in the clan, Peter, Mary, and Bridget, played no identifiable role in the church insurrection.

The eldest brother James lived on for six years after the interdict was lifted, dying in 1868 at age seventy-three.

Anthony Sr., with sons James and Anthony, Jr., along with surviving triplet Cornelia, boarded for a long time with his daughter Rose Ann and son-in-law Martin Leach, also an Irish Settlement farmer. Anthony never remarried after his wife Mary died in 1844 due to complications after giving birth to the famous triplets. He spent his final years living with son James and his wife Alegia (nee Neary) and their five children, until his death in 1882 at age seventy-eight.

Anthony, Jr. interrupted his shoemaker occupation with his father for a stint in the Civil War. He joined M Co. of the New York 14th Heavy Artillery Battalion at Utica, and served from December 1863 until he was discharged for disability in August of 1865. While serving under Gen. Ambrose Burnside, Anthony's Battalion engaged in heavy battles that in just one year resulted in over 500 deaths due to cannon, cartridge, or contagion. It was reported that, of all the men who enlisted with him at Utica, Anthony was the only soldier not taken prisoner or killed. At the battle of Spotsylvania Court House he suffered a shell wound to his left hand, losing a finger and ending up in a military hospital in Baltimore, Maryland. In 1887, some twenty-two years after the war ended, the veteran was awarded a pension in the "handsome sum" of $72 per month. Prior to that raise, he had received the paltry sum of between $2 and $6 per month.

Unlike his brother James, Anthony did not revel in parades and celebrations after the war ended. His disability curtailed some of his shoemaking activities but didn't deter him from successfully expanding his shoe-making business. He worked at his profession until a couple of years before his death in 1913 at age seventy-six.

James, as we saw, had begun learning his undertaker's profession at age twelve. He was quite ambitious and left his benefactor's employ to partner with another of Gallagher's former apprentices, George Kapfer, and opened their own undertaking parlor and furniture store in 1861. James also answered the patriotic call and became a Civil War soldier, enlisting in A Co. of the 186th Infantry Regiment in August 1864. He served a total of nine months and was mustered out as a sergeant in September of the following year. His unit saw action in the Petersburg, Virginia campaign, a ten day battle not nearly as fierce as his brother's Spotsylvania Court House experience. His unit suffered less than a fifth of the casualties of Anthony's unit. (Gallagher's brother-in-law William A. Sherwood also served with the 59th NY Infantry Regiment at Spotsylvania Court House.)

In his obituary, it was reported James was the "dean" of the Carthage undertakers, having officiated at more funerals during his lifetime than any of his peers, including all the surrounding vicinity. He was a zealous member of the GAR (Grand Army of the Republic) veterans, marching in many parades and delivering many a "graceful" Decoration Day speech. He died in 1907 at age sixty-eight after suffering for a year with a "stomach disorder."

Henry and Juliana Haberer

Originally from Utica, Haberer first arrived at Carthage in May 1850, but only stayed five months before returning home. His decision was heavily influenced by the inability to find permanent lodging in the village due to the severe housing shortage. He reappeared in Carthage a year or so later and remained there for another twenty-five years.

Haberer had mixed emotions about the squabble that developed at St. James Church. At times he supported the priest, and at others he realized the pastor's position was untenable and felt changes had to be made. He also was uncomfortable at having found himself in the middle of the conflict between priest and parishioners.

Both Henry and his wife, as noted, were accomplished musicians and as a result had many friends. Parlor music recitals, a major form of entertainment in those times, put the couple much in demand as performers.

A few months after the onset of the Civil War, forty-one year-old Henry decided to enlist in the 35th NY Infantry Regiment. Surprisingly, he left his wife and six children behind to serve his country. As was the practice then, a unit was enlisted for a fixed period of time, and no matter the progress of the war, would be disbanded when their time was up. Haberer's unit was mustered out in June of 1863, but he hadn't yet exhausted his patriotic fervor. At age forty-four he reenlisted in the 186th Infantry Regiment after it was formed in August of 1864. He served with that unit until the end of the war and was awarded a small pension.

A few years later Henry tried his hand in the grocery business, a venture that lasted less than three months. In 1876, he left Carthage for good and moved to Lowville where he lived out his days applying his cabinetmaking-undertaking skills. He died of painful "inflammation of the bowels" on October 28, 1887 at sixty-six years of age. James Walsh was retained to handle the undertaking duties for Haberer's funeral. His remains were transported by rail to Carthage for internment, alongside his son Henry Jr. who had died prematurely in 1869. His Alsatian wife Juliana outlived Henry by six years, passing away in 1893 at the age of sixty-eight. A special train transported her remains to Carthage for burial in St. James Cemetery.

Squire George O'Leary

O'Leary had completed his shoemaking apprenticeship in Ireland before immigrating to Canada in 1832 at age nineteen. He immediately crossed the border to the States and found a job with a man by the name of Joshua Babcock at Felts Mills, New York. An avid student who prized education highly, it was said he was never without a book next to his shoe bench so he could read and work at the same time. He devoted years to studying law and history and was said to have a remarkable memory. He resided in Jefferson County for a total of sixty-three years and was a dedicated and respected politician and public servant, holding numerous and various offices for forty-three of those years. At times he was a justice of the peace, deputy sheriff, postmaster, constable, and school trustee. Although never admitted to the bar, a prominent lawyer once remarked of the Squire that, "He knew of no one outside of the legal profession who had a finer idea on a question of law." Over the years, O'Leary's docket handed down over 2,000 judgments, several of which were appealed to a higher court, but none was ever reversed, a distinction of which he was quite proud. His motto was, "Equal and exact justice for all."

That O'Leary was an avowed patriot of his adopted country is unquestioned. He gave stirring speeches at the drop of a tam-o-shanter to a variety of audiences. His antipathy for his English oppressors was well known and spurred him to participate in the Patriot War of 1837, a short-lived conflict whose aim was to persuade Canadians to secede from British rule. His patriotic cheerleading often helped to recruit soldiers for the Civil War for he was as devoted to the preservation of the Union as any native-born citizen.

Like many an immigrant of the time, O'Leary came to America as a penniless and friendless youth, but succeeded beyond all expectation. He became wealthy from his astute business endeavors and dabbled in land speculation in places as far away as Omaha, Nebraska. Two of his children even took up permanent residence there.

O'Leary's family did not escape a heavy dose of tragedy. Their accomplished and well-educated daughter Josephine, who lived for a time in New Orleans, La., was a teacher and writer of some note. She returned to Carthage from the South due to illness and died of consumption in 1878. A son George Jr., whom the Squire had set up in the real estate business in Omaha, died suddenly and prematurely in 1890 at thirty-six, the same age as his sister at her death.

In 1887, the Squire and wife Alice celebrated fifty years of marriage. Three years later Alice became seriously ill with a malady called "typhoid pneumonia." The disease supposedly resulted from her having caught a simple cold and plagued her for well over a year before she succumbed in 1891.

The Squire, although he had been ill for some time, lived on for four more years after Alice's demise. The newspapers reported in 1889 the esteemed community member had long been doctoring in Watertown. A year before his death in 1895, he suffered a "stroke of paralysis" from which he never recovered, and passed away at age eighty-two. At the time of his death, he was living with his daughter Maria in Carthage.

Bishop John McCloskey

Above all else, Bishop McCloskey could not bring himself to accept the despised trustee system. The highly educated, well-traveled cleric's frail appearance belied a strong will, one that continually surprised his fellow clergy.

In his first parish assignment at St. Joseph's in Greenwich Village, he encountered great resistance to his appointment. Parish leader Charles Casserly, a man who had no truck with native born clergy, vowed "no child of mine will kneel before an American priest." McCloskey eventually instructed all the Casserly children, one of whom was elected a Senator from California in 1869. The bishop often mentioned that, "Senator Eugene Casserly wrote me after his election and reminded me that it was I who prepared him for his first communion, and he credited me with an essential hand in his subsequent success. I treasure that letter to this day."

McCloskey served as Bishop of Albany from 1847 until Archbishop Hughes died in New York in 1864. Everyone expected that he would succeed "Dagger" Hughes, but he demurred, writing Rome to humbly request he not be considered because of his health. The request was denied and in May of that year McCloskey took his place in New York City as only the second ever American Archbishop.

McCloskey was an indefatigable fundraiser, and one of his first acts as archbishop was to mount a campaign to complete

St. Patrick's Cathedral, begun by his predecessor Hughes. His mission was finally realized when the church was dedicated on May 25, 1879. He was also responsible for building numerous other churches, schools, a seminary, hospitals, and orphanages.

McCloskey's antipathy for the trustee system was fierce and was exacerbated by the enactment of the *Putnam Bill,* passed by the New York Assembly in 1855-a piece of legislation that was instigated by the Know Nothing Party's Joseph Putnam, a Senator from Buffalo. The bill claimed to champion the separation of church and state, and concerned the vesting of church property to trustees, per the 1784 Act, which governed the organization of religious societies. It provided for the confiscation of said property in the case of non-compliance. Bishop McCloskey worked tirelessly behind the scenes with Irish members of state government to finally have the offensive legislation repealed in 1863.

Rumors of naming an American Cardinal had begun as early as 1850 and despite President Lincoln's encouragement to the Pope to act in 1860, official notice of such did not come until March 15, 1875, when Pius IX named McCloskey as the first American Cardinal.

Shortly after celebrating his 50th jubilee as a priest, McCloskey's health took a turn for the worse and in October of 1886, he passed away at age seventy-six. His remains are interred in a crypt at St. Patrick's Cathedral.

Vicar General John Conroy

The Irish born Conroy arrived in America in 1833 at age fourteen. He was younger than McCloskey by nine years, and his career followed a similar arc. The young Conroy studied at Emmitsburg, and St. John's College at Fordham when McCloskey was president, and where he would also later serve in the same capacity. Appointed vicar general of the

Albany Diocese in 1857, he was ready to succeed McCloskey and did so upon the latter's elevation as archbishop of New York. He was consecrated bishop of Albany in October 1865 by Pope Pius IX.

Conroy knew well the number of secular priests being ordained could not keep up with the rapid Catholic population increase in his vast See. He thus began a program to encourage other religious orders, such as the Augustinians, to come into his diocese and alleviate the shortage. Growth in the North Country caused the Albany See to be split in 1872 when the Ogdensburg Diocese was formed. The St. James Parish then came under the control of the new Bishop Edgar P. Wadhams, a former Episcopal priest. Two years later the Augustinian Fathers were put in charge of running the parish in Carthage, causing some to whisper that the new bishop didn't want to put up with the fractious Irish of Carthage, a contention hotly disputed by St. James historians.

Conroy also set about attracting communities of nuns to serve the increasing number of schools and hospitals in his Episcopal See. Among them were the Sisters of St. Joseph of Carondelet, Missouri. This decision would turn out to have a grim consequence for Conroy.

Well before he became bishop, Conroy had a known drinking problem. In 1874, he was asked to resign as Bishop of Albany because of it and he refused. His situation became exacerbated when a rumored relationship with a nun from the above mentioned Carondelet order surfaced.

Margaret Lacy, originally born in Cohoes, New York in 1839, had joined the Sisters of St. Joseph in St. Louis, Missouri where she became known as Sr. Mary Herman of the Carondelet Community of nuns. Sent to work at a mission at St. Joseph's Church in Troy, New York, she took her final vows there in 1863. The nun drifted in and out of the Albany Diocese over the next dozen years, coming in contact with Bishop Conroy on numerous occasions. Rumors of a relationship between the two caused Cardinal McCloskey in

1877, despite Conroy's refusal to resign, to abruptly order him back to New York. He was given the honorific title of Bishop of Curium (bishop at large) and lived out his days there until he died in November of 1895 at age seventy-six.

Margaret Lacy's reputation, deserved or not, followed her wherever she went and, after being refused audiences in both Troy and St. Louis, she ended up in Watertown, NY, starting a convent there with a small group of young women. While there, she sent the first teaching nuns to Carthage. Those nuns eventually founded what became the Augustinian Academy parochial school, which celebrated its 125th anniversary in the year 2011. Not one to stay too long in one place, and thinking the Watertown convent had no future, Lacy forsook the place to return to the Midwest. She arrived in Kalamazoo, Michigan with nine other nuns whom she had persuaded to leave Watertown with her. In Kalamazoo she is fondly remembered as the foundress of the Sisters of St. Joseph of that city and is credited with establishing an orphanage and school.

FATHER MICHAEL CLARKE

Early on in his career, Father Clarke displayed an ability to seize opportunity whenever and wherever it was presented. He relinquished his first assignment at St. Paul's in Oswego after only nine months when he wangled a transfer to St. John's in Utica. He was unconcerned the parish might feel abandoned after so short a stay, and it turned out they didn't mind, at least officially. Years later, a St. Paul's Church historian would write a glowing obituary of Clarke, mentioning that during his term there he was a "...very holy priest and many wonderful cures were attributed to him." Clarke had, in a very short time, acquired the reputation of being a mystic, an attribute talked about wherever he went.

Clarke's good friend and benefactor, Nicholas Devereux, did not fare well after their European tour concluded. He certainly had no reason to be included in McCloskey's Curse but eight months after the party returned to Utica, he suddenly became deathly ill. He came down with a fever followed by symptoms of an "apoplectic nature," dying at age sixty-four shortly afterwards in December of 1855.

After Father Clarke was permitted his last, face-saving Mass in Carthage, he went off to become pastor of St. Mary's Church in Amsterdam, New York. Three years later he assumed the pastorate of St. John's Church in Schenectady and remained there until his death in 1872 at age sixty-four. He left behind a considerable sum of money and had no will. The local newspaper printed a notice of search for relatives, but neither the size of the estate, nor whether his brother William laid claim to it, was ever reported.

Another deed that outlived the priest came to light when his brother, William, a seemingly confirmed bachelor, died in June of 1874. A squabble arose after his passing when his will revealed he had left nearly a third of his estimated $75,000 estate to the Society of St. James Church. He stipulated the bequeathed property was to be used by the parish for a new parochial school.

A lady named Catherine Foley, who claimed to be living at the Clarke farm as a housekeeper, went to court to assert she was secretly married to William some four years before his death. She claimed that none other than his brother Father Michael performed the ceremony in 1870. The former pastor failed to record any such marriage, either with civic or church officials, and as he was dead, could not attest to its validity. It took three years after "husband" William's death for the case to be tried in 1877. In her legal brief, Miss Foley alleged cohabitation with William for eighteen years while his housekeeper. The Census of 1860 showed only her sister as a servant living in the household. Since she wasn't there in 1860, and he died in 1874, she must have been living in sin for ten years and cohabiting with his ghost for four of those eighteen years.

During the trial a total of sixty-nine witnesses were called, several of whom supported Foley's claim. The jury found in her favor, but since she was not named in the will, nor was there any issue from the union, the law held she was entitled to but one-half of the spouse's remaining personal property. She also was awarded the use of one-third of his real estate. In any event, an out of court settlement was made with St. James and they acquired the property necessary to build their adjoining parochial school, which they did in 1885.

ADELAIDE MASURY GALLAGHER

Addie Gallagher had seven children with husband Richard, six of whom survived into adulthood. Her last child, a son named after her brother George, was born in 1879 when her husband was sixty-one years-old.

Addie's father, Dr. John Masury, died at age seventy-four in Watertown in 1864 at which time the family purchased a plot in Brookside Cemetery. Her mother, Mary, lived until 1895 when she passed away at eighty-seven and was interred with her husband at the Watertown cemetery.

As we saw, Addie's three younger brothers, John, George and William, went off to do their duty in the Civil War. John was the oldest at eighteen and served in A Co 106th Infantry Regiment. He was wounded at Spotsylvania Court House, the same battle at which Anthony Walsh lost a finger. Her two youngest brothers served in the 60th New York Heavy Artillery Regiment as drummer boys and saw action in the battle of Antietam. Both held the rank of musician when they were mustered out because of disability, one year after enlistment. George reenlisted a year later at Rochester in L Co. of the 14th Heavy Artillery Regiment (his name was recorded as Massuary) in which he served until the war ended eighteen months later.

William Masury died at age forty-nine in 1896 at brother George's home in Chicago. A short time before his death he was in treatment at the National Soldier's Home in Dayton, Ohio. The cause of his demise was due to complications from unnamed diseases contracted while serving in the Civil War.

Addie's sister Harriet Chase, the baker's wife with whom she was living when she first met Richard Gallagher, died in 1898 at age sixty-three. Harriet's husband, Justus, had an entrepreneurial bent and in 1868 received a patent for a Bake Pan, which was "a great improvement," *The Tribune* reported. "Superior to any bread we have eaten... highly commended by some of the best physicians and hotel keepers in the country." It is fairly certain Chase had given a few loaves of freshly baked bread to *The Tribune* in order to secure that endorsement.

Brother George, in his obituary, was incorrectly touted by several newspapers as the youngest Union Army drummer boy to serve in the Civil War (historical sources name a boy of nine years as the youngest). He moved around a bit after leaving Ogdensburg, going to Watertown and on to Chicago. He finally ended up in East Long Meadow, Mass., where, as the town's last surviving veteran of the Civil War, he passed away in 1932 at age eighty-three. Among the jobs George held was as a "chemist" (bartender) at various resorts including the St. Lawrence Hotel and the Woodruff House in Watertown.

In 1864, two years after the interdict was lifted, Addie was attending St. James Church with her husband and sponsoring baptisms. But, she didn't embrace Catholicism nearly as eagerly as did her predecessor, Maria Sherwood.

After Richard's death, Addie was unable to maintain the large house on State Street. She moved in with her daughter Alice Gallagher Coburn and rejoined the Episcopal Church. Addie outlived her husband by twenty-four years, passing away at age seventy-two in 1914.

Adelaide Masury Gallagher's funeral was held in Carthage at the Grace Episcopal Church with her remains taken to Watertown to be buried in the family plot at Brookside Cemetery-some 18 miles from where her husband Richard was resting.

Richard Gallagher

Our protagonist, Gallagher, was truly what one would call a mover and shaker in Carthage's early civic development. He promoted the need for a school and became one its first board members. He was one of only two announced abolitionists at a time when that stand was not at all popular. When opened, his furniture emporium was the first and largest of its kind in Jefferson County. Never one to stand still, he had an eye for economic opportunities and tried his hand at other business ventures besides furniture. On one occasion, he formed a partnership in the clothing business, advertising fine silk suits for sale.

A few months before the church interdict was lifted in 1862, Gallagher was reelected president of the village of Carthage board of trustees. He would serve as a trustee four more times, the last being in 1877.

After the church dispute was settled, and his nemesis Clarke vanquished, Richard finally buried the hatchet and went back to his Catholic upbringings.

Gallagher sold furniture on the installment plan and often had difficulty collecting payment. An ominous ad appeared from time to time under his name in *The Tribune* warning: "Unless I get money soon, someone will be hurt." What he meant by "hurt" isn't specified, but it sounded like a cry of financial desperation.

After the church dispute ended, Gallagher's furniture business began to decline in earnest as residual shunning and competition from the very people he had trained in his cabinetmaking shop increased.

Not unusual for the time, Gallagher had a large garden and henhouse behind his State Street home. In the name of friendly competition, it became common practice for gardeners to drop off produce of an exemplary nature to *The*

Tribune office. The paper reported on April 7, 1868 that, "Richard Gallagher left at our office one day last week, an egg which measured 7¼ x 5¼ inches, and weighed 3 ozs.-the production of a pullet of 9 months growth." That was a large egg indeed!

Oddly perhaps, of all his children, Richard Sherwood Gallagher (RS), whose birth triggered his mother's death, was his father's favorite child. He was at the Gallagher store learning the business at a very early age. Addie often chided her husband that he was spoiling the boy, but it was the patriarch's intent from the first to pass the business down to Maria's final child.

In his later years, Richard gave up his temperate ways and began drinking heavily. When he turned sixty-four he began having back pains, which the doctors said was from kidney disease, assumedly brought on by over-consumption of alcohol. He struggled with the malady for another year before deciding to turn over the business to his putative heir RS in 1883. He retired to his home where he spent the next six years consulting different doctors and trying various health cures in hopes of getting better. He often traveled to a spa at Avon Springs in western New York, trusting and praying the mineral waters there would help. Alas, they did not.

Meanwhile, RS proved to be much less astute in business than his dad. He required infusions of cash from the patriarch to keep the store afloat, thereby helping sap his father's fortune. He took a man named Perry Fargo in as his partner only one year after assuming control, hoping this would keep the business solvent. It wasn't long, however, before the partner had to take over the furniture emporium to protect his investment. In due course, the Gallagher name was erased from the marquee. RS left town, traveling to Gloversville to take a sales job. He later moved to Lowville and ironically ended up working for the Haberer brothers, the sons of Henry and Juliana. His next stop was Watertown, where his wife Frankie (Frances) nee Culberson divorced him in 1903.

He died one year later of typhoid fever at age 44 and was buried in St. James Cemetery next to his mother and father. No one saw fit to employ a stone carver to note his presence there, and his grave remains unmarked to this day.

The patriarch of the large Gallagher clan was a driven man who had overcome many obstacles to become a prominent and wealthy citizen of Carthage. He never really believed in the bishop's curse but many of his friends (and enemies) did. They mentioned that he had been warned by Bishop McCloskey well before the tragic death of his first wife. His business decline was also attributed by many to his stubborn battle with the Church. He suffered greatly as he saw his son squander away his wealth, which no doubt accelerated the downward spiral of his health. He died in June of 1890, a virtually penniless and broken man. The obituary in *The Tribune* said he had suffered terribly for the last two years of his life. The funeral was held on June 11 at 9:00 am and every store in Carthage closed its doors for an hour and a half to honor the passing of the former pillar of their community. His many old friends sadly shook their heads during the eulogy delivered by Squire O'Leary. "He came with nothing, and is leaving with nothing," observed the Squire.

Perhaps Bishop McCloskey was smiling from a perch on high, ready to forgive and welcome his old enemy. One can only hope.

Carthage

Our little village, which sits on the banks of the Black River, got its start some 180 years after the Pilgrims landed at Plymouth Rock. It was erected on a small portion of the Onondaga Indian Nation lands that became available as a result of various wars and subsequent treaties with the Native Americans.

Although several pioneers had passed through the area before him, Jean Baptiste Bossout is credited as the first permanent resident of the wilderness area that eventually became Carthage. In the early 1800s, the fledgling settlement showed great promise, but that promise would not be fulfilled. The combination of geography and an overly conservative approach to the adoption of technological advances limited the village's growth.

Although perhaps coincidental, from the moment the St. James insurrection broke into the open, village economic activities began to slow. Meanwhile Watertown, its neighbor to the west, grew to be a city ten times Carthage's size. The village didn't embrace the telegraph until after the Civil War ended. Railroads, which came to Watertown in 1851, took another 21 years before arriving at Carthage.

Many smaller towns along the tardy Black River Canal prospered, but the anticipated boom at its terminus in Carthage was never realized. In addition, the slow pace of canal delivery limited its use for perishable products. The cost of maintenance for the artery was high due to sinkholes, leakage, and washouts of the soft earth beneath the Canal bed. In November of 1876, when it was drained for cleaning, workers found three wagonloads of eels, 28 drowned mules, 82 dead dogs, and countless demised cats. The canal, used mostly for transport of the diminishing supply of Adirondack lumber, limped along until 1922 when it was officially abandoned by the State.

Carthage firefighting equipment was eventually updated in 1875 with a second-hand Silsby steam rotary pumper, along with two carts holding 100 feet of rubber hose. The upgrade arrived well in advance of the second great fire of 1884, but this equipment also proved no match for a large conflagration. Although help arrived from Watertown and Lowville, the blaze consumed over seventy acres of both business and residential real estate before it burned itself out. The Gallagher block, however, was spared a second time.

A few years later, a bank teller absconded with significant funds, nearly bankrupting the institution where he worked.

And because of the lack of growth and subsequent career opportunities, its youth necessarily and regularly abandoned the place for better futures elsewhere.

The affair at St. James is talked about in the village even to the present day, although few know the true story. Whether McCloskey's "curse" was ever really levied, or even lifted, is open to conjecture.

We close our story with an anecdote that has been passed down through the decades and which gives us an idea of just how primitive life was back when Carthage began.

In 1803, a young Washington Irving,* while traveling with New York lawyer Josiah Ogden Hoffman, stopped at the inn in Long Falls** on the Black River. Hoffman was a land speculator on his way to Ogdensburg, New York, to visit his uncle Col. Samuel G. Ogden, for whom that city is named.

As a twenty-year-old law clerk, with New York City merchant class breeding, Irving had little experience with life in the bush. Consequently he had nothing good to say about the inn kept by the only inhabitants of Long Falls, M. & Mme. Bossout. He later wrote his recollection of the visit in vol. 4 of his *Life and Letters*.

> *In the evening we arrived at B's, at the head of Long Falls. A dirtier house was never seen. We dubbed it the 'Temple of Dirt,' but we contrived to have our venison* [hunted en route] *cooked in a cleanly manner by Mr. Ogden's servant, and it made very fine steaks, which, after living for two days on crackers and ginger bread, were highly acceptable.*
>
> *Friday, the 13th - We prepared to leave the Temple of Dirt, and set out about 60 miles through woods to Ogdensburg. We ate an uncomfortable breakfast, for indeed it was impossible to relish anything in a house so completely filthy. The landlady herself was in perfect character with the house, - a little squat Frenchwoman, with a red face, and a little black hat stuck upon her head, her hair greasy and uncombed, hanging about her ears, and the rest of her*

dress and person in similar style. We were heartily glad to make our escape.

Before leaving, Irving took his pencil and wrote over the fireplace the following piece of doggerel:

Here sovereign dirt erects her sable throne,
The house, the host, the hostess all her own.

Some years later, Judge William Cooper, father of famed novelist James Fennimore Cooper, passed by the inn, and taking note of Irving's still legible inscription, decided to add this postscript:

Learn hence, young man, and teach it to your sons,
The wisest way is to take it as it comes.

THE END

References

Bruner, Sister Nola; Archives of Roman Catholic Diocese of Albany, Repository of Bishop McCloskey correspondence used in this work.

Bickford, Marcus, Publisher; *The Carthage Republican Tribune* (Carthage, N.Y., 1860-1865)

Durant, Samuel W.; *History of Jefferson County 1797-1878* (New York, 1878)

Smith, Rev. J. Talbot; *History of the Ogdensburg Diocese* (New York, 1885)

Child, Hamilton; *Geographical Gazetteer of Jefferson County, N.Y. 1684-1890* (Syracuse, N.Y., 1890)

Haddock, John A.; *History of Jefferson County, New York, From 1793 To 1894* (Philadelphia, Pa., 1894)

Emerson, Edgar C.; *Our County and its People, AS Descriptive Work on Jefferson County New York* (New York, 1898)

Middleton, Rev. Thomas C., O.S.A. *Records of the American Catholic Society of Philadelphia, An Early Catholic Settlement*, pp. 17-77 (Philadelphia, Pa., 1899)

Farley, John Cardinal. *The Life of John Cardinal McCloskey: first prince of the Church in America,* (New York, 1918)

Guilday, Peter; *The Life and Times of John Carroll* (New York, 1922)

Dignan, Patrick J.; *History of the Legal Incorporation of Catholic Church Property in the United States* (New York, 1935)

Brownell, Charles M.; *They Called Me Chuckie* (New York, 1943)

Taylor, Sister Mary Christine, SSJ; *A History of Catholicism in the North Country* (Camden, N.Y., 1972)

Becker, Martin; *A History of Catholic Life in the Diocese of Albany 1609-1864,* The Interdict in Carthage, pp. 132-168, (New York, 1975)

Giblin, Joseph; *Random Sketches of the History of St. James Parish* (Carthage, N.Y., 1977)

Giblin, Joseph; *Renaissance at St. James Parish* (Carthage, N.Y., 1979)

Books by Raff Ellis

Kisses from a Distance—A memoir that begins in 1895 at a remote convent in the mountains of Lebanon, where a young postulant, the author's grandmother, is abducted and given into an unanticipated, and undesired marriage. An engaging, true story that examines the Lebanese ethos through the lives and travails of three families before and after their journey and being caught up in world-shaking events such as WWI.

- *You are a wonderful story teller, Kisses was one of the rare books I read from cover to cover.*
- *I thoroughly ENJOYED it. For me it was a "page turner."*
- *I loved the book. It reads like a suspense novel.*
- *Your book is awesome! A Lebanese* Gone with the Wind!

Dam Foolishness is a memoir that weaves tales about interesting people the author met on his journey through life with his personal experiences. Here's what readers had to say:

- *Really enjoyed the book. Brought back memories of growing up in a small town.*
- *I couldn't put the book down. It took me back to Carthage and a lot of great and funny times...*
- *I read the book twice and laughed as much at the antics of Peewee and you on the second reading as the first.*
- *... the writing was so engrossing and descriptive it brought the reader straight into the story. I felt I was there!*
- *I thoroughly enjoyed* Dam Foolishness. *It was a relaxed fast read for me. So many things I never knew...*

To order autographed copies of these titles by Raff Ellis, simply go to the web site:

www.raffellis.com

Kisses from a Distance—$15 (includes S&H)

Dam Foolishness—$20 (includes S&H)